THE REIGN OF GOD

T&T Clark Enquiries in Theological Ethics

Series editors
Brian Brock
Susan F. Parsons

THE REIGN OF GOD

A Critical Engagement with Oliver O'Donovan's Theology of Political Authority

Jonathan Cole

LONDON • NEW YORK • OXFORD • NEW DELHI • SYDNEY

T&T CLARK

Bloomsbury Publishing Plc

50 Bedford Square, London, WC1B 3DP, UK
1385 Broadway, New York, NY 10018, USA
29 Earlsfort Terrace, Dublin 2, Ireland

BLOOMSBURY, T&T CLARK and the T&T Clark logo are trademarks of
Bloomsbury Publishing Plc

First published in Great Britain 2022
Paperback edition published 2024

Copyright © Jonathan Cole, 2022

Jonathan Cole has asserted his right under the Copyright, Designs and Patents Act,
1988, to be identified as Author of this work.

For legal purposes the Acknowledgments on p. viii constitute an
extension of this copyright page.

All rights reserved. No part of this publication may be reproduced or transmitted
in any form or by any means, electronic or mechanical, including photocopying,
recording, or any information storage or retrieval system, without prior permission
in writing from the publishers.

Bloomsbury Publishing Plc does not have any control over, or responsibility for, any
third-party websites referred to or in this book. All internet addresses given in this
book were correct at the time of going to press. The author and publisher regret any
inconvenience caused if addresses have changed or sites have ceased to exist,
but can accept no responsibility for any such changes.

A catalogue record for this book is available from the British Library.

Library of Congress Cataloging-in-Publication Data
Names: Cole, Jonathan (Theology, Charles Sturt University), author.
Title: The reign of God: a critical engagement with Oliver O'donovan's
theology of political authority / Jonathan Cole.
Description: London; New York: T&T Clark, 2022. |
Series: T&T Clark enquiries in theological ethics |
Includes bibliographical references and index. |
Identifiers: LCCN 2022004135 (print) | LCCN 2022004136 (ebook) |
ISBN 9780567707468 (hb) | ISBN 9780567707505 (paperback) |
ISBN 9780567707475 (epdf) | ISBN 9780567707499 (epub)
Subjects: LCSH: O'Donovan, Oliver. | Christianity and politics.
Classification: LCC BR115.P7 C6155 2022 (print) |
LCC BR115.P7 (ebook) | DDC 261.7–dc23/eng/20220511
LC record available at https://lccn.loc.gov/2022004135
LC ebook record available at https://lccn.loc.gov/2022004136

ISBN: HB: 978-0-5677-0746-8
PB: 978-0-5677-0750-5
ePDF: 978-0-5677-0747-5
eBook: 978-0-5677-0749-9

Series: T&T Clark Enquiries in Theological Ethics

Typeset by Integra Software Services Pvt. Ltd.

To find out more about our authors and books visit www.bloomsbury.com
and sign up for our newsletters.

For Eva

CONTENTS

Acknowledgments	viii
Introduction	1
Chapter 1 OLIVER O'DONOVAN'S ENGLISH-LANGUAGE RECEPTION AND THEOPOLITICAL INFLUENCES	3
Chapter 2 GOVERNMENT-AS-JUDGMENT: AN EXPOSITION OF O'DONOVAN'S THEOLOGY OF POLITICAL AUTHORITY	17
Chapter 3 DOES ISRAEL REVEAL THE ESSENCE OF POLITICAL AUTHORITY?	37
Chapter 4 ROMANS 13: 1–7 AND THE CHRISTOLOGICAL "RE-AUTHORIZATION" OF POLITICAL AUTHORITY	57
Chapter 5 SALVATION-HISTORY, BIBLICAL THEOLOGY, AND POLITICAL AUTHORITY	69
Chapter 6 THE "PROVIDENCE THESIS" AND ITS THEODICY IMPLICATIONS	79
Chapter 7 O'DONOVAN'S (CONSERVATIVE) CHRISTIAN LIBERALISM	101
Chapter 8 PROVIDENCE AND THE CREATED ORDER: THE ONTOLOGICAL TENSION IN THE ACCOUNTS OF POLITICAL AUTHORITY IN *RESURRECTION* AND *DESIRE*	111
Chapter 9 THE REDEMPTION OF POLITICAL AUTHORITY AND ITS NEW HISTORICAL *BENE ESSE* AS THE WORK OF DIVINE PROVIDENCE	123
Conclusion	137
Bibliography	139
Index	149

ACKNOWLEDGMENTS

There is something perfunctory, yet unavoidable (because appropriate), about the inclusion of acknowledgments at the beginning of a work such as this. In aid of avoiding the pretense of making acknowledgments more interesting than they can, or ought to, be, I simply name the persons who have contributed to my journey with Oliver O'Donovan's political theology, which began with a PhD in 2014 (completed in 2017), and then evolved into the present work some seven years later. With thanks and appreciation, I acknowledge Stephen Pickard, Wayne Hudson, Andrew Cameron, Geoff Broughton, Nicholas Aroney, Guido de Graaff, Simon Kennedy, Mike Mawson, Brian Brock, and Susan Parsons. Finally, I acknowledge a special debt of gratitude to Oliver O'Donovan for teaching me what a genuine political theology can and ought to be, one which manages to say something of substance about both politics and theology and their connection.

INTRODUCTION

It is an understatement to say that we live in interesting times. Troubling, worrying, disconcerting, uncertain might be more apposite adjectives to describe the current trials and tribulations afflicting Western liberal political order. Even before the *annus horribilis* of 2020 (and again in 2021), serious thinkers had begun to contemplate post-liberal alternatives to a Western liberalism perceived to be in terminal decline. John Milbank and Adrian Pabst, in *The Politics of Virtue: Post-Liberalism and the Human Future*, written before the disorienting arrival of Trumpism, examined what they describe as "metacrises" in the culture, economics, and politics of Western liberalism. Their book opens with the observation that "the twenty-first century quickly revealed the recommencement of history that called into question both the complacency and the character of the West."[1] Indeed, the twentieth-century prophet of the end of history himself, Francis Fukuyama, now fears for the future of democracy.[2]

Celebrated Anglican political theologian Oliver O'Donovan's seminal works in political theology, *The Desire of the Nations: Rediscovering the Roots of Political Theology* (hereafter *Desire*) and *The Ways of Judgment: The Bampton Lectures, 2003* (hereafter *Judgment*), straddle the intersection standing between the post–Cold War "end of history" and its "recommencement," published, as they were, in 1996 and 2005, respectively.[3] As early as 1996, O'Donovan sensed that liberalism was at risk of descending into unintelligibility and going the way of the "prodigal" as a consequence of the West's rejection of the "theological horizons" that had facilitated the emergence of liberalism.[4] O'Donovan averred that the solution to

---

1. John Milbank and Adrian Pabst, *The Politics of Virtue: Post-liberalism and the Human Future* (London: Rowman and Littlefield, 2016), 1.

2. Ishaan Tharoor, "The Man Who Declared the 'End of History' Fears for Democracy's Future," *The Washington Post*, February 9, 2017, https://www.washingtonpost.com/news/worldviews/wp/2017/02/09/the-man-who-declared-the-end-of-history-fears-for-democracys-future/?utm_term=.eef0fd23428f.

3. Oliver O'Donovan, *The Desire of the Nations: Rediscovering the Roots of Political Theology* (Cambridge: Cambridge University Press, 1996); Oliver O'Donovan, *The Ways of Judgment: The Bampton Lectures, 2003* (Grand Rapids: Eerdmans, 2005).

4. O'Donovan, *The Desire of the Nations*, 20.

liberalism's weakening foundations lay in "recover[ing] the ground traditionally held by the notion of authority," an authority that found both its origin and legitimacy in God's kingly rule over history.[5] O'Donovan sought to retrieve a theological account of political authority—a "theology of political authority"—capable of restoring a version of Christian liberalism that could forestall secular liberalism's descent into ruin, or in O'Donovan's inimitably evocative language, "anti-Christ," which is to say, "a parodic and corrupt development of Christian social order."[6]

The purpose of the present study is to undertake a systematic critical evaluation of O'Donovan's theology of political authority that arrives at a comprehensive evaluation of its cogency and tenability. To pre-empt the study's conclusion at this early juncture, I argue that the foundational propositions in O'Donovan's theology of political authority are untenable in the form in which they are articulated and on the basis of the argumentation adduced in support of them. I also conclude, however, that O'Donovan's conception of political authority is insightful and bears the potential of empirical efficacy and, for those reasons, that it is compelling. The overarching aim of the book is to propose some refinements to O'Donovan's theology of political authority capable of resolving, or at least avoiding, the problems that attend its present formulation identified in this study, while preserving its genuine fruits. This is to say that the goal in this context is to make O'Donovan work, not demonstrate that his project is irretrievable. I do so by integrating and developing certain insights from O'Donovan's moral theology that are missing in his political theology.

My critical engagement with O'Donovan's theology of political theology comes from a place of genuine sympathy for his concerns regarding the fate and fortunes of liberalism, as well as his diagnosis that its current foreboding trajectory stems, at least in part, from the abandonment of its erstwhile theological horizons. I also approach the project at hand from a sympathetic theological perspective, one which could be described as broadly Evangelical, to use a problematic and contestable theological label. Above all, my approach is guided by O'Donovan's own wise aphorism that "the lover of truth has no truer friend than an intelligent critic."[7]

The book consists of three modes which follow a logical path of development: descriptive, critical, and constructive. The first two chapters are descriptive and provide an overview of O'Donovan's reception and influences and an exposition of his theology of political authority. Chapters 3–8 mark a shift to the book's critical mode where the primary task of critical engagement with O'Donovan's theological account of political authority is undertaken. Chapter 9 marks a shift to the book's final constructive mode, where I introduce the foreshadowed refinements and endeavor to convince readers of their virtues. This is followed by a conclusion, drawing the work to a close.

5. Ibid., 19.
6. Ibid., 275. "Theology of political authority" is my phrase, not O'Donovan's.
7. Ibid., ix. (Preface to the paperback edition, 1999).

Chapter 1

OLIVER O'DONOVAN'S ENGLISH-LANGUAGE RECEPTION AND THEOPOLITICAL INFLUENCES

Impact and Reception

O'Donovan has had a significant impact on contemporary Western Christian political theology.[1] Nicholas Wolterstorff has described *Desire* as no less than the twentieth century's "most important contribution to political theology."[2] In Richard Neuhaus' view, it was that rare book that "interrupts the conversation and sets it off in new directions."[3] For Philip Lorish and Charles Mathewes, it "recast the field of 'political theology'" and "inaugurated a new era in theological thinking on politics."[4] Jonathan Chaplin found *Desire* "the most arresting, challenging and rewarding work of political theology to have appeared in a long time."[5] David Novak went so far as to credit O'Donovan with having "revived political theology

---

1. "Western" in the theological sense of the term. O'Donovan's work in political theology appears to have found negligible traction in the Orthodox world, although it is difficult to be definitive in this regard without surveying literature in Russian, Romanian, Greek, Serbian, and Arabic. For a rare exception, see Evaggelos Ganas, "Η πολιτική τοῦ Ἰησοῦ καὶ ἡ προσδοκία τῶν ἐθνῶν: Θέτοντας τον Τζόν Χάουαρντ Γιόντερ καί τόν Ὄλιβερ Ο' Ντόνοβαν σέ διάλογο" [*The Politics of Jesus and The Desire of the Nations: Bringing John Howard Yoder and Oliver O'Donovan into Conversation*] in Θρησκεία καί πολιτική [*Religion and Politics*], ed. Stavros Zoumboulakis, 322–55 (Athens: Artos Zois, 2016).
2. Nicholas Wolterstorff, "A Discussion of Oliver O'Donovan's *The Desire of the Nations*," *Scottish Journal of Theology* 54, no.1 (2001): 100.
3. Richard John Neuhaus, "Commentary on *The Desire of the Nations*," *Studies in Christian Ethics* 11, no.2 (1998): 56.
4. Philip Lorish and Charles Mathewes, "Theology as Counsel: The Work of Oliver O'Donovan and Nigel Biggar," *Anglican Theological Review* 94, no.4 (2012): 725.
5. Jonathan Chaplin, "Political Eschatology and Responsible Government: Oliver O'Donovan's 'Christian Liberalism,'" in *A Royal Priesthood? The Use of the Bible Ethically and Politically: A Dialogue with Oliver O'Donovan*, ed. Craig Bartholomew et al. (Carlisle, Cumbria: Paternoster, 2002), 265.

as a field of enquiry."[6] "Even O'Donovan's strongest critics," James McEvoy notes, "acknowledge the significance of his contribution to political theology."[7]

Desire and *Judgment* (the latter described by O'Donovan as *Desire's* "sequel" and the second phase in "a single extended train of thought") in particular have elicited substantial scholarly interest and engagement.[8] The journal *Studies in Christian Ethics* devoted an entire edition in 1998 to *Desire*, which included a response from O'Donovan.[9] In 2001, *The Scottish Journal of Theology* published articles engaging *Desire* by Wolterstorff and William Schweiker along with a response from O'Donovan.[10] In 2002, the Scripture and Hermeneutics Seminar published the results of a dialogue with O'Donovan called *A Royal Priesthood? The Use of the Bible Ethically and Politically: A Dialogue with Oliver O'Donovan*.[11] The journal *Political Theology* dedicated an entire edition in 2008 to *Judgment*, including a response from O'Donovan.[12] The latest addition to this growing body of work engaging O'Donovan's political theology is the 2015 *festschrift* edited by Robert Song and Brent Waters, *The Authority of the Gospel: Explorations in Moral and Political Theology in Honor of Oliver O'Donovan*.[13]

O'Donovan's political theology has also been the subject of several book-length comparative studies. These include Paul Doerksen's *Beyond Suspicion: Post-Christendom Protestant Political Theology in John Howard Yoder and Oliver O'Donovan*, David McIlroy's *A Trinitarian Theology of Law: In Conversation with Jurgen Moltmann, Oliver O'Donovan and Thomas Aquinas*, and Dorothea Bertschmann's *Bowing Before Christ—Nodding to the State? Reading Paul Politically with Oliver O'Donovan and John Howard Yoder*.[14] O'Donovan's political theology

---

6. David Novak, "Oliver O'Donovan's Critique of Autonomy," *Political Theology* 9, no.3 (2008): 327.

7. James Gerard McEvoy, "A Dialogue with Oliver O'Donovan about Church and Government," *The Heythrop Journal* 48, no.6 (2007): 953.

8. O'Donovan *The Ways of Judgment*, x.

9. *Studies in Christian Ethics* 11, no.2 (1998).

10. Wolterstorff, "A Discussion of Oliver O'Donovan's *The Desire of the Nations*"; William Schweiker, "Freedom and Authority in Political Theology: A Response to Oliver O'Donovan's *The Desire of the Nations*," *Scottish Journal of Theology* 54, no.1 (2001); Oliver O'Donovan, "Deliberation, History and Reading: A Response to Schweiker and Wolterstorff," *Scottish Journal of Theology* 51, no.1 (2001).

11. Craig Bartholomew et al., *A Royal Priesthood?*

12. *Political Theology* 9, no.3 (2008).

13. Robert Song and Brent Waters, eds., *The Authority of the Gospel: Explorations in Moral and Political Theology in Honor of Oliver O'Donovan* (Grand Rapids: Eerdmans, 2015).

14. Paul G. Doerksen, *Beyond Suspicion: Post-Christendom Protestant Political Theology in John Howard Yoder and Oliver O'Donovan* (Colorado Springs: Paternoster, 2009); David H. McIlroy, A Trinitarian "Theology of Law," in *Conversation with Jurgen Moltmann*, ed. Oliver O'Donovan and Thomas Aquinas (Carlisle, Cumbria: Paternoster, 2009); and Dorothea H. Bertschmann, *Bowing Before Christ—Nodding to the State? Reading Paul Politically with Oliver O'Donovan and John Howard Yoder* (London: Bloomsbury T&T Clark, 2014).

has also been the focus of, or featured substantively in, a growing number of essays, many of which again bring him into dialogue with other scholars.[15] *Desire* is also regularly cited in prominent works in political theology and O'Donovan's name has appeared in introductory texts to the field.[16]

It is interesting to observe that, while O'Donovan has been the subject of several comparative studies, his political theology has not been the subject of a dedicated book-length study.[17] It is also noteworthy that a significant proportion of the comparative studies brings O'Donovan into conversation with John Howard

---

15. See, for example, Paul Doerksen, "Christology in the Political Theology of Oliver O'Donovan," *Mennonite Quarterly Review* 78, no.3 (2004); McEvoy, "A Dialogue with Oliver O'Donovan about Church and Government"; David McIlroy, "The Right Reason for Caesar to Confess Christ as Lord: Oliver O'Donovan and Arguments for the Christian State," *Studies in Christian Ethics* 23, no.3 (2010); Guido de Graaff, "To Judge or Not to Judge: Engaging with Oliver O'Donovan's Political Ethics," *Studies in Christian Ethics* 25, no.3 (2012); Andrew Ross Errington, "Between Justice and Tradition: Oliver O'Donovan's Political Theory and the Challenge of Multiculturalism," *Studies in Christian Ethics* 27, no.4 (2014); Therese Feiler, "From Dialectics to Theo-Logic: The Ethics of War from Paul Ramsey to Oliver O'Donovan," *Studies in Christian Ethics* 28, no.3 (2015); Andrew Errington, "Authority and Reality in the Work of Oliver O'Donovan," *Studies in Christian Ethics* 29, no.4 (2016); Jonathan Chaplin, "Towards a Monotheistic Democratic Constitutionalism? Convergent Themes in Oliver O'Donovan, Sajjad Rizvi and Paul Heck," *Studies in Christian Ethics* 29, no.2 (2016).

16. See, for example, William T. Cavanaugh, *Migrations of the Holy: God, State, and the Political Meaning of the Church* (Grand Rapids: Eerdmans, 2011); Michael Walzer, *In God's Shadow: Politics in the Hebrew Bible* (New Haven: Yale University Press, 2012); Kristen Deede Johnson, *Theology, Political Theory, and Pluralism: Beyond Tolerance and Difference* (Cambridge: Cambridge University Press, 2007); Elizabeth Phillips, *Political Theology: A Guide for the Perplexed* (London: T&T Clark, 2012). O'Donovan has an essay in William T. Cavanaugh, Jeffrey W. Bailey, and Craig Hovey, eds., *An Eerdmans Reader in Contemporary Political Theology* (Grand Rapids: Eerdmans, 2012).

17. Tranter has written a book-length critical engagement with O'Donovan's moral theology (the first of its kind), which, while incorporating discussion of O'Donovan's political theology, is not primarily focused on it. Samuel Tranter, *Oliver O'Donovan's Moral Theology: Tensions and Triumphs* (London: T&T Clark, 2020). Errington's recent book in Christian ethics includes a substantive critical engagement with O'Donovan's moral theology, which Like Tranter's, only makes occasional references to O'Donovan's political theology. Andrew Errington, *Every Good Path: Wisdom and Practical Reason in Christian Ethics and the Book of Proverbs* (London: T&T Clark, 2020).

Yoder.[18] This trend testifies to the level of interest O'Donovan's political theology has generated amongst Mennonite scholars and/or those sympathetic to Yoder's political theology, no doubt as a consequence of the implicit, and sometimes explicit, rebuttal of Yoder's political theology entailed in O'Donovan's.[19]

Like all significant thinkers, O'Donovan's thought has elicited both praise and criticism, often from the same voice.[20] Although criticisms of O'Donovan's political theology are substantial and widespread, they have generally tended to be tentative and somewhat inconclusive. Several reasons can be adduced for this tendency. Some respondents have probably found themselves reluctant to follow criticisms to their logical conclusions on account of their genuine respect and sympathy for O'Donovan and his project. Others might have found themselves reticent to make conclusive pronouncements on O'Donovan's subtle and complex thought within the confines of journal articles, the main vehicle for critical responses to date.

---

18. In addition to the aforementioned books, see also Travis Kroeker, "Why O'Donovan's Christendom Is Not Constantinian and Yoder's Voluntariety Is Not Hobbesian: A Debate in Theological Politics Re-defined," *The Annual of the Society of Christian Ethics* 20 (2000); Justin Neufeld, "Just War Theory, the Authorization of the State, and the Hermeneutics of Peoplehood: How John Howard Yoder Can Save Oliver O'Donovan from Himself," *International Journal of Systematic Theology* 8, no.4 (2006); Mike Mawson, "The Understandings of Christendom in Yoder and O'Donovan," *The New Zealand Journal of Christian Thought and Practice* 15, no.3 (2007); Dorothea Bertschmann, "The Rule of Christ and Human Politics—Two Proposals: A Comparison of the Political Theology of Oliver O'Donovan and John Howard Yoder," *The Heythrop Journal* 56, no.3 (2015); Phillips brings O'Donovan and Yoder into critical dialogue (*Political Theology*, 19–23).

19. In his interview with Rupert Shortt, O'Donovan said that "in *The Desire of the Nations* [he] took issue with the late John Howard Yoder." Oliver O'Donovan and Joan Lockwood O'Donovan with Rupert Shortt, "Political Theology," in *God's Advocates: Christian Thinkers in Conversation*, ed. Rupert Shortt (London: Darton, Longman and Todd, 2005), 255.

20. Neuhaus, for example, describes *Desire* as a "*tour de force* that nobody writing on political theology or the public nature of the Gospel can responsibly ignore," but then criticizes the book for "weakening ... the felt pressure of the eschatological horizon," contending that it suffers from a weak "punctiliar" ecclesiology: Neuhaus, "Commentary on *The Desire of the Nations*," 58, 61; Hauerwas and Fodor said of *Desire* that, "despite O'Donovan's failure to produce a consistent hermeneutical theory, he has nevertheless advanced important theological work and insight." Stanley Hauerwas and James Fodor, "Remaining in Babylon: Oliver O'Donovan's "Defense of Christendom," *Studies in Christian Ethics* 11, no.2 (1998): 43; Chaplin says: "While I part with some of O'Donovan's most fundamental claims, I believe that *DN* performs an invaluable service to those seeking to ground their Christian political reflections as deeply as possible in biblical and theological foundations and to avoid capitulation to secular modernity" ("Political Eschatology and Responsible Government," 265–6).

A further possible reason is O'Donovan's discursive style, which is liable to frustrate the best efforts to arrive at definitive judgments of his work. *Desire*, by way of example, contains a self-described "central thesis," namely, that "theology, by developing its account of the reign of God, may recover the ground traditionally held by the notion of authority."[21] But that thesis is enmeshed in a web of sub-theses and elaborated amidst wide-ranging discussions that at times do more to obscure than clarify the book's central thesis. Chaplin has surely spoken for many when he observed of *Desire* that "what the text says, with its dense prose and multiple, interlocking themes, is not obvious even after repeated readings."[22] The way that O'Donovan's discursive mind might have frustrated attempts by interlocutors to comprehensively and conclusively evaluate his work can be illustrated by the controversy over his alleged defense of Christendom in *Desire*.[23] O'Donovan's sympathetic account of Christendom—"Christendom is *response* to mission, and as such a sign that God has blessed it"—has been the subject of a number of critical essays.[24] Yet O'Donovan has expressed surprise at this critical focus on his reading of Christendom given what he describes as "its modest thesis," even describing it as "an afterthought."[25] To that end, he subsequently sought to clarify for critics that he does not, in fact, advocate a return to Christendom.[26] However, describing the chapter on Christendom (Chapter 6—"The Obedience of Rulers")

---

21. O'Donovan, *The Desire of the Nations*, 19.

22. Chaplin, "Political Eschatology and Responsible Government," 266.

23. In the preface to the paperback edition of *Desire* (1999) O'Donovan wryly observed that he "set out to discover the kingship of Christ, and ended up, as [he is] told, with a 'defence of Christendom,'" (preface to paperback edition of *The Desire of the Nations*, ix).

24. O'Donovan, *The Desire of the Nations*, 195. Emphasis original. For critical responses, see Arne Rasmusson, "Not All Justifications of Christendom Are Created Equal: A Response to Oliver O'Donovan," *Studies in Christian Ethics* 11, no.2 (1998); Hauerwas and Fodor, "Remaining in Babylon"; McIlroy, "The Right Reason for Caesar to Confess Christ as Lord"; Kroeker, "Why O'Donovan's Christendom Is Not Constantinian and Yoder's Voluntariety Is not Hobbesian."

25. O'Donovan, "Deliberation, History and Reading," 140. In an interview with Rupert Shortt conducted with wife Joan Lockwood O'Donovan, O'Donovan told Shortt that "some reviewers have suspected my interest in Christendom as carrying a hint of reactionary conservatism about it. As I say, I have no agenda for the restoration of Christendom, and cannot even conceive what such an agenda might look like if I were to have it." Oliver O'Donovan and Joan Lockwood O'Donovan, "Political Theology," in *God's Advocates: Christian Thinkers in Conversation*, ed. Rupert Shortt (London: Darton, Longman and Todd, 2005), 255.

26. Oliver O'Donovan, "Response to the Respondents: Behold, The Lamb!" *Studies in Christian Ethics* 11, no.2 (1998): 103. "I am puzzled, at any rate, by my readers' reluctance to take me at my word when I say that the important thing is not to be *for* Christendom or *against* it ... but to have such a sympathetic understanding of it that we profit from its politico-theological gains and avoid repeating its politico-theological mistakes [original emphasis]."

in a book with seven chapters as an "afterthought" is perhaps the epitome of English understatement. The final chapter, "The Redemption of Society," deals with the transition from Christendom to liberalism, in which case it would be accurate to say that two of the seven chapters of *Desire* deal substantively with the meaning and legacy of Christendom. Even so, O'Donovan makes a valid point with respect to the "modest thesis" of these chapters, for they do not advance his *theory* of political authority. That work is completed by the end of Chapter 4 (the fifth chapter deals with the status of the church in light of the normative conception of political authority developed in the first four chapters). This is why O'Donovan can characterize Chapter 6 as an "afterthought," given the book is, as Andrew Shanks rightly observed, "quite unambivalently focused on the political-theological issue of *authority*."[27]

Lorish and Mathewes have speculated that O'Donovan's impact has "perhaps [been] unduly limited by the impression of rebarbative indirectness and obliqueness that marks his prose."[28] Separately and more recently, Mathewes has described O'Donovan's prose as "intricate," "famously chewy," "dense," and "demanding a serious effort of decryption by the reader."[29] While judgments of this nature are unavoidably subjective, they do reflect something of a consensus about the difficulty of O'Donovan's prose. There is really no point in tip-toing around the issue; O'Donovan is "difficult," as no less than Rowan Williams has noted.[30] Or, as Lorish and Mathewes wryly put it, O'Donovan has never been accused of "writing too simplistically."[31] In fact, O'Donovan himself has conceded that some might find his English "too involved."[32] The widely acknowledged difficulty of O'Donovan's work might have frustrated, perhaps even deterred, some of O'Donovan's potential interlocutors from engaging his work more systematically, or even at all. Still, the density of O'Donovan's prose, a reflection of the density of his thought, has proved no impediment to him deservedly acquiring a reputation as one of the most important figures in contemporary Christian political theology. Moreover, as Williams, again, has rightly noted, O'Donovan's writing is "enriching" and provides extraordinary "stimulus ... for all who have engaged with it."[33]

---

27. Andrew Shanks, "Response to *The Desire of the Nations*," *Studies in Christian Ethics* 11, no.2 (1998): 86. Emphasis original.

28. Lorish and Mathewes, "Theology as Counsel," 721.

29. Charles Mathewes, "A Response to Oliver O'Donovan's *Ethics as Theology* Trilogy," *Modern Theology* 36, no.1 (2020): 165.

30. Rowan Williams, foreword to *The Authority of the Gospel*, viii.

31. Lorish and Mathewes, "Theology as Counsel," 721.

32. Oliver O'Donovan, *Resurrection and Moral Order: An Outline for Evangelical Ethics*, 2nd ed. (Grand Rapids: Eerdmans, 1994), ix.

33. Williams, foreword to *The Authority of the Gospel*, viii.

Theopolitical Influences

A full intellectual history of O'Donovan is beyond the scope of the present work. However, an embryonic intellectual history is offered here by way of further contextualizing his political theology and reception. I have restricted myself to the influences nominated by O'Donovan himself and those identified by his readers, which diverge in some interesting ways. A comprehensive and more critical evaluation of O'Donovan's intellectual influences properly awaits a systematic intellectual history, currently a gap in the scholarship on O'Donovan and something which would represent a valuable contribution in due course.

It is no secret that O'Donovan is deeply influenced by Augustine. In the preface to his first book, *The Problem of Self-Love in St. Augustine,* O'Donovan said that "to live with [Augustine] intermittently for ten years, to think, to pray, to preach, to teach under his tutelage, has been a life-shaping experience of which, I fear, the reader of this study will gain barely an idea."[34] O'Donovan has acknowledged that his account of government-as-judgment can "claim to speak from the Augustinian tradition."[35] And when asked in an interview to nominate "the best article or essay a young paster could read on politics," he suggested book XIX of *City of God.*[36]

Many scholars have noted the profound influence of Augustine on O'Donovan's political thought and his political theology is widely characterized as "Augustinian." William Cavanaugh places O'Donovan within a "current revival of Augustine's political thought" and Peter Leithart describes O'Donovan's political thought as a "revived Augustinian political theology."[37] Bretherton characterizes O'Donovan's political theology as a "self-conscious re-statement of Augustine" and Waters detects an "Augustinian framework" in it.[38] Stanley Hauerwas and James Fodor argue that "in order to understand (something) of O'Donovan's project, one has to be cognisant of the central importance of Augustine in his political theology."[39]

---

34. Oliver O'Donovan, *The Problem of Self-Love in St. Augustine* (Eugene, OR: Wipf & Stock, 1980), viii.

35. O'Donovan, "Judgment, Tradition and Reason: A Response," *Political Theology* 9, no.3 (2008): 396.

36. Center for Pastor Theologians, "SAET Interviews in Politics and Theology #5: Oliver O'Donovan," October 29, 2010, question 9, http://www.pastortheologians.com/saet-interviews-in-politics-and-theology-5-oliver-odonovan/.

37. Cavanaugh, *Migrations of the Holy*, 57; Peter J. Leithart, "Good Rule," in *The Cambridge Companion to Political Theology*, 269.

38. Luke Bretherton, "Introduction: Oliver O'Donovan's Political Theology and the Liberal Imperative," *Political Theology* 9, no.3 (2008): 267.; Brent Waters, "*The Desire of the Nations*: An Overview," *Studies in Christian Ethics* 11, no.2 (1998): 2.

39. Hauerwas and Fodor, "Remaining in Babylon," 39 (footnote 5).

And finally, McIlroy identifies six foundational propositions in O'Donovan's political theology that "derive" from Augustine.[40]

With the exception of Eric Gregory, however, none of O'Donovan's readers has attempted to locate him within wider currents of political Augustinianism. Gregory places O'Donovan within a category he calls "Augustinian liberalism," which in turn has three types. The type O'Donovan belongs to is said to have "emerge[d] in the 1990s, when suspicions about realism and Rawlsianism led to a revival of concepts of civic virtue." Gregory associates this form of Augustinian liberalism with the likes of Paul Tillich, Martin Luther King Jr, Paul Ramsey, and Gustavo Gutierrez.[41]

It is striking, however, just how infrequently *Desire* draws explicitly on Augustine given O'Donovan's own nomination of him as a profound influence and a similar observation on the part of many readers. One of the few explicit Augustinian debts is the concept of "dual authority," which O'Donovan attributes to Augustine's "two cities" motif.[42] O'Donovan, it must be said, is no romantic Augustinian. Despite his open sympathy for Augustine, O'Donovan reads him with a critical eye.[43] In an interview with Rupert Shortt, for instance, he indicated that he "can sympathise with what [Augustine] gets *wrong* as well as with what he gets right."[44] While there can

---

40. They are: 1. "The Church, not the political community, is the true society." 2. "Societies are united by their common objects of love … " 3. "Worship, including the ascription of ultimate worth, offered to that which is not God is worship of the demonic." 4. "There can be no right in a society that does not acknowledge the right of God." 5. "Government action is only justified when, in the absence of such action, wrong would be done … " 6. "Government may legitimately offer deliberate assistance to the church" ("The Right Reason for Caesar to Confess Christ as Lord," 301–2).

41. Eric Gregory, *Politics and the Order of Love: An Augustinian Ethic of Democratic Citizenship* (Chicago: University of Chicago Press, 2008), 1; Eric Gregory and Joseph Clair, "Augustinianisms and Thomisms," in *The Cambridge Companion to Political Theology*, ed. Craig Hovey and Elizabeth Phillips (Cambridge: Cambridge University Press, 2015), 10–12. Gregory does not give a name to the "type" of "Augustinian liberalism" to which O'Donovan is thought to belong. The second type is labelled "Augustinian realism" and the third type, like the first type, is not given a name, although it is associated with the work of John Rawls.

42. O'Donovan, *The Desire of the Nations*, 159. The lack of substantial and sustained engagement with Augustine in *Desire* reflects a general characteristic of the book, which is that it is fundamentally an exercise in biblical theology. It relies principally on exegesis of Scripture rather than the work of any political theorist or theologian, though thinkers in both categories are engaged in the extensive small print in-text notes. The book that is most clearly and explicitly indebted to the political thought of Augustine is Oliver O'Donovan, *Common Objects of Love: Moral Reflection and the Shaping of Community* (Grand Rapids: Eerdmans, 2002) in which O'Donovan develops an account of community from Augustine's understanding of community being formed by a people's "common objects of love."

43. For a critical engagement with Augustine's political theology, see Oliver O'Donovan, "The Political Thought of *City of God* 19," in *Bonds of Imperfection*.

44. Shortt, "Political Theology," 267. Emphasis mine.

be no doubt that O'Donovan's political theology is "Augustinian" in some sense, it is much more than a mere restatement of Augustine, and in that vein it is imperative that the Augustinian influence not be exaggerated.[45] O'Donovan's self-confessed Augustinianism must be read in conjunction with the additional influences identified below, some of which have not received due recognition in the secondary scholarship, leading perhaps to an overemphasis on the influence of Augustine. The Augustinian influence in O'Donovan's political theology is one area of O'Donovan scholarship that could do with more considered and subtle treatment, reinforcing the need for a proper systematic intellectual history of O'Donovan's thought in time.

After Augustine, Barth is the name most frequently associated with O'Donovan in the secondary literature. However, while many scholars have detected the influence of Barth in O'Donovan's political theology, there is little agreement about what that influence has been. Bretherton, who declares Barth a "key influence" in O'Donovan's political theology, has discerned "the faint trace of Barth's inner-outer ground duality in *Desire* ... as well as Barth's method ... of seeing political goods such as 'equality' as the corollary or analogy of Christological affirmations."[46] He has further suggested that O'Donovan has followed Barth in maintaining that "the relationship between theological and political conceptualisations of life together is not simply epistemological but ontological."[47] Travis Kroeker sees the "clear" influence of Barth's "anti-liberal and exegetical, apocalyptic messianism" in O'Donovan, while Bartholomew sees a "Barthian epistemology" in his work.[48] O'Donovan has acknowledged a debt to Barth—"a precise but important influence"—explaining that he learned from Barth "how the theological endeavour had to understand its intellectual responsibilities and its authority."[49] At one stage early in his career, O'Donovan said he "was in danger of being branded a Barthian" by colleagues.[50] O'Donovan offers this, admittedly enigmatic, verdict on Barth's political theology in *Desire*: "a magnificent, but incomplete, beckoning movement."[51]

---

45. O'Donovan has said, for example, that "one pillar of my account of government can admittedly claim no Augustinian parentage, and that is my view of government's representative status ... Its ancestry may be traced back in the first instance to St. Thomas" ("Judgment, Tradition and Reason," 396).

46. Bretherton, "Introduction," 267.

47. Luke Bretherton, "Coming to Judgment: Methodological Reflections on the Relationship between Ecclesiology, Ethnography and Political Theory," *Modern Theology* 28, no.2 (2012): 172.

48. Travis Kroeker, foreword to *Beyond Suspicion*, xiii; Craig G. Bartholomew, "A Time for War, and a Time for Peace: Old Testament Wisdom, Creation and O'Donovan's Theological Ethics," in *A Royal Priesthood?* 101.

49. Shortt, "Political Theology," 267.

50. Ibid.

51. O'Donovan, *The Desire of the Nations*, 286. O'Donovan thinks Barth correctly understood that the hope of the Christian community consists in a *polis* rather than an eternal church, but that he "fail[ed] to acknowledge the political character of the church itself" (*The Desire of the Nations*, 285).

In O'Donovan's own telling, he ultimately abandoned Barth's moral theology for that of Paul Ramsey, who was to become one of his seminal influences, his most important after, or perhaps alongside, Augustine.[52] In *Desire*, he describes Ramsey as the "teacher from whom, one other person apart, I have learned the most about the subjects dealt with in the book."[53] Elsewhere, O'Donovan has said that he had his "first introduction to Christian political thought through the teaching of … Ramsey."[54] He also credits Ramsey with helping him to find his "way back to the thinkers of the sixteenth and seventeenth century, which was a high period of Christian political thought."[55]

O'Donovan singles out Hugo Grotius from amongst the figures of this "high period" as someone he particularly "treasures."[56] He has said that his "enthusiasm" for Grotius strikes many as "rather eccentric."[57] Secondary scholarship, however, has not shown any substantive interest in the influence of Ramsey and Grotius on O'Donovan's political theology, in spite of his open indebtedness to the former and high regard for the latter.[58] In the case of Grotius, the silence in the secondary literature might, if anything, testify to the eccentricity of his interest.[59]

O'Donovan does not identify the other political "teacher" alongside Ramsey mentioned in *Desire*, but it may well be his wife Joan Lockwood O'Donovan (also a scholar and political theologian), whom he describes in the acknowledgments as "the most important intellectual influence" on that book.[60] He goes on to say that

---

52. Shortt, "Political Theology," 267. O'Donovan has written an essay that brings Barth's and Ramsey's political theologies into critical dialogue. Oliver O'Donovan, "Karl Barth and Paul Ramsey's 'Uses of Power,'" in *Bonds of Imperfection*. O'Donovan acknowledges a debt to Ramsey in the prefaces to both *The Problem of Self-Love in St. Augustine*, vii and Oliver O'Donovan, *Peace and Certainty: A Theological Essay on Deterrence* (Grand Rapids: Eerdmans, 1989), viii.

53. O'Donovan, *The Desire of the Nations*, 20.

54. Center for Pastor Theology, "SAET Interviews in Politics and Theology," question 3.

55. Ibid.

56. Ibid. O'Donovan has written an essay on Grotius. Oliver O'Donovan, "The Justice of Assignment and Subjective Rights in Grotius," in *Bonds of Imperfection*.

57. Shortt, "Political Theology," 267. In another interview, O'Donovan named Ramsey and Grotius when asked to identify "two influential thinkers" to whom he responds in his political theology. Center for Pastor Theology, "SAET Interviews in Politics and Theology," question 3.

58. For a rare exception, see Feiler, "From Dialectics to Theo-Logic," *Studies in Christian Ethics* 28, no.3 (2015). This essay, as the title suggests, is focused on Ramsey and O'Donovan's Just War theories rather than their view of political authority.

59. O'Donovan has indicated that "much of [his] preferred reading has been in older texts—almost any generation but our own," which may help clarify the Grotius interest. Eerdword: the Eerdmans blog, "Five Questions with Oliver O'Donovan," March 17, 2015, http://eerdword.com/2015/03/17/five-questions-with-oliver-odonovan/, question 5.

60. O'Donovan, *The Desire of the Nations*, xii. O'Donovan also appears to suggest in the acknowledgments that Hobbes' *Leviathan* had a profound impact on his thinking as he wrote *Desire*, although there are only five references to Hobbes in the index, xi.

Joan "opened up questions I never knew were there, and [her] careful interpretive skills unravelled questions I never thought I could understand."[61] Bretherton has observed that "the O'Donovan project," as he dubs it, is "developed in close collaboration with ... wife Joan Lockwood O'Donovan."[62]

Bretherton and Chaplin have both identified Canadian philosopher George Grant as an influence on O'Donovan's political theology.[63] Neither elaborates as to the precise nature of this perceived influence and no other scholar has discerned or noted a Grant connection. However, it is perhaps significant that Joan "came under the influence" of Grant at one stage, as she describes it.[64] O'Donovan has not publicly nominated Grant as one of his influences and Grant's work is cited only a handful of times in *Desire*.

A curiously under-analyzed aspect of O'Donovan's thought is his evangelicalism. O'Donovan is a first-generation Anglican, having Roman Catholic relatives on one side of the family and Methodists on the other[65] As he explained in his interview with Shortt, he "found ... [his] ... way into the Church of England" in childhood and "received ... catechesis there in an Evangelical context," something for which he is grateful.[66] O'Donovan's evangelicalism manifests, in his own words, in a commitment to "the Scriptures as the norm of all theology" and "a central emphasis on the atoning death of Christ."[67] These evangelical convictions suffuse O'Donovan's political theology, which seeks to identify a normative conception of political authority authorized from Scripture and which is thoroughly "Christocentric" in nature.[68]

In light of O'Donovan's evident comfort with the moniker "evangelical"—he appears in the volume *Evangelical Anglicans*, after all—it is striking just how little he talks about it in his work.[69] The term "evangelical" is recurring, but always has

---

61. Ibid., xi. Unpicking the influence of Joan on Oliver's theology of political authority ideally requires a joint interview as she is not explicitly credited with any of the key ideas in *Desire*, although judging by the acknowledgments she was profoundly influential. Joan, like Oliver, has written on political authority and in such a way that displays great convergence of thought. See, for example, Joan Lockwood O'Donovan, *Theology of Law and Authority in the English Reformation* (Atlanta: Scholars Press, 1991); and Joan Lockwood O'Donovan, "Subsidiarity and Political Authority in Theological Perspective," in *Bonds of Imperfection*.

62. Bretherton, "Introduction," 266.

63. Ibid., 267; Chaplin, "Political Eschatology and Responsible Government," 266.

64. Shortt, "Political Theology," 252.

65. Ibid., 265. The fact that one side of O'Donovan's family is Catholic might be relevant to his "philo-Catholic" Protestantism.

66. Ibid.

67. Ibid.

68. It is probably more than coincidence that O'Donovan's political mentor Ramsey wrote that "Christian political theory must be decisively and entirely Christocentric." Paul Ramsey, *Basic Christian Ethics* (Louisville: Westminster John Knox Press, 1993), 17.

69. Oliver O'Donovan, "Evangelicalism and the Foundation of Ethics," in *Evangelical Anglicans: Their Role and Influence in the Church Today*, ed. R. T. France and A. E. McGrath (London: SPCK, 1993).

the sense of "proclamation"[70] rather than the interdenominational movement famously defined by Bebbington as "conversionism, activism, biblicism and crucicentrism."[71] It is noteworthy that the secondary literature on O'Donovan has barely noted, let alone discussed, his evangelicalism, though this might simply reflect the fact that O'Donovan makes so little of it in his published work.

O'Donovan is best characterized as a quiet, ecumenical evangelical. He does not reject the descriptor "evangelical," and nor do his writings exhibit any concern with promoting or defending evangelical orthodoxy, particularly in relation to sectarian theological and political debates. Nor does he write exclusively *to* or *for* evangelicals. Eminent evangelical scholar Mark Noll has observed that the term "evangelical" is "plastic."[72] So while it is possible to describe O'Donovan as an "evangelical" theologian without controversy, that appellation only reveals so much in the absence of further qualification. Much like the case with O'Donovan's Augustinianism, his evangelicalism is an area of influence that warrants a much more thorough analysis than is possible here, or than currently exists.

Some Anglican theologians have described O'Donovan as "reformed," rather than "evangelical." Williams, for example, locates O'Donovan in the tradition of "classical Reformed divinity which, like Calvin's own thinking, is imbued with the insights of the patristic age as well as the result of painstaking scriptural exegesis."[73] Timothy Gorringe discerns "three styles of Anglican political thought" and identifies O'Donovan as a modern representative of the "Reformed" style ("Broad Church" and "Anglo Catholic" are the other two).[74] This, according to Gorringe, places O'Donovan within the tradition that traces its origins to Richard Hooker via S.T. Coleridge and F.D. Maurice.[75] Interestingly, Gorringe suggests that "the evangelical wing" of the Anglican Church could represent a fourth and different style.[76]

---

70. See, for example, O'Donovan, *Resurrection and Moral Order*, 11; O'Donovan, *Self, World, and Time: Ethics as Theology Volume 1* (Grand Rapids: Eerdmans, 2013), 91; and Oliver O'Donovan, *Finding and Seeking: Ethics as Theology Volume 2* (Grand Rapids: Eerdmans, 2014), 2.

71. Timothy Larsen, "Defining and Locating Evangelicalism," in *The Cambridge Companion to Evangelical Theology*, ed. Timothy Larsen and Daniel J. Treier (Cambridge: Cambridge University Press, 2007), 1. Larsen says that "no other definition comes close to rivalling its [Bebbington's] level of general acceptance." Bebbington's definition first appeared in David W. Bebbington, *Evangelicalism in Modern Britain: A History from the 1730s to the 1980s* (London: Unwin Hyman, 1989).

72. Mark A. Noll. *Between Faith and Criticism: Evangelicals, Scholarship, and the Bible in America*, 2nd ed. (Grand Rapids: Baker Book House, 1991), 1.

73. Williams, foreword to *The Authority of the Gospels*, vii. O'Donovan's "philo-Catholicism" is a sharp point of difference with Calvin though.

74. Timothy Gorringe, "Anglican Political Thought," *The Expository Times* 124, no.3 (2012): 105, 107.

75. Ibid.

76. Ibid. Contrast this, however, with O'Donovan's statement to Shortt that he received catechesis in an "Evangelical context" ("Political Theology," 267).

Another important influence on O'Donovan's political theology, one which has received no attention in secondary scholarship, is Catholic tradition.[77] O'Donovan describes the period 1100–1650 as the "High Tradition" of Christian political thought.[78] This gives O'Donovan what can be described aptly as a "philo-Catholic" disposition toward Christian history and theology.[79] This philo-Catholicism is the product of a sensitive ecumenism that pervades his work, which liberally and approvingly draws on the insights of catholic medieval political thinkers in a way that is rare in many evangelical circles. I made reference above to O'Donovan's sympathetic account of Christendom in *Desire* and the controversy this generated for some Protestant critics. O'Donovan has gone so far as to state that he "believe[s] in the authority of Catholic tradition and though [he] will not restrict its exercise to its Roman representatives, [he is] grateful for the contribution Roman tradition has made to maintaining it."[80] O'Donovan also recounts an anecdote that testifies to his "philo-Catholic" ecumenism. While teaching a course on the Thirty Nine Articles of Religion of the Church of England in Toronto in the 1980s, he invited Catholic colleague George Schner to attend the class and provide a Catholic response to each article.[81] He has even quipped that he "learned how to read Karl Barth from a Jesuit."[82]

The question of the provenance of this "philo-Catholicism" is something properly left to an intellectual history of O'Donovan. He has said that he is "deeply thankful to have been born in a generation of ecumenical progress," and that his time teaching in Canada in the late 1970s and early 1980s "exposed [him] for the first time to intensive interaction with Roman Catholic theologians," an interaction he found very fruitful.[83] It is also probably worth noting that his PhD supervisor at Oxford, Henry Chadwick, was a prominent figure in Anglican-Catholic ecumenical

77. Westberg is a rare exception. Commenting on O'Donovan's moral theology, he notes that "Oliver O'Donovan, as an Anglican, provides a clear model (and challenge) in keeping before us the call to be evangelical and Christocentric, but at the same time to have the patience to work through the detail of practical reasoning and analysis of action associated with Roman Catholic ethics," Daniel A. Westberg, *Renewing Moral Theology: Christian Ethics as Action, Character and Grace* (Downers Grove, IL: IVP Academic, 2015), 27–8.

78. O'Donovan, *The Desire of the Nations*, 4; In *Judgment*, O'Donovan refers to this period specifically as a "high period of political theology" (*The Ways of Judgment*, 168); He has lamented the "ignorance" of this High Tradition characteristic of so much contemporary political theology in Oliver O'Donovan, "Political Theology, Tradition, and Modernity," in *The Cambridge Companion to Liberation Theology*, ed. Christopher Rowland (Cambridge: Cambridge University Press, 2007), 235.

79. I have coined this term by analogy with the Greek term "φιλορθόδοξος" (philorthodoxos), which denotes a non-Orthodox Christian who is favorably disposed to Orthodox theology and tradition.

80. O'Donovan, "Judgment, Tradition and Reason," 404.
81. Ibid., 10.
82. Shortt, "Political Theology," 265.
83. Ibid.

rapprochement in the second half of the twentieth century.[84] O'Donovan's work on Augustine also appears to have contributed to his "philo-Catholic" ecumenism. He regards Augustine as "a crucial focus for Western ecumenism" because "his influence has been so great both on Catholics and Protestants."[85] It might also have something to do with the influence of his wife Joan, who could also be described aptly as "philo-Catholic." She has explained that her "Catholic leanings are towards a medieval tradition of Christocentric Platonic 'realism'" and has opined that "contemporary Roman Catholicism has the unequalled pedagogical tool of the papal encyclical for renewing the theological framework of political thought," adding that they "deserve to be used more extensively by other Churches than they have been."[86]

O'Donovan's "philo-Catholicism" is one aspect of his theology that qualifies his evangelicalism, and in ways that make it difficult to comfortably fit him into some current definitions of the movement. Timothy Larsen, for example, has provided an updated version of Bebbington's famous "quadrilateral" that locates the origins of evangelicalism in "the cross-pollinating revivalistic and evangelistic atmosphere of Britain and North America in the 1730s."[87] But O'Donovan identifies the period 1100–1650 as the "High Christian tradition" and it is this tradition, along with Augustine, that does so much to inform his theology of political authority.[88]

The task of explaining the complex ways in which Augustine, Barth, Ramsey, Grotius, Joan Lockwood O'Donovan, medieval Catholic tradition, and Anglican evangelicalism interact and shape the thought of O'Donovan is properly left to a systematic and detailed intellectual history. But two pertinent observations can be made here. In the first place, it is a rather eclectic set of influences, making it difficult to classify O'Donovan comfortably within existing theological taxonomies. This eclecticism might go a long way to explaining his idiosyncrasy, but also the difficulty of trying to locate him within any existing tradition or current of thought. The other side of eclecticism is originality. The truth is that O'Donovan is one of the most original and creative theological minds of his generation. Thus, while many and varied influences can be identified, some nominated by O'Donovan himself, the fact remains that many of O'Donovan's most important insights are actually the product of ingenuity, albeit an ingenuity informed by an impressive depth and breadth of reading.

---

84. Rowan Williams, "Obituary: Henry Chadwick," *The Guardian*, June 19, 2008, https://www.theguardian.com/world/2008/jun/19/religion; G. R. Evans, "Henry Chadwick," in *Key Theological Thinkers: From Modern to Postmodern*, ed. Staale Johannes Kristiansen and Svein Rise (Surrey: Ashgate, 2012), 477.

85. Shortt, "Political Theology," 267. If Augustine helped pave the way to O'Donovan's "philo-Catholic" ecumenism, then he might also explain the commensurate lack of interest in or engagement with the Orthodox tradition given Augustine's thought and legacy has been a source of deep conflict between the East and West.

86. Ibid., 265–6.

87. Larsen, "Defining and Locating Evangelicalism," 5.

88. Note also that Oliver and Joan's tour de force *From Irenaeus to Grotius* covers the period 100–1625. Oliver O'Donovan and Joan Lockwood O'Donovan, eds., *From Irenaeus to Grotius: A Sourcebook in Christian Political Thought 100–1625* (Grand Rapids: Eerdmans, 1999).

Chapter 2

GOVERNMENT-AS-JUDGMENT: AN EXPOSITION OF O'DONOVAN'S THEOLOGY OF POLITICAL AUTHORITY

A project of this nature of necessity must begin with an exposition of the material to be critically evaluated, in this case O'Donovan's theology of political authority. Scholars who have responded to O'Donovan's work have noted the challenge of summarizing his arguments without doing injustice to their "thick," "dense," and "rich" composition.[1] As such, it is necessary to provide a sufficiently detailed exposition to ensure that the arguments critically evaluated in the following chapters are set out fully and accurately. Readers well-versed in O'Donovan's political theology may wish to proceed directly to the critical discussion that begins in Chapter 3.

The ensuing exposition is primarily based on the account of political authority offered in O'Donovan's aforementioned seminal works *Desire* and *Judgment*. It begins, however, with an earlier book, *Resurrection and Moral Order: An Outline for Evangelical Ethics* (hereafter *Resurrection*). I begin with *Resurrection* because chronologically it constitutes O'Donovan's first, albeit brief, foray into the topic of political authority. It also foreshadows some of the central ideas given fuller development in *Desire* and *Judgment*. Finally, it provides insights that I will draw on in subsequent chapters to resolve some of the tensions and problems I will identify in the theological account of political authority provided in *Desire* and *Judgment*. Other works in the O'Donovan corpus touch on the question of political authority, but not in such a way that either rivals the level of detail provided in *Desire* and *Judgment*, or that significantly alters the account of political authority provided therein. While not included in the exposition below, such works will be drawn into the discussion in subsequent chapters as required.

---

1. Neuhaus, "Commentary on *The Desire of the Nations*," 77. Doerksen attributes the difficulty of summarizing O'Donovan's arguments to "the richly nuanced structure and content" of the work ("Christology in the Political Theology of Oliver O'Donovan," 436). Tranter puts the "challenge" of responding to O'Donovan's arguments accurately and fairly down to what he describes as O'Donovan's "dialectical argumentation" (*Oliver O'Donovan's Moral Theology*, 12).

Resurrection and Moral Order (1986)

Resurrection is divided into three parts: Part 1—"The objective reality," Part 2—"The subjective reality," and Part 3—"The form of the moral life." A large portion of Part 2 is devoted to the issue of "authority," and it is within this context that O'Donovan's first discussion of political authority emerges.[2] Authority is defined as "something which, by virtue of its kind, constitutes an immediate and sufficient ground for acting."[3] In short, authority is what makes human action meaningful and intelligible.[4] The concept of authority is integral to morality, according to O'Donovan, because it forms the grounds for humankind's proper participation in the moral order through Christ's redemption. Christ's resurrection redeems the place of men and women in the created order, allowing them to "subject" themselves to "God's order" and to assume once again "the place of dominion which God assigned to Adam."[5]

O'Donovan argues that authorities are "natural" in the sense that they derive their authority from the fact that they are grounded in the created order. O'Donovan provides three archetypical examples of natural authorities in this regard: beauty, community, and truth.[6] As O'Donovan explains, listening to music, joining a club, and reading philosophy are self-explanatory grounds for action that are immediately intelligible.[7] Their intelligibility derives from their existence as "aspect[s] of the teleological structure of the universe."[8]

Humans are able to "evoke free action" in other human beings by virtue of their possession of naturally endowed authority.[9] In fact, "many characteristic features of human society arise because some human beings have this authority to evoke human action."[10] O'Donovan provides several illustrations of this principle: "the young accept the recommendations of their elders," "those who have physical beauty or charm of speech influence other people," "forceful personalities gather a following," "widely-held opinions are more likely to win new adherents than those held by only a few," and "customary practices are maintained because they are customary."[11]

---

2. O'Donovan's understanding of "authority," which is central to his moral theology, has generated less interest than his work on political authority. For a recent exception, see Errington, "Authority and Reality in the Work of Oliver O'Donovan."

3. O'Donovan, *Resurrection and Moral Order*, 122.

4. Ibid. This is a theme to which I return in due course as it proves to be vital to resolving a significant problem in O'Donovan's theology of political authority as it is propounded in *Desire/Judgment*.

5. Ibid., 24.
6. Ibid., 122.
7. Ibid.
8. Ibid.
9. Ibid., 124.
10. Ibid.
11. Ibid.

2. Government-as-Judgment

Chapter 6, called "Authority," contains a four-page self-titled discussion of political authority that is introduced by O'Donovan as a "digression."[12] It is in this "digression" that O'Donovan ventures a first definition of political authority:

> The distinctive form of authority which we call 'political' is, then, at its simplest, a concurrence of the natural authorities of might and tradition with that other 'relatively natural' authority, the authority of injured right. When these three authorities are exercised together by one subject, then they are endorsed by a moral authority which requires that we defer to them.[13]

Might and tradition derive their natural authority from their "strength" and "age," respectively.[14] Injured right relates to the "righting of wrongs" and is described as "relatively natural" because it "belongs to the natural order as it is encountered under the conditions brought about by Adam's sin."[15] O'Donovan explains that these authorities are "exercised together" when "might" and "tradition" are placed at the "disposal" of "injured right."[16] Thus, the three constitutive authorities that together make up political authority operate in something of a teleological hierarchy: the function of might and tradition is to redress injured right, i.e., to effect justice. "For justice," O'Donovan maintains, "in the relative sense in which it is appropriate to speak of it in human communities, can be realised only by this triad of authorities in combination."[17] Justice therefore constitutes the purpose of political authority.

O'Donovan further says that "we should not only obey an institution which unites these three authorities in itself, but we should make every effort to sustain it."[18] The political task of a community, society, or nation, then, is to establish and sustain institutions which allow political authority to function in the way outlined in the definition above—might and tradition supporting injured right—for the purposes of realizing justice. It will become clear in subsequent work that O'Donovan believes that a range of institutional and legal arrangements can achieve this end.

O'Donovan emphasizes the "relative" nature of the justice effected by political authority by drawing a distinction between the options available to the individual moral agent, in the sense of a private citizen, on the one hand, and the political leader as a public moral agent, on the other.[19] The latter, unlike the former, is "constrained by the limited possibilities for action in the public sphere," limitations that emerge as a consequence of the public moral agent's dependence on tradition and might, which imposes an obligation "not to strain those possibilities to their

---

12. Ibid., 127.
13. Ibid., 128.
14. Ibid., 127.
15. Ibid., 124.
16. Ibid., 128.
17. Ibid., 129.
18. Ibid.
19. Ibid., 130.

breaking-point."[20] As such, "even at its best, public right action can bear only an indirect relation to the demands of truth and goodness considered absolutely."[21] The fallen context in which humans must exercise political authority (the coordination of might and tradition in support of injured right in a single subject) in aid of justice entails "the search for a compromise which, while bearing the fullest witness to the truth that can in the circumstances be borne, will, nevertheless, lie within the scope of possible public action in the particular community of fallen men which it has to serve."[22]

The Desire of the Nations (1996)

Desire develops an elaborate theological account of political authority, which is then used to interpret Western political history, and in particular to critique "late-modern liberalism."[23] As indicated earlier, its "central thesis" is that "theology, by developing its account of the reign of God, may recover the ground traditionally held by the notion of authority."[24] O'Donovan maintains that the notion of authority became unintelligible in the late-modern period, and along with it "the idea of political activity as kingly," on account of the fateful separation of politics and theology.[25] He contends that recapturing the "theological horizon" of politics, one which situates human politics "within the history of God's reign," can restore political authority's lost intelligibility.[26]

In particular, O'Donovan believes that an account of politics that begins with the concept of divine rule can restore three critical elements that have disappeared from contemporary political thought: (1) it can "safeguard and redeem the goods of creation"; (2) "strip away the institutional fashions with which the Western ... tradition has clothed the idea of authority"; and (3) recapture the history of Israel as "revealed history" and the "measure" of "our understanding of general and universal history."[27] *Desire* is therefore fundamentally a project of retrieval.[28] By returning to Scripture, the history of Israel and what O'Donovan terms the "High Tradition" of Christian political thought (1100–1650), political theology can revive the notion that political authority performs a vital service within the history of God's rule.[29]

20. Ibid.
21. Ibid.
22. Ibid.
23. Schweiker, "Freedom and Authority in Political Theology," 111. Schweiker has observed that "even a cursory look at *The Desire of the Nations* shows that its central concern is with the question of authority."
24. O'Donovan, *The Desire of the Nations*, 19.
25. Ibid.
26. Ibid., 6, 19.
27. Ibid., 19–21.
28. Doerksen has observed that O'Donovan's "historical project is one of retrieval of the Christian tradition" (*Beyond Suspicion*, 129).
29. O'Donovan, *The Desire of the Nations*, 4.

2. Government-as-Judgment

If *Desire* is fundamentally a work of retrieval from the High Christian tradition, it is also fundamentally an exercise in biblical theology. Political theology, in O'Donovan's view, only arises as both possibility and necessity by virtue of the correspondence—grounded in reality—that exists between the "political vocabulary of salvation" and secular political vocabulary.[30] At the heart of this correspondence are political terms such as "king" and "judge," both of which are central to the political theology O'Donovan develops in *Desire*.[31] What gives form in reality to the conceptual correspondence in question is the "political act."[32] The political act is a "divinely authorized" human act that "witnesses faithfully to the presence and future of what God has undertaken for all."[33] Terms such as "king" and "judge" therefore correspond in reality to the extent that they reference acts, both divine and human, which occur "within the one public history which is the theatre of god's saving purposes and mankind's social undertakings."[34] A central task of political theology, then, is to "understand how and why God's rule confers authority upon human political acts," something O'Donovan hopes to achieve in *Desire*.[35] As a consequence of the conceptual correspondence between the political vocabulary of salvation and the vocabulary of the human political act, O'Donovan believes that theology can be regarded as "political simply by responding to the dynamics of its own proper themes."[36] It is impossible to talk about "Christ," "salvation," "the church," or "the Trinity," he maintains, without speaking also about society, or indeed, without developing "normative political ends."[37] The goal of political theology is not to reduce speech about the acts of God to "commonplace political discussion," but rather to expand the semantic field of secular political speech by opening it to the activity of God.[38]

This explains why O'Donovan also characterizes political theology as an "exegetical task."[39] But more than mere conceptual analysis is required in this regard. Political theology must contend with "the Scriptures in their entirety."[40] It

---

30. Ibid., 2. "Secular," in the context of O'Donovan's political theology, always has a temporal sense, that is, the present age, and is contrasted with "eternal" (211).

31. Ibid., other such terms include, according to O'Donovan, "kingdom," "deliver," "servants," "numbered," "saints," and "glory."

32. Ibid., 20.

33. Ibid.

34. Ibid., 2.

35. Ibid., 20.

36. Ibid., 3.

37. Ibid.

38. Ibid., 2. This is an inversion, or perhaps reversal, of Carl Schmitt's famous argument that "all significant concepts of the modern theory of the state are secularized theological concepts," Carl Schmitt, *Political Theology: Four Chapters on the Concept of Sovereignty*, trans and introduction George Schwab, foreword by Tracy B. Strong (Chicago: University of Chicago Press, 2005), 36.

39. Ibid., 15–16. Moberly maintains that "the whole book [*Desire*] is an exposition and application of Scripture—in conjunction with a robust sense of tradition." R. W. L. Moberly, "The Use of Scripture in *The Desire of the Nations*," in *A Royal Priesthood?* 46.

40. O'Donovan, *The Desire of the Nations*, 22.

cannot lay its foundation merely in several cherished texts, a key failing of political theology (liberation theology, in particular) in the twentieth century: "Political theology grew weaker as [its] exegetical foundations shrank."[41] "If the Scriptures are to be read as a proclamation, not merely as a mine for random sociological analogies dug out from the ancient world," O'Donovan contends, "then a unifying conceptual structure is necessary that will connect political themes with the history of salvation as a whole."[42] Connecting Scripture's political themes with the history of salvation as a whole requires an "architectonic hermeneutic," and it is "salvation-history" that serves as *Desire*'s architectonic hermeneutic: Scripture is to be read as the authoritative testimony of God's salvific acts in history.[43] O'Donovan's emphasis on understanding human political history through the lens of God's divine rule, and on Scripture as testimony to God's saving acts in history, makes history the integral framework within which his political theology is developed. Thus, in addition to political theology being an exegetical task, it is also a historical task. Indeed, O'Donovan has characterized *Desire* as a "historico-theological" exploration of God's kingship.[44]

A Christian account of the reign of God begins with Israel's political categories, according to O'Donovan.[45] "Israel's knowledge of God's blessing was," he avers, "from beginning to end, a political knowledge and it was out of that knowledge that the evangelists and apostles spoke about Jesus."[46] The biblical political concept that stands as the cornerstone in the unified conceptual structure of which O'Donovan is in pursuit is "divine kingship," as expressed in the refrain *Yhwh mālak* found in the "enthronement psalms" (93, 97, and 99 specifically).[47] O'Donovan describes these Psalms as the "leading texts" for an exposition of the concept of divine kingship.

O'Donovan identifies three terms "habitually grouped" with Yhwh's kingship: salvation, judgment, and possession.[48] These each correspond to one or more Hebrew terms in Scripture.[49] There is actually a fourth concept, "praise," which, O'Donovan explains, is not constitutive of kingly rule in the way that the aforementioned three are.[50] Praise, rather, provides "demonstrative proof" of

41. Ibid.
42. Ibid.
43. Ibid.
44. O'Donovan, "Response to the Respondents," 92. Hauerwas and Fodor have described *Desire* as "historical theology" ("Remaining in Babylon," 31).
45. O'Donovan, *The Desire of the Nations*, 22. Emphasis mine.
46. Ibid., 123.
47. Ibid., 33–4. O'Donovan has suggested that "*Yhwh malak*" is best translated as "Yhwh has exerted his rule" or "has proved his royal authority." Goldingay gives the following translation: "Yahweh has succeeded to the kingship and reigns in the present." John Goldingay, *Psalms: Volume 3; Psalms 90–150* (Grand Rapids: Baker Academic, 2008), 67.
48. O'Donovan, *The Desire of the Nations*, 36.
49. Ibid., 36–41. The corresponding Hebrew terms are $y^e sh\bar{u}^c\bar{a}h$ (salvation), $tsedeq'$ and $mishp\bar{a}t$ (judgment), and $nah^al\bar{a}h$ and $\d{h}\bar{e}leq$ (possession).
50. Ibid., 47.

kingship.[51] In reality, praise plays no significant role in O'Donovan's theology of political authority and as a consequence it is not discussed here further.

"Salvation" is understood as the establishment of God's kingship through his deliverance of "his people from peril in conflict with their enemies."[52] The paradigmatic instance of this salvation is the Exodus, the miraculous and providential deliverance of the Hebrew people from their bondage. However, O'Donovan contends that the primary political implication of salvation is "Israel's power to win military engagements."[53] "Judgment" denotes making a "distinction between the just and the unjust" and bringing this distinction into "the daylight of public observation."[54] Judgment in the Old Testament is an "activity" rather than a "state of affairs that obtains."[55] "Possession" relates to the law as a tradition handed down through the generations. It is the means by which "the judgments of God … give order and structure to a community and sustain it in being."[56] Possession also relates to land, though this is of secondary importance on O'Donovan's account.[57] "Possessing the land," he explains, "was a matter of observing that order of life which was established by Yhwh's judgments."[58] These three "affirmations"—salvation, judgment, and possession—forge Israel's distinctive political identity and give meaning to the idea of God's divine kingship over Israel: "Yhwh's authority as king is established by the accomplishment of victorious deliverance, by the presence of judicial discrimination and by the continuity of a community-possession."[59]

O'Donovan then uses this conceptual triad to "provide a framework for exploring the major questions about authority posed by the Western tradition."[60] For God's kingship over Israel, O'Donovan maintains, "can be seen as a point of disclosure from which the nature of all political authority comes into view."[61] O'Donovan's analysis of the concepts associated with divine kingship in Scripture (salvation, judgment, and possession) produce six theorems of political authority, the first two of which are:

Theorem 1—Political authority arises where power, the execution of right and the perpetuation of tradition are assured together in one coordinated agency.[62]

---

51. Ibid., 113.
52. Ibid., 36.
53. Ibid.
54. Ibid., 38.
55. Ibid., 39.
56. Ibid., 41.
57. Ibid.
58. Ibid.
59. Ibid., 36.
60. Ibid., 45.
61. Ibid.
62. Ibid., 46.

Theorem 2—That any regime should actually come to hold authority, and should continue to hold it, is a work of divine providence in history, not a mere accomplishment of the human task of political service.[63]

Theorems 3–6 emerge at various intervals in a lengthy discussion of divine kingship in the Old Testament.[64] But they play no significant role in the further development of O'Donovan's theory of political authority. They are not repeated, nor referred to subsequently, either in *Desire* or in any other book. The only significant element to emerge from amongst these theorems is the first part of Theorem 4: "The authority of a human regime mediates divine authority."[65] The place of the six theorems in O'Donovan's theology of political authority has understandably perplexed some readers.[66] O'Donovan does provide an explanation of sorts regarding the status of the theorems, although that explanation strays perilously close to the "rebarbative indirectness and obliqueness" of which Lorish and Mathewes charge him.[67] He explains that "the six general theorems ... drawn from Israel's political experience provide an outline of what theology may need to put in the place traditionally held by a notion of political authority."[68] He further explains that in the theorems he has "abstract[ed] from Israel's experience a general understanding of what the divine rule is which is to be the subject of the proclamation [of an evangelical political theology]."[69]

O'Donovan then shifts focus to the New Testament where the Christ-event (advent, passion, restoration, and exaltation) marks a seminal transition in the function of political authority in human history.[70] According to O'Donovan,

63. Ibid.
64. **Theorem 3**—In acknowledging political authority, society proves its political identity. **Theorem 4**—The authority of a human regime mediates divine authority in a unitary structure, but is subject to the authority of law within the community, which bears independent witness to the divine command. **Theorem 5**—The appropriate unifying element in international order is law rather than government. **Theorem 6**—The conscience of the individual member of a community is a repository of the moral understanding which shaped it, and may serve to perpetuate it in a crisis of collapsing morale or institution (*The Desire of the Nations*, 47, 65, 72, 80).
65. Ibid., 65.
66. Chaplin, for example, has said of the theorems that "their hermeneutical status and conceptual connection remain unclear" ("Political Eschatology and Responsible Government," 299, footnote 138). Hauerwas and Fodor have opined that they produce "a rather complex formal configuration" which appears to blur the distinction between exegesis and theory ("Remaining in Babylon," 37). For Doerksen, the link between the theorems and the "exegetical work" lacks clarity (*Beyond Suspicion*, 59–60).
67. Lorish and Mathewes, "Theology as Counsel," 721.
68. O'Donovan, *The Desire of the Nations*, 80–1.
69. Ibid., 81. "Evangelical" here has the sense of proclamation.
70. Hauerwas and Fodor found the transition from the Old Testament to the New Testament confusing ("Remaining in Babylon," 37), as did Doerksen (*Beyond Suspicion*, 59–60).

Jesus "stands at the moment of transition between the ages where the passing and coming authorities confront one another."[71] This transition is characterized by both continuity and discontinuity with respect to the function of political authority in salvation-history.

O'Donovan argues that the concept of divine kingship that was so "fundamental to Israel's political self-awareness" was also fundamental to "Jesus' proclamation of the fullness of time."[72] This is most evident in Christ's role as the fulfillment of Israel's hopes for a new king in the line of David.[73] "The ascended Christ," he writes, "takes his throne, as the Davidide monarch was summoned to do in the ancient psalm (2:1)."[74] But O'Donovan is also cognizant of discontinuity between the political categories of Israel, as he exegetes them, and their relevance and application to the Christ-event. On the basis of his exegesis of Rom. 13:1–7, he argues that the Christ-event results in what he calls the "re-authorization" of political authority (also articulated as "reconception" and "refashioning") such that judgment (the execution of right) becomes the sole function of secular political authority in the present age.[75] As he explains,

> secular authorities are no longer in the fullest sense mediators of the rule of God. They mediate his judgments only ... No government has a right to exist, no nation has a right to defend itself. Such claims are overwhelmed by the immediate claim of the Kingdom. There remains simply the rump of political authority which cannot be dispensed with yet, the exercise of judgment.[76]

O'Donovan explains this significant change in the function and purpose of political authority through the distinction between *esse* and *bene esse*. The coordination of power, the execution of right and the perpetuation of tradition in one coordinated agency remains unchanged as the *esse* of political authority in the wake of the Christ-event. Judgment, however, becomes the new *bene esse* of political authority as a consequence of Christ's triumph over the nations:

> The subjection of all authorities to Christ's authority does not mean the dissolution of authority. The conjunction of power, judgment and tradition defines what political authority *is* ... Power and community tradition are still essential to establish authority; the new development is that they are subordinated to just judgment as means to an end.[77]

71. O'Donovan, *The Desire of the Nations*, 158.
72. Ibid., 32. Recall that O'Donovan has already developed a conception of political authority from his analysis of "political terms" associated with divine kingship in the Old Testament (Theorem 1): "political authority arises where power, the execution of right and the perpetuation of tradition are assured together in one coordinated agency" (46).
73. Ibid., 123.
74. Ibid., 144.
75. Ibid., 106, 147.
76. Ibid., 151.
77. Ibid., 233. Emphasis original.

The rationale and function of government had a wider scope in the Old Testament period, according to O'Donovan, in contrast to its reduced ("re-authorized") scope following Christ's exaltation. In the history retold in the Old Testament, for example, the purpose of government included "safeguarding Israel's existence in relation to the land and law," a purpose that has ceased to exist (or to be legitimate) following the Christ-event.[78] However, instead of the Christ-event re-instating the Davidic monarchy, "it carries the rule forward to a moment of revelation that is of a different order entirely."[79] In the post-Easter phase of salvation-history "the whole rationale of government" is reduced to "its capacity to effect the judicial task."[80] At its most succinct, O'Donovan's political theology contends that "the state exists in order to give judgment."[81]

O'Donovan's thesis about the "re-authorization" of political authority does not emerge purely out of an exegesis of passages in the New Testament that speak to the issue of political authority.[82] He argues that "a theological account of how this world is ruled ... must proceed from and through an account of the church."[83] O'Donovan construes the church as a "political society" by analogy.[84] Unlike other institutions in secular society, the church is "not brought into being and held in being ... by a special function ... but by a government that it obeys in everything."[85] This government is "ruled and authorized by the ascended Christ alone and supremely."[86] However, the church's government is "hidden," and thus to be "discerned by faith."[87] The marks of the church's "political character as a community ruled by Christ" are its catholicity and its order.[88]

O'Donovan clarifies that the church and society do not form separate, independent entities. There is, he says, "but one structured human community."[89] Rather, the church exists as a "sanctuary" in the "midst" of society, representing God's kingdom "by living under its rule, and by welcoming the world under its rule."[90] It is through the church that humankind is able to "participate in God's rule."[91] However, the church has no mandate to "philosophise about the future world," nor to exercise political authority, a task for which it is not "consecrated."[92]

78. Ibid., 148.
79. Ibid., 24.
80. Ibid., 148.
81. Ibid., 233.
82. In response to criticisms of *Desire* by Schweiker and Wolterstorff, O'Donovan explained that his "re-authorization thesis" is driven in part by the emergence of "the church as a community acknowledging the kingly rule of Christ" ("Deliberation, History and Reading," 132).
83. O'Donovan, *The Desire of the Nations*, 159.
84. Ibid.
85. Ibid., 132.
86. Ibid.
87. Ibid., 166.
88. Ibid., 169.
89. Ibid., 156.
90. Ibid., 156, 174.
91. Ibid., 181.
92. Ibid., 187, 217.

The church therefore has a dialectical relationship with society and secular government, marked by "martyrdom" and "mutual service" depending on the circumstances.[93]

A key function of the secular governmental task of judgment is to help facilitate the church's mission by creating "a certain social space ... for men and women of every nation to be drawn into the governed community of God's Kingdom."[94] Political authorities, O'Donovan explains, have been "thrust back by Christ's victory to the margins ... to perform a single function of which the church ... [and] ... the world [stand] in need for the time being."[95]

The Ways of Judgment (2005)

In the introduction to *Desire*, O'Donovan made a distinction between the theoretical discipline of political theology and the practical discipline of political ethics. *Desire* was cast as a work in political theology and the promised companion to *Desire*, which came in the form of *Judgment* (its "sequel"), was conceived as a work in political ethics.[96] By the time he came to write *Judgment*, however, he had begun to doubt the validity of this distinction, describing them as "pseudo-disciplinary designations."[97] He questioned whether such a clear methodological distinction between "theory" and "practice" could, in fact, be made. He thus concluded in *Judgment* that the two books were in reality a mixture of both theory and practice.[98] This prompted a reconception of the differences and relationship between the two books: while they both share a common subject matter in the correspondence of theological and political concepts, *Desire* approaches the correspondence more from the theological side and *Judgment* more from the political side.[99]

Chaplin makes a useful distinction between political theology and Christian political philosophy that can help illuminate the relationship between *Desire* and *Judgment*. This is to conceive political theology as "reflection on political material in (or the political implications of) *biblical and theological sources*" and Christian political philosophy as "reflection on *political reality* in the light of those sources."[100] *Desire* is self-consciously a work in Christian political theology, and

---

93. Ibid., 217.
94. Ibid., 146. 1 Tim. 2:1–3 is cited as warrant for this view. Blount maintains that O'Donovan argues that "government exists to promote the extension of the Gospel." Brian K. Blount, "Response to *The Desire of the Nations*," *Studies in Christian Ethics* 11, no.2 (1998): 11.
95. O'Donovan, *The Desire of the Nations*, 156.
96. Ibid., 15; O'Donovan, *The Ways of Judgment*, ix–x.
97. O'Donovan, *The Ways of Judgment*, ix.
98. Ibid., ix–x.
99. Ibid., x.
100. Chaplin, "Political Eschatology and Responsible Government," 265 (footnote 2). Emphasis original.

while O'Donovan conceives *Judgment* as a work in Christian political ethics, it comfortably meets the definition of Christian political philosophy in the sense articulated by Chaplin, and can helpfully be thought of as such. *Desire* is concerned with developing an account of political authority from "biblical and theological sources" (as well as from Christian history) and *Judgment* represents an examination of "political reality" in light of the theological and exegetical findings of *Desire*. This distinction helps to explain the very different ways that the question of political authority is handled in both works. *Judgment* does not revisit or substantively elaborate the theological and exegetical foundations of political authority developed in *Desire*. Rather, it augments and nuances the account of political authority given in *Desire* as O'Donovan explores its application to contemporary Western liberal political order. This is to say that O'Donovan's *theology* of political authority is developed in *Desire* and then carried through unaltered to *Judgment*. This helps to clarify that *Desire* will be the primary text of the present study with *Judgment* and *Resurrection* used primarily for what they clarify, or problematize, as the case may be, regarding O'Donovan's definitive *theological* account of political authority set out in *Desire*.

In *Judgment*, O'Donovan reaffirms (verbatim) the definition of political authority he introduced in *Desire*: "Political authority arises where power, the execution of right, and the perpetuation of tradition are assured together in one coordinated agency."[101] (This definition has remained remarkably consistent throughout O'Donovan's work, reiterated as recently as 2016.)[102] O'Donovan also reaffirms the idea set out in *Desire* that political authority is "re-authorized" by Christ's exaltation, which sees it function on "*new* terms" within the context of salvation-history: "the triumph of God in Christ has not left these authorities just where they were, exercising the same right as before. It imposes the shape of salvation-history upon politics."[103] Again, like *Desire*, *Judgment* maintains that "the authority of secular government resides in the practice of judgment."[104] However, whereas the central "thesis" of *Desire* is that "theology, by developing its account of the reign of God, may recover the ground traditionally held by the notion

---

101. O'Donovan, *The Ways of Judgment*, 142. This is a verbatim reproduction of theorem 1 from *Desire*. It is also characterized as a "theorem" in *Judgment*.

102. Oliver O'Donovan, "Representation," *Studies in Christian Ethics* 29, no.2 (2016): 135 (footnote 1): "I have defended elsewhere the thesis that 'the authority of government is constituted by the coincidence in one agency of power, representation and the exercise of judgment.'" Note, however, that "representation" here is substituted for "execution of right" ("injured right" in *Resurrection*).

103. O'Donovan, *The Ways of Judgment*, 5.

104. Ibid. O'Donovan also propounded this conclusion in an essay published prior to *Judgment*, but after *Desire*, in which he said: "The reign of Christ in heaven has left *judgment* as the single remaining political deed." Oliver O'Donovan, "Government as Judgment," *First Things* 92 (1999), https://www.firstthings.com/article/1999/04/004-government-as-judgment.

of authority," the central thesis that *Judgment* seeks to "sustain" is simply: "the authority of government resides in the practice of judgment."[105]

Although the concept of judgment was first introduced in *Desire*, it was not until *Judgment* that it received sustained treatment and elaboration.[106] Judgment is defined as "an act of moral discrimination that pronounces upon a preceding act or existing state of affairs to establish a new public context."[107] Moral discrimination consists of clarifying and resolving the "moral ambiguity" regarding the right and wrong of a given situation, and doing so in such a way that establishes a new "public moral context."[108] The purpose of making such moral discriminations (judgments) is "establishing, or maintaining, a just social order."[109] Judgment is "reactive" by nature.[110] It can never be "a forward-looking action," for "to pronounce a judgment is always to speak about something that already is the case."[111] However, the fact that acts of judgment are intrinsically "retrospective" does not mean that they cannot be performed "without a prospective object of action."[112] This is where the new "public moral context" is relevant. By retroactively, yet publicly, resolving the moral ambiguity of a preceding act or current state of affairs, governments are able to establish "a practical context ... in which succeeding acts, private and public, may be performed."[113] This delineation of judgment clarifies that not every government act constitutes an act of judgment, because some acts make no "reflective pronouncement," nor create "new public space."[114] For example, when a government decides the outcome of a tender and then signs a contract with the successful company, or when a prime minister reshuffles cabinet, no reflective moral discrimination is made. Similarly, when governments issue public health warnings, no new public context is created.[115] The importance of judgment being a "public act" is predicated on a distinction between private and public acts of judgment. O'Donovan regards some private acts as judgment, but only in a marginal sense. This is because private acts of judgment, unlike those performed by magistrates and judges, are not representative, that is, done "on behalf of the public," and therefore are incapable of creating a new public context that shapes succeeding public *and* private acts.[116]

---

105. O'Donovan, *The Ways of Judgment*, 3.
106. O'Donovan, *The Desire of the Nations*, 38: "To judge is to make a distinction between the just and the unjust, or, more precisely, to bring the distinction which already exists between them into the daylight of public observation."
107. O'Donovan, *The Ways of Judgment*, 7.
108. Ibid.
109. Ibid., 93.
110. Ibid., 8.
111. Ibid.
112. Ibid.
113. Ibid. The function and operation of the common law might be informing O'Donovan's view here.
114. Ibid., 9.
115. Ibid.
116. Ibid., 10–11.

While *Judgment* reaffirms and proceeds from the theology of political authority set out in *Desire*, it does add some notable additional nuance. For example, O'Donovan identifies "non-reciprocality" as "the stumbling block from which the dominant problematics of modern politics have arisen."[117] The modern contractarian conception of political authority is based on the notion that citizens participate in "the reciprocal relations of self-government."[118] But the "myth" that "political subjection was owed not to the rulers themselves but to the collective whole" was nothing more than the "failed attempt to resolve the paradox of political subjection."[119] O'Donovan maintains that political subjection, *contra* modern contractarian orthodoxy, is not "servitude."[120] Rather, "the political subject is freer *as* a subject."[121] The conception of freedom O'Donovan has in view here relates to "the self-realisation of the individual within social forms," an idea found in both *Resurrection* and *Desire*: "the objective correlate of freedom is authority."[122]

At the heart of the non-reciprocal nature of political authority is the idea that it creates an obligation to act on the part of subjects. O'Donovan explains that obligation is often erroneously conflated with power. Power entails compulsion, whereas obligation is the ability to get someone to do something freely.[123] Political authority is a form of obligation rather than power, although it does depend on the latter for its effectiveness.[124] In order for political authority to oblige someone to act, it must, O'Donovan argues, "present us with a reason for doing it."[125] "Action," he says, "is free only as it is intelligible."[126] It is important to understand that O'Donovan's contention is not that *blind* obedience leads to our freedom. On the contrary, the relationship of freedom to political obligation turns on "an element of discretion that can never be removed from the obedient subject."[127] The subject is to "always … be clear in his or her own mind that this or that command actually *requires* obedience."[128] The obligation to act commanded by political authority is

---

117. Ibid., 127.
118. Ibid., 128.
119. Ibid.
120. Ibid.
121. Ibid. Emphasis original.
122. Ibid., 68–9. O'Donovan, *Resurrection and Moral Order*, 122; O'Donovan, *The Desire of the Nations*, 30; and again, more recently, in O'Donovan, *Self, World, and Time*, 53.
123. O'Donovan, *The Ways of Judgment*, 129–30.
124. Ibid., 130.
125. Ibid.
126. Ibid. O'Donovan further clarifies that obligation to act can be differentiated from spontaneous action, which is an act entirely owned by the actor. In contrast, when a person is obliged to act by some political authority, the action is "laid upon" that person, "even though it is still free action." He also stipulates that political authority is not the only kind of authority that is non-reciprocal. There is, he notes, "a multitude of non-political authorities … which direct us to perform certain actions: doctors, teachers, parents, employers … ."
127. Ibid., 136.
128. Ibid. Emphasis original.

further tempered by the obligation created by membership of a society: "something owed to the neighbour before anything is owed to the ruler."[129]

O'Donovan expands on the mediated nature of political authority in *Judgment* by arguing that recognition of political authority entails recognition of "a *particular bearer* of political authority," that is, "we hear the summons to defend the common good mediated through this or that political actor."[130] O'Donovan clarifies that political obligation does not necessarily imply approval of "the way the bearer acquired authority," nor a judgment regarding whether there is one better suited to bear political authority.[131] There is a further obligation, which can be thought of as a communal obligation, although O'Donovan does not couch it in such terms. This is the obligation "to sustain that bearer in place, to achieve continuity of regime."[132] This obligation relates to the promotion of "political institutions," construed as "a series of common practices in which the exercise of political authority has a regular position."[133] Political authority is therefore borne, and mediated, by human individuals (or groups), as well as institutions.

There is an interesting difference of emphasis in the respective accounts of political authority offered in *Judgment* and *Desire*. Whereas *Desire*, like *Resurrection*, places the emphasis on political authority serving the purposes of addressing injured right, *Judgment* stresses the connection between political authority and the "common good."[134] *Judgment* presents defending the common good as one of the tasks of government, served by its acts of judgment. However, this task is purely "reflexive" on O'Donovan's account.[135] A government's judgments are restricted to *defending* the common good, not pursing it "directly"; direct pursuit of the common good is more appropriately a task for public activity.[136] The execution of right and the perpetuation of tradition are aspects of the common good that form "the essential ground of political authority."[137] To say that political authority must "defend" the common good is to imply "the good and the right *of a community*, that is, the sphere of social communications in which each member communicates within the whole."[138] Further, the common good "implies the flourishing of a particular society with a particular identity," which

---

129. Ibid., 137.
130. Ibid., 135. Emphasis original.
131. Ibid.
132. Ibid.
133. Ibid. O'Donovan clarifies that sustaining a regime can accommodate changes in administration and in democracies "loyal opposition."
134. Ibid., 138. The "common good" is mentioned several times in *Desire*, but it is nowhere explicitly linked to the definition or function of political authority. See, for example, O'Donovan, *The Desire of the Nations*, 17, 94, 282-3.
135. O'Donovan, *The Ways of Judgment*, 56.
136. Ibid. "Governments," O'Donovan clarified in his response to Wolterstorff and Schweiker (in the context of *Desire*), "react to wrong, actual or threatened; they do not determine our pursuit of the good" ("Deliberation, History and Reading," 136).
137. O'Donovan, *The Ways of Judgment*, 140.
138. Ibid., 139. Emphasis original.

is to say a "tradition," and the authority of tradition is "that of its *continuity with immediate history*."[139] This is all to say that in order for a government to make the kinds of moral discriminations that can successfully create new public contexts, more just than the contexts preceding them, the moral discrimination (judgment) must be made in respect of the community's right and within the context of a representative tradition.

O'Donovan's Political Theology Method

O'Donovan outlines an embryonic method for political theology in *Desire*. The method begins with recognition that political theology is a "theoretic discipline," followed by the insight that "true concepts" are constitutive of theory.[140] As political theology is also a *theological* discipline, the "true political concepts" that are constitutive of *theo*political theory "must be authorized, as any datum of theology must be, from Holy Scripture."[141] Finally, political theology requires more than simply authorized political concepts; it requires "a unifying conceptual structure" to "connect political themes with the history of salvation as a whole."[142] The interplay between theory, concepts, and Scripture in the context of political theology entails the following process, according to O'Donovan:

> Identifying concepts comes before constructing theory; but it comes after reading the text, for it is not a matter of simply emphasising key words in the text ... the words themselves are not the concepts but are like flags on a map which signal their presence.[143]

This makes it clear that political theology, in O'Donovan's view, begins with Scripture, but is much more than the mere analysis of biblical vocabulary. The task of the political theologian is to identify "true political concepts" in Scripture, but then also to tie them together in a unifying conceptual structure in an act of theorizing. "A commentary on a unique particular is not a theory," O'Donovan has clarified, "so that neither exegesis nor narrative in themselves are theoretical, though they could never be of much interest unless they also interacted with theory."[144]

It is important to note that the principles of this theopolitical method are treated as axiomatic by O'Donovan. In principle, all axioms are contestable.

---

139. Ibid., 140.
140. O'Donovan, *The Desire of the Nations*, 15.
141. Ibid.
142. Ibid., 22. This criterion is designed to counter the danger of Scripture becoming "a mine for random sociological analogies dug out from the ancient world."
143. Ibid., 15–16.
144. O'Donovan, "Response to the Respondents," 97.

However, while all axioms are intrinsically contestable, not all axioms are, in practice, controversial. Some of the axioms in O'Donovan's method can safely be regarded as uncontroversial. It is difficult, for example, to conceive of a political theology that is not "theoretic" in the sense meant by O'Donovan. It is likewise difficult to conceive of a kind of "theory" that does not involve "concepts," since, as O'Donovan correctly points out, "true concepts are an essential prerequisite for organised theory."[145] Moreover, the notion that political theology requires "a unifying conceptual structure" seems to follow from the previous two axioms. In contrast, the axiom that "true political concepts" must be "authorized" from Scripture is contentious and in practice is not followed by many writers in political theology. Aside from the light these explicit methodological principles shed on the process that O'Donovan seeks to follow in *Desire*, they also constitute a criterion that can be an aid to evaluating O'Donovan's theopolitical arguments: those arguments can be evaluated according to the extent to which they can be regarded as "authorized from" Scripture. This is a test I apply throughout the critical chapters that follow.

Kelsey: The Uses of Scripture in Recent Theology

There is a degree of ambiguity in O'Donovan's use of the term "authorize" in the methodological schema outlined above. O'Donovan does not clarify precisely what he means by "authorize." Moreover, its conjunction with the preposition "from," as in true political concepts "authorized *from* ... Holy Scripture," is a slightly odd turn of phrase, and certainly more ambiguous than either "authorized *in*" or "authorized *by*" might have been. The closest thing to clarification provided by O'Donovan is the statement that "nothing assures us a priori that politico-theological concepts are to be found; the question of their existence must be put to Scripture itself."[146] This appears to give "authorized from" a strong sense, akin perhaps to "verify," particularly if we are to assume that the very existence of politico-theological concepts is something that can only be confirmed by (or from) Scripture. Notwithstanding this acknowledged ambiguity, it is clear that the Bible performs a controlling epistemological function in the formation of political theology (or theopolitical theory) in O'Donovan's view, to the extent that it is the ultimate arbiter of true political concepts. It is equally clear that O'Donovan aspires to offer a theological account of political authority that is itself "authorized from" Scripture.

To help navigate this ambiguity and to aid in the examination of the extent to which O'Donovan's own theopolitical arguments regarding political authority rely on "true concepts ... authorized from ... Holy Scripture," I turn to David Kelsey's book *The Uses of Scripture in Recent Theology*. This book is suitable to the task at hand because it investigates the notion of "Scriptural authority" in the

---

145. O'Donovan, *The Desire of the Nations*, 15.
146. Ibid.

context of theological arguments.¹⁴⁷ Kelsey's central insight is that "theologians use scripture in the *context* of an argument in support of a theological proposal" in distinct ways.¹⁴⁸ He identifies five ways in which Scripture is generally construed as "authoritative" in the context of theological arguments: (1) the content of Scripture—"the authoritative element in scripture is its doctrinal or conceptual *content*"; (2) the concepts of Scripture—"lay[ing] out the distinctively biblical concepts of one thing and another"; (3) narrative as authoritative—"narrative ... construed as confessional recital"; (4) narrative as identity descriptions—"biblical narrative ... rendering an agent whose identity and actions theology is then to discuss"; and (5) biblical images—by "expressing" the occurrence of the revealing and saving event, scripture somehow links us with that event.¹⁴⁹

Kelsey suggests that "scripture may properly be said to be 'authority' for a theological proposal when appeal is made to it in the course of making a *case* for the proposal."¹⁵⁰ He identifies the following technical functions that Scripture can perform in a theological argument: "data," "warrant" (an "inference-license"), "backing" (backing for the warrant), and "rebuttal" (demonstrating that the conditions of rebuttal are excluded).¹⁵¹ Kelsey observes that theologians can and do use Scripture in one or more of these roles in the course of making theological arguments.¹⁵² This provides us with a model for identifying the formal ways in which O'Donovan uses Scripture in the course of developing the arguments that constitute his theology of political authority. Kelsey's model can also help to overcome the ambiguity surrounding O'Donovan's use of the phrase "authorized from," for irrespective of what O'Donovan understands by the term, Kelsey's model will help us to identify the formal role Scripture plays, for example, data or warrant, in O'Donovan's arguments.

Three Foundational Theses Regarding Political Authority

The preceding exposition demonstrates that O'Donovan's theology of political authority is both extensive and complex. There is naturally much more that can, and will, be said regarding the details of the arguments O'Donovan develops in relation to political authority. However, the discursive nature of O'Donovan's thought, the size of his corpus, and the self-professed "involved" nature of its prose necessitates a refinement of scope before embarking on the critical phase of this study in the chapters to follow. I propose to restrict my critical focus in coming

---

147. David H. Kelsey, *The Use of Scripture in Recent Theology* (London: SCMS Press, 1975), 1.
148. Ibid., 3. Emphasis original.
149. Ibid. Emphasis original.
150. Ibid., 125. Emphasis original.
151. Ibid., 126–8. An argument also formally requires a conclusion.
152. Ibid., 128–9.

chapters to what in my judgment are three foundational theses in O'Donovan's theological account of political authority:

Thesis 1—Political authority arises where power, the execution of right, and the perpetuation of tradition are assured together in one coordinated agency (theorem 1 in *Desire*, reiterated verbatim in *Judgment*).

Thesis 2—The authority of secular government resides in the practice of judgment (articulation taken from *Judgment*, but theoretical work concluded in *Desire*).[153]

Thesis 3—That any regime should actually come to hold authority, and should continue to hold it, is a work of divine providence in history, not an accomplishment of the human task of political service (Theorem 2 in *Desire*, reaffirmed, albeit in different formulation, in *Judgment*).

Hereafter I use "essence of political authority thesis," "re-authorization thesis," and "providence thesis" as shorthand descriptors for the three theses, respectively.[154] The three have been selected on the basis of the twin aims of manageability and substance. Reducing O'Donovan's complex theology of political authority to just three theses provides a manageable scope that enables, on the one hand, detailed analysis of his work in a way that can arrive at clear and definite conclusions, conclusions that can then be readily assessed by others, while, on the other hand, isolating and focusing on the most substantive claims involved in that theology.[155]

---

153. O'Donovan, *The Ways of Judgment*, 3.
154. Apropos the influence of wife Joan Lockwood O'Donovan on Oliver's political theology, it is worth noting, *en passant*, that both the "essence of political authority thesis" and the "re-authorization thesis" can be seen in her own work:

> The nation is a concrete territorial order of *political power, judgment and tradition* that sustains a space within the sinful human condition for the gathering of Christ's faithful people through the work of the Holy Spirit … In a sense, the nation remains what Israel revealed it to be—its constitutive elements have not changed … But its *theological significance has changed* … it is no longer revealed to be the vehicle of salvation, but merely the guaranteed social space within which God's saving work proceeds [emphasis mine].

Joan Lockwood O'Donovan, "Nation, State, and Civil Society in the Western Biblical Tradition," in *Bonds of Imperfection*, 285–6.
155. As Moberly has noted, "it is difficult … to know how best to comment on a project such as O'Donovan's without appearing merely to nit-pick" ("The Use of Scripture in *The Desire of the Nations*," 61).

The following chapters examine and critique each of the three theses identified above (with an intervening excursus in Chapter 5 that examines O'Donovan's salvation-history biblical hermeneutic). Specifically, these chapters problematize each one of these theses, concluding that they are untenable in their present formulation and on the basis of their present argumentation. The foreshadowed constructive chapter that concludes the work will endeavor to resolve the problems identified in relation to these three foundational theses.

Chapter 3

DOES ISRAEL REVEAL THE ESSENCE OF POLITICAL AUTHORITY?

The "essence of political authority thesis" states that "political authority arises where power, the execution of right and the perpetuation of tradition are assured together in one coordinated agency." Below I question the tenability of this thesis, contending that O'Donovan fails to substantiate that it can be regarded as "authorized from" Scripture in the way that he implies. I further question the tenability of the notion that Israel reveals the essence of political authority through the way that its political forms mediated God's rule (specifically in the Davidic monarchy).

The Missing Biblical Warrant for the Constitutive Concepts in the "Essence of Political Authority Thesis"

As indicated in the previous chapter, the path to the "the essence of political authority thesis" begins with O'Donovan's analysis of political concepts "habitually grouped" with divine kingship in the Old Testament. The concepts that O'Donovan identified in this regard were: salvation, judgment, and possession. Salvation, we recall, related principally to military victory, while judgment pertained to the act of making public moral distinctions between right and wrong. Possession entailed a tradition of law and the possession of a land. These "three affirmations," as O'Donovan characterizes them, "shape Israel's sense of political identity and define what is meant by saying that Yhwh rules as king."[1] Each of these concepts is tied to a Hebrew term(s) in the text of the Old Testament: Salvation corresponds with *yᵉshūʿāh*, judgment with *tsedeq'* and *mishpāt*, and possession with *naḥᵃlāh* and *ḥēleq*. For ease of reference, I henceforth refer to this triadic conceptual schema as the "divine kingship as salvation, judgment and possession paradigm."

It is instructive to pay attention to how O'Donovan describes the analytical process by which he develops the "divine kingship as salvation, judgment and possession paradigm." In a move that *prima facie* appears to traduce one of his central methodological axioms, he says that "this analysis of concepts cannot, of course, claim to be directly *authorized* by the text of the Hebrew Scripture."[2] Rather,

1. O'Donovan, *The Desire of the Nations*, 45.
2. Ibid. Emphasis original.

like all "exegetical structures," it seeks to "apprehend the text and illuminate it by allowing one aspect to shed light upon another."[3] The concession that the "divine kingship as salvation, judgment and possession paradigm" is *not* authorized directly from Scripture likely reflects O'Donovan's cognizance that, while the text associates these concepts with divine kingship, it is O'Donovan who draws the conclusion that together they shape Israel's sense of political identity and define what it means to say that Yhwh rules as king.[4] The original authors/editors/redactors of the Old Testament, as well as rulers and officials in ancient Israel, and even the populace of Israel more broadly, might have recognized this articulation of divine kingship and perhaps even have embraced it, but it is not a paradigm presented explicitly in the Old Testament. This is to say that, while the Hebrew terms that stand for "salvation," "judgment," and "possession" might indeed be "habitually grouped" with the concept of "divine kingship," as O'Donovan contends, it is in fact O'Donovan, and not Scripture per se, who makes them constitutive concepts in a paradigm of God's kingly rule over Israel.

Still, O'Donovan is able to adduce ample evidence that salvation, judgment, and possession are prominent biblical concepts that are indeed closely associated with the concept of divine kingship.[5] He can also claim without controversy that divine kingship is a biblical concept, one "fundamental to Israel's political self-awareness."[6] Moreover, there is no reason to question the characterization of these concepts as "political" in a rather conventional Western sense of the term, that is, "the practice of the art or science of directing and administrating states or other political units."[7]

Thus, while the paradigm itself technically might not be "authorized" from Scripture, at least not directly in the way formulated by O'Donovan, it is nevertheless developed from concepts that are genuinely biblical and political. Recalling that the second criterion in O'Donovan's methodological schema is to

3. Ibid.
4. Ibid.
5. Ibid., 37–41. Note, however, that McConville questions O'Donovan's rendering of *tsedeq*' and *mishpāt* as "judgment," maintaining that they are better understood as "justice-righteousness." J. G. McConville, *God and Earthly Power: An Old Testament Political Theology Genesis–Kings* (London: T&T Clark, 2006), 171.
6. Ibid., 30. Provan, Long and Longman note that "the understanding that God is king lies at the heart of the biblical tradition." Iain Provan, V. Philips Long, and Tremper Longman III, *A Biblical History of Israel* (Louisville: Westminster John Knox Press, 2003), 208. Not all agree, however, with Preuss arguing that "one cannot say that the conception of kingship of YHWH is very central and really basic for the Old Testament." Horst Dietrich Preuss, *Old Testament Theology Volume 1*, trans. Leo G. Perdue (Louisville: Westminster John Knox Press, 1995), 159. Goldingay takes a more nuanced middle view, maintaining that the Pentateuch very rarely speaks of Yhwh as king, but that it grew in prominence in Jerusalem and thereafter. Goldingay, *Psalms*, 67.
7. Iain McLean and Alistair McMillan, eds., *Oxford Concise Dictionary of Politics*, 3rd ed. (Oxford: Oxford University Press, 2009), s.v. "politics."

establish a "unifying conceptual structure" that "connects political themes with the history of salvation as a whole," it is possible to conclude that the paradigm can be construed as "authorized" from Scripture in the sense that it unifies in a coherent fashion "true political concepts ... authorized from ... Holy Scripture," namely divine kingship, salvation, judgment, and possession. Using Kelsey's model, we might say that Scripture provides the (conceptual) data, in the first place, for the development of a theopolitical paradigm, and partial warrant, in the second place, on account of the habitual association of those concepts with the concept of divine kingship in the text of Scripture.[8]

However, O'Donovan makes a subtle, unacknowledged conceptual move in the transition from the "divine kingship as salvation, judgment and possession paradigm" to the "essence of political authority thesis," undermining the notion that the latter could be deemed as "authorized from" or "revealed" in Scripture. The significance of this conceptual move for the cogency of O'Donovan's "essence of political authority thesis" has escaped the notice and attention of the secondary literature on O'Donovan's political theology.[9] The conceptual move in question is the substitution of power for salvation, judgment for execution of right, and tradition for possession in the "essence of political authority thesis": *political authority arises where power, the execution of right and the perpetuation of tradition are assured together in one coordinated agency.* The "essence of political authority thesis" also introduces the concept of "one coordinated agency," something absent in the "divine kingship as salvation, judgment and possession paradigm," although it is arguably implied in the concept of divine kingship.

It is difficult to infer or reconstruct a rationale for these conceptual substitutions, particularly as they are, as I note, unacknowledged and therefore unexplained. In the discussion that immediately precedes the introduction of "the essence of political authority thesis" in *Desire*, O'Donovan states that "our view here," ostensibly in reference to the "divine kingship as salvation, judgment and possession paradigm," "stretches beyond this exegetical claim to a *theoretical* one," from context a reference to the "essence of political authority thesis."[10] O'Donovan

---

8. It is noteworthy that the "divine kingship as salvation, judgment and possession paradigm" has not come under serious criticism in the critical secondary literature. Moberly and Gordon McConville, for example, who both find much to criticize in O'Donovan's analysis of the Old Testament's political categories, nevertheless acknowledge the centrality of divine kingship in the Old (and New) Testament and the validity of associating "salvation," "judgment," and "possession" with it. See Moberly, "The Use of Scripture in *The Desire of the Nations*," 61–2; and J. Gordon Mcconville, "Law and Monarchy in the Old Testament," in *A Royal Priesthood?* 80.

9. Hauerwas and Fodor questioned the general move from exegesis to theory, finding it "curious" and "puzzling." However, they did not notice, or note, the conceptual move and its implications identified here. They did observe, however, that O'Donovan "owes the reader a clearer explanation of how his move from exegesis to theoretical description is warranted" ("Remaining in Babylon," 38).

10. O'Donovan, *The Desire of the Nations*, 45. Emphasis original.

further intimates that the "divine kingship as salvation, judgment and possession paradigm" (my description not his) is to "provide a *framework* for exploring the major questions about authority posed by the Western tradition."[11] The "essence of political authority thesis" (described as "theorem 1" in this context) is then introduced with the following somewhat opaque preamble:

> The direction to be taken can be indicated at this point in two theorems, to which we shall quickly add a third, which appropriate [sic], in terms *adapted* for general theoretical use, the threefold analysis of kingship [the "divine kingship as salvation, judgment and possession] on the one hand and the ascription of kingship to Yhwh on the other.[12]

The apposite terms here are "theoretical," "framework," and "adapted." These provide some insight into the relationship between the "divine kingship as salvation, judgment and possession paradigm" and the "essence of political authority thesis," at least as O'Donovan understands it. The "essence of political authority thesis" appears to be a *theory adapted* from the *framework* that is "the divine kingship as salvation, judgment and possession paradigm," which in turn is based on an exegesis of terms habitually associated with the concept of divine kingship in the Old Testament.[13] In the context of the critical discussion that followed publication of *Desire,* O'Donovan clarified that "the analysis of political authority in terms of power, right and tradition" is the "theoretical form" of the "exegetical form" of "salvation, judgment and possession."[14] He has also acknowledged that "the theory about the components of political authority is not discovered by exegesis—which is to say, it is not the theory of any biblical author, but mine."[15]

What O'Donovan presents us with, then, appears to be a "theory" of political authority extrapolated from a paradigm of divine kingship "authorized" from Scripture (in the indirect sense understood by O'Donovan and outlined above—data and partial warrant). This immediately gives rise to the following question: Does, and indeed *can*, O'Donovan cogently show that his *theory* of political authority, as opposed to the *paradigm* from which it is extrapolated, is "authorized from" Scripture, as he apparently believes to be the case given the way he uses the thesis subsequently in the development of his theology of political authority?

---

11. Ibid. Emphasis mine.
12. Ibid., 46. The "third" theorem referenced is: "In acknowledging political authority, society proves its political identity" (*The Desire of the Nations,* 47). Emphasis mine.
13. Hauerwas and Fodor have drawn attention to the disparity in the way that many of the moving parts of O'Donovan's theology of political authority are characterized by him for example "frameworks," and the way that they are actually used. They concluded, for example, that, "despite O'Donovan's disclaimer that his exegetical framework has little more than heuristic value, he nonetheless wants to 'stretch' beyond the insights thereby gained and use them to make strong theoretical claims" ("Remaining in Babylon," 38).
14. O'Donovan, "Response to the Respondents," 97.
15. Ibid., 98.

The first thing to note in regard to answering this question is that power, right, and tradition are not described by O'Donovan as biblical concepts, and indeed no exegesis is conducted to justify their appearance in the discussion; they are not tied to any Hebrew terms in Scripture, for example, in the way that the concepts that constitute the "divine kingship as salvation, judgment and possession paradigm" are. This omission alone appears to leave two of the three constitutive concepts of the "essence of political authority thesis" without ostensible biblical warrant.

It is incumbent upon us at this point to ask whether O'Donovan might intend the pairs salvation and power, judgment and right, and possession and tradition to be understood as synonyms, respectively. If what we have before us are English synonyms for the same Hebrew terms, rather than substantive conceptual substitutions, then O'Donovan might be able to argue that his "essence of political authority thesis" is, in some sense, grounded in "true political concepts" authorized from Scripture. If, on the other hand, they are not in fact synonyms in this context, then the actual concepts "authorized from Scripture" have been inexplicably substituted for new concepts that are not, leaving a critical thesis in O'Donovan's theology of political authority without ostensible biblical warrant, or even the support of biblical data. This would be a critical problem in the face of the methodological standard O'Donovan sets for political theology.

It is my contention that two of these conceptual pairs are indeed substantively different and therefore not synonymous (judgment and injured right can be regarded as synonymous). The most obvious and consequential difference between salvation and power, as both are explicated by O'Donovan, is that military victory is not constitutive of O'Donovan's conception of power in this context. Recall that O'Donovan defines salvation in the context of divine kingship in the Old Testament principally in terms of the military victory God grants to Israel: "Yhwh's kingship is established by the fact that he delivers his people from peril in conflict with their enemies."[16] One could reasonably argue that warfare, and perhaps even military victory, are implicit to some degree in the concept power. Indeed, O'Donovan makes clear in his book *The Just War Revisited* that armed conflict can be a legitimate use of power in support of a just judgment in certain circumstances.[17] But in truth, warfare, and in particular military victory, does not play the constitutive role in the "essence of political authority thesis" that it does in the "divine kingship as salvation, judgment and possession paradigm." In fact, it plays no explicit role whatsoever. In the account of political authority given in *Desire* following introduction of the "essence of political authority thesis," it is clear that political authority can exist without a regime ever having to engage in armed conflict—it need merely exercise power, execute right, and perpetuate tradition in one coordinated agency under peaceful conditions. Moreover, a regime can conceivably lose a military conflict and still retain political authority on

---

16. O'Donovan, *The Desire of the Nations*, 36.

17. Oliver O'Donovan, *The Just War Revisited* (Cambridge: Cambridge University Press, 2003). A central tenet of *The Just War Revisited* is that "armed conflict is to be reconceived as an extraordinary extension of ordinary acts of judgment" (14).

O'Donovan's definition, perhaps via the terms of an armistice or peace treaty, even one that favors the victorious party in the conflict. So the move from salvation to power appears to presage a change of conceptual substance.

There is a close connection between possession and tradition, with the former construed, *inter alia*, as "a tradition of law." However, the overt link between the possession of land in O'Donovan's explication of that concept as it appears in Scripture is quietly dropped when it comes to the concept of tradition in the "essence of political authority thesis." When discussing possession, for example, O'Donovan says that "originally and fundamentally the existence of Israel as a people was mediated through the land" and "possessing the land was a matter of observing that order of life which was established by Yhwh's judgments."[18] According to O'Donovan, "we may say that the land was the material cause of Yhwh's kingly rule."[19]

So the important connection between land and law disappears with the move to tradition in the "essence of political authority thesis." It is not difficult to see why. In Israel's case land was tied to a specific covenant, whereas the human exercise of political authority post-Easter has no such covenant with any specific land following Christ's exaltation. Given that the "essence of political authority thesis" purports to describe the nature of *all* political authority, tradition naturally loses the connection to land explicitly contained in the notion of possession, where Israel's possession of a specific promised land was constitutive of God's rule over Israel.

That said, O'Donovan could reasonably counter that the whole thesis presupposes the possession of *some* territory in order to give effect to the exercise of power, execution of right, and perpetuation of tradition. Indeed, he implies as much in *Judgment*, where he suggests that "no political authority is possessed by a 'government in exile,' since a government that does not govern is nothing."[20] Yet, on the other hand, the history of the Jewish diaspora, the main vessel of Jewish identity and tradition for much of Jewish history, teaches that a tradition does not require possession of a sovereign territory, nor power for that matter, in order to be preserved and maintained.

The central problematic for O'Donovan is the matter of how he can escape a charge of arbitrary conceptual change in this context. It is difficult to discern, for example, a warrant for making *these* conceptual changes rather than some *other* conceptual changes. In fact, it is difficult to discern the rationale for making any conceptual move at all. If salvation and possession, with their connection to warfare and land, are the *actual* political concepts associated with divine kingship in the Old Testament, and God's divine kingship over Israel is to be construed as providing the basis for an understanding of the generic nature of political authority, then why depart at all from the exegeted concepts that constitute the paradigm,

---

18. Ibid., 41.
19. Ibid.
20. O'Donovan, *The Ways of Judgment*, 141.

which, after all, can claim to be authorized from Scripture?[21] This unacknowledged and unexplained conceptual move from Hebrew concepts habitually associated with divine kingship in the text of the Old Testament to English concepts that O'Donovan has not shown to correspond to Hebrew terms habitually associated with divine kingship in the Old Testament appears to leave the "essence of political authority thesis" without biblical warrant, at least according to the high standard that O'Donovan sets in his theopolitical method: a unified conceptual structure based on "true political concepts … authorized from … Holy Scripture."

The Ramsey Factor

Jonathan Chaplin was the first to observe that the "essence of political authority thesis" is "simply a reformulation" of the definition of political authority O'Donovan provided ten years prior in *Resurrection* (the definition of political authority in *Resurrection* consisted of the conjunction of "might," "injured right," and "tradition" "exercised by one subject").[22] Chaplin further perceptively observed that O'Donovan "was able to propose this formulation … without dependence upon the extensive exegetical work of justification he presented only in [*Desire*]."[23] This observation prompted Chaplin to question whether the "essence of political authority thesis" (as I have called it) was "*derived from* biblical exegesis or rather *brought to* it."[24] O'Donovan responded to Chaplin's observations in *Judgment*, conceding that "the source of this triad"—"power," "right," and "tradition"—as he now realized, "was Paul Ramsey's analysis of authority as *lex, iustitia* and *ordo*."[25] These terms appear in Ramsey's 1968 essay "The Uses of Power" in the following context:

> This leads to a final characterisation of the good of politics, this time involving three terms: *lex, ordo* and *iustitia*—or law, the order of power, and justice. A Christian understanding of politics will be one that makes use of the concept of order (the order of power) in its relation to justitia on the one hand and to lex on the other.[26]

---

21. James W. Skillen, "Acting Politically in Biblical Obedience?" in *A Royal Priesthood?* 413. Skillen thinks even the concepts "salvation," "judgment," and "possession" are "arbitrarily abstract[ed]" to represent the way that Israel's political order was constituted. But this is a little unfair given their correspondence to Hebrew terms and O'Donovan's ability to demonstrate that they are indeed habitually grouped with "divine kingship."

22. Chaplin, "Political Eschatology and Responsible Government," 299–300. Note that, in the prologue to the second edition of *Resurrection* (1994), O'Donovan indicated that he had come to prefer "power" instead of "might" (*Resurrection and Moral Order*, xx).

23. Chaplin, "Political Eschatology and Responsible Government," 298. In fact, O'Donovan ostensibly conducted no exegesis to arrive at his conception of political authority in *Resurrection*, there being no single reference to Scripture in the context of that discussion.

24. Ibid., 298–9. Emphases original.

25. O'Donovan, *The Ways of Judgment*, 142. O'Donovan clarifies that Ramsey used "*ordo*" in the sense of "control of the situation" and therefore "something more like power."

26. Paul Ramsey, "The Uses of Power," in *The Essential Paul Ramsey: A Collection*, ed. William Werpehowski and Stephen D. Crocco (New Haven: Yale University Press, 1994), 93.

It is noteworthy that the triad *lex, ordo,* and *iustitia* are not adduced with any biblical exegesis, nor supported by any biblical warrants in "The Uses of Power," in which case the concession that O'Donovan apparently acquired these central concepts from Ramsey only succeeds in further undermining the notion that the "essence of political authority thesis" could be construed as "authorized" from Scripture. Turning again to Kelsey's model, O'Donovan's concession raises the possibility that Ramsey actually provides both the data and warrant for the "essence of political authority thesis" and, as Chaplin has suggested, that the thesis might have been *brought* to Scripture in this case, not extrapolated from it, as suggested in *Desire.*[27]

In sum, the "essence of political authority thesis" appears to be a theoretical extrapolation from an analysis of biblical concepts closely associated with the notion of divine kingship in the Old Testament, an extrapolation shaped, to some extent, by the work of Paul Ramsey, which in turn does not appear to be predicated specifically on any exegetical analysis.

Israel Reveals the Essence of Political Authority

O'Donovan repeatedly makes it clear in *Desire* that he regards Israel as politically normative for Christian political theology: "If political theologians are to treat ancient Israel's political tradition as normative, they must observe the discipline of treating it *as history*"; "It is a clear illustration of the principle that, to treat Israel's political tradition as normative, we have to wrestle with its history"; "If Israel's experience of government is to be taken as a model for other societies, then we must allow that divine providence is ready to protect other national traditions besides the sacred one"; "This means that any question about social forms and structures must be referred to a normative critical standard: do they fulfil that will of God for human society to which Israel's forms authoritatively point us?"; and "From those concepts we may derive an orientation of political principle through which the legacy of Israel regulates our own political analysis and deliberation."[28] O'Donovan further notes that "the history of divine rule is presented to us as *revealed* history which takes form quite particularly as the history of Israel."[29] O'Donovan's most revealing remark, however, in relation to both the normative and revelatory function of Israel in relation to political authority is this: "the unique covenant of Yhwh and Israel can be seen as a point of disclosure from which the nature of *all* political authority comes into view."[30] It is similarly revealing that this contention appears moments before the introduction of the "essence of political authority

---

27. It is, of course, possible that Ramsey derived these concepts from his own study of Scripture, but that this was not acknowledged in the essay in question. However, in the absence of further evidence we are only left with conjecture in that regard.
28. O'Donovan, *The Desire of the Nations*, 25, 27, 29, 73–4. Emphasis original.
29. Ibid., 21. Emphasis original.
30. Ibid., 45. Emphasis mine.

thesis" in *Desire* and is located in the section that explains (albeit less than clearly) the movement from the exegetical analysis of leading political concepts habitually associated with divine kingship in the Old Testament (the "divine kingship as salvation, judgment and possession paradigm") to the "essence of political authority thesis." This leads to the unavoidable conclusion that O'Donovan regards the "essence of political authority thesis" to be revealed, in some sense, in Israel's history, the authoritative account of which is found in Scripture. In other words, O'Donovan appears to suggest that the Old Testament reveals that the essence of political authority is the conjunction of power, the execution of right and the perpetuation of tradition in one coordinated agency.

The same unwarranted conceptual move that undermines the biblical authorization of the "essence of political authority thesis," discussed above, similarly undermines any notion that the Bible's account of Israel could be said to have revealed the essence of political authority, for the simple fact that the thesis is O'Donovan's own theory extrapolated from an association of biblical concepts, not a theory presented *in* Scripture. There are additional grounds to question the cogency of the idea that Israel reveals the essence of political authority.

O'Donovan's Ambiguous Conception of Divine Kingship and Its Implications

Divine kingship sits at the epicenter of O'Donovan's theological account of political authority. However, on closer inspection it becomes apparent that divine kingship has three distinct senses in that account. After clarifying that God's divine rule in history is an "expression" of God's *potentia ordinata* ("the covenant that is established through creation"), to be contrasted, following medieval tradition, with his *potentia absoluta* ("the bare fact of creation itself"), O'Donovan proceeds to distinguish three aspects of God's *potentia ordinata*.[31] The first aspect I will call "universal kingship." This relates to God's general rule over creation and history. O'Donovan says that "Yhwh's kingship is ... an act of providence, keeping faith with creation once made."[32] He adds that God's kingship "offered a geophysical reassurance about the stability of the natural order" and "reassurance about the international political order."[33] He further says that God's authority was "shown forth on earth through cataclysmic events, not only of a natural but also of a political order," and that it "secured the relations of the nations and directed them towards peace."[34] "Universal kingship," then, relates to God's providential rule over the natural world and the global political order in a generic sense.

The second aspect relates to what I will dub God's "covenantal kingship"— Israel's unique experience, expression, and mediation of God's kingship in

31. Ibid., 19, 32.
32. Ibid.
33. Ibid.
34. Ibid., 49, 71.

history. O'Donovan describes God's divine rule over Israel as a form of "special providence" in contrast to God's more general "universal kingship" outlined above.[35] God's "covenantal kingship" and "universal kingship" appear to have something of a dialectical relationship in O'Donovan's mind, although this idea is not developed in *Desire*. There, he simply alludes to a "difference between the ways in which Yhwh's national and international sovereignties were understood, the one mediated by the monarch, the other not susceptible of unitary mediation at all."[36] Thus, God rules as king of the "international order" and also specifically and uniquely as the king of one nation, Israel.

The third aspect in which O'Donovan talks about "divine kingship" relates specifically to the Davidic monarchy, which, on his account, expresses God's kingship in a way that other periods in Israel's covenantal history did not: "for the claims of monarchy were precisely to hold together military, judicial and, ultimately, tradition-bearing functions in one pair of hands."[37] "The strategy of David and Solomon," according to O'Donovan, "in moving the Ark to Jerusalem and housing it in a temple adjoining the royal palace had been to create a unified centre of worship and government."[38] Recall that "one coordinated agency" is a constitutive element of O'Donovan's "essence of political authority thesis." O'Donovan thus appears to make a third distinction between God's more general "covenantal kingship" over Israel, which traversed a diverse set of political orders and circumstances, from slavery in Egypt to second temple priestly rule, and between the way that the Davidic monarchy uniquely mediated God's kingship. I refer to the latter as "mediated Davidic kingship." "Universal kingship," "covenantal kingship," and "mediated Davidic kingship" mark a movement from the generic to the progressively more particular.

There is reason to think that the "divine kingship as salvation, judgment and possession paradigm" comes from O'Donovan's reading of God's "covenantal kingship" and not the Davidic monarchy *per se*. The clearest indication is the way O'Donovan applies the paradigm to the Exodus and Moses' leadership over the Hebrew people more generally. He says, for instance: "Indeed, Moses' role throughout the Book of Exodus, as we now have it, corresponds to the same pattern: he leads the people out of Egypt to the *victory* of the Red Sea; he *judges* their cases in the wilderness; he lays before them the pattern of their new life in *possession* of their land at Sinai."[39] This single citation illustrates two important features of the "divine kingship as salvation, judgment and possession paradigm": (1) it is not dependent on the Davidic monarchy in the way that I will shortly argue the

---

35. Ibid., 72.

36. Ibid. In *Judgment*, O'Donovan argues against the coherence of the notion of a world government, noting that "a world-government would have to be predicated on a world-people, but a world-people could come into existence only, one might say, when Martians arrived" (*The Ways of Judgment*, 208).

37. O'Donovan, *The Desire of the Nations*, 52.

38. Ibid., 43.

39. Ibid., 52. Emphasis mine.

"essence of political authority thesis" is; and (2) it clearly covers a range of different political circumstances and periods in Israel's history. It is not difficult to see how the paradigm might justifiably be applied to other periods in Israel's political history, such as the priestly rule of the Ezra–Nehemiah period.[40] O'Donovan could argue that God "saved" the Israelite people by liberating them from exile and returning them to their possession where he restored their tradition.[41]

In contrast, the "essence of political authority thesis" is much more difficult to apply consistently to all of the periods that span Israel's covenant with God. Moses does not appear to have exercised "power" in the sense meant by O'Donovan, at least not in Egypt. Indeed, Israel's bondage in Egypt would appear to represent the very essence of powerlessness. The Judges period appears to be in complete conflict with the "essence of pollical authority thesis": "In those days there was no king in Israel; all the people did what was right in their own eyes" (Judges 21:25). "Power" again seems to be an awkward fit for Israel's period of exile in Babylon.[42] Even upon being released from exile in Babylon, the Israelites were only able to exercise a limited, delegated "authority" in Judah under Persian suzerainty.[43] In fact, in a sermon of O'Donovan's published in the collection *The Word in Small Boats*, he observed that "Ezra still complains of political dependence upon Persia."[44]

The disparity between the "essence of political authority thesis" and Israel's pre- and post-monarchical political forms is evident in the language O'Donovan uses to describe those periods. He describes, for instance, the Israelites' post-exilic political experience as one of "dual authority," in recognition that following the downfall of the monarchy Israel never again held "power," "executed right," and

---

40. "For we are slaves; yet our God has not forsaken us in our slavery, but has extended to us his steadfast love before the kings of Persia, to give us new life to set up the house of our God, to repair its ruins, and to give us a wall in Judea and Jerusalem" (Ezra 8:9).

41. Ezra 9, for example.

42. Ester shows that the Israelites found ways to exercise power in an informal sense, but this does not seem to rise to the definition of political authority in O'Donovan's sense of the term.

43. Bishop, Moore, and Kelle argue that Sheshbazzar, Nehemiah, and Ezra probably functioned as "acknowledged officials in the Persian system" and that the Jewish elite who ruled the Persian satrapy of Judah likely collected tax on behalf of the Persian rulers. Megan Bishop Moore and Brad E. Kelle, *Biblical History and Israel's Past: The Changing Study of the Bible and History* (Grand Rapids: Eerdmans, 2011), 438. Bimson describes the Israelite attitude toward Persian kings as "ambivalent," torn between the view that those kings were agents of God yet also the source of their bondage. John J. Bimson, "Ezra," in *Theological Interpretations of the Old Testament: A Book-by-Book Survey*, ed. Kevin J. Vanhoozer (Grand Rapids: Baker Academic, 2008), 135. Miller, however, notes that the returned exiles nevertheless exercised a degree of self-government. Maxwell J. Miller, *A History of Israel and Judah*, 2nd ed. (Louisville: Westminster John Knox Press, 2006), 523.

44. Oliver O'Donovan, *The Word in Small Boats: Sermons from Oxford*, ed. Andy Draycott (Grand Rapids: Eerdmans, 2010), 14.

"perpetuated tradition" in "*one coordinated agency,*" at least not until the formation of the state of Israel in 1948. Of the Judges period, O'Donovan says:

> In the pre-monarchical period the nearest approximation to a continuous governmental function that can be discerned was provided by 'the judges', and it was a crucial element in the case for a monarchy that they had failed to provide not only the security necessary for Israel's identity but even a consistent standard of justice itself.[45]

One is drawn to another unavoidable conclusion at this point: O'Donovan's "essence of political authority thesis" is actually derived from the Davidic monarchy rather than Israel's history per se. O'Donovan does not make such an argument explicitly. Indeed, it is clear that he does not regard God's kingship to be restricted to the period of the Davidic monarchy: "David and the Davidides are only a small part of what is implied" by the theme *Yhwh mālak* and monarchy is "only one of the mediations of YHWH's kingship," the law being "a much larger part."[46] However, it is implicit in the fact that the definition of political authority that he offers, following an exegetical analysis of divine kingship in the Bible, only appears to apply to the monarchy from within the long and variegated constitutional history of the people of Israel (the duration of which God's "covenantal kingship" was in effect). As Wolterstorff has noted, according to O'Donovan's definition of political authority, there appears to have been "no genuine human political authority" during either the Babylonian exile or upon its return to the land of Judah.[47] It seems reasonable to conclude that "the essence of political authority thesis" is in actual fact derived solely and exclusively from O'Donovan's analysis and understanding of the Davidic monarchy, rather than Scripture's account of Israel's history *per se*.

The Problematic Notion That the Davidic Monarchy Reveals the Essence of Political Authority

The insight that O'Donovan's "essence of political authority thesis" is in fact derived from the Davidic monarchy might go some way to explaining the unacknowledged and unexplained conceptual move from the "divine kingship as salvation, judgment and possession paradigm" to "the essence of political authority thesis." The latter appears to be derived from a general analysis of the way that O'Donovan understands the Davidic monarchy to have mediated God's rule ("mediated Davidic kingship"), whereas the former, based on an exegetical analysis of leading Hebrew concepts associated with divine kingship in the Old Testament, appears to describe the way that God's rule was mediated throughout

---

45. O'Donovan, *The Desire of the Nations*, 56.
46. O'Donovan, "Response to Gordon McConville," 89.
47. Wolterstorff, "A Discussion of Oliver O'Donovan's *The Desire of the Nations*," 93–4.

Israel's history ("covenantal kingship"), transcending any single specific political form or circumstance.

O'Donovan does not claim that monarchy *per se* is the normative political model for all societies in all times. He contends, for example, that "political institutions are ... too fluid to assume an ideal form, since they are the work of Providence in the changing affairs of successive generations."[48] Rather, it is the way that Israel's monarchy combined "power," "right," and "tradition" in "one coordinated agency" that revealed the essence of political authority. The "one coordinated agency" could just as well have been an oligarchy or a democracy, provided such an agency assured power, executed right and perpetuated a representative tradition. Israel's monarchy thus served as the constitutional *vehicle* through which the essence of political authority was revealed, in O'Donovan's account. Monarchy itself is not a constitutive concept in the essence of political authority; it is but one constitutional form in which political authority can legitimately and efficaciously exist.

The immediate question that arises from the insight that O'Donovan appears to believe that the Davidic monarchy reveals the essence of political authority is this: on what grounds are we to accept that the Davidic monarchy, as presented in Scripture, *reveals* the essence of political authority as opposed to merely *reflects* the essence of political authority? There are three reasons to doubt the tenability of the former: first, there is no suggestion in the Bible itself that the Davidic monarchy reveals the essence of political authority, nor even that it is in any way to be regarded as politically normative; second, God's covenant with his chosen people does not appear to be in any way dependent on the Davidic monarchy's mediation of his rule; and third, O'Donovan's own account of the political impact of the Christ-event sees the emergence of a new *bene esse* of political authority that departs from the Davidic model in significant ways, which seems to relativize its importance.

Biblical Ambivalence Regarding the Rise of Monarchy in Israel

O'Donovan provides no scriptural warrant for the idea that the Davidic monarchy reveals the essence of political authority. This might have something to do with the fact that this part of the thesis is made implicitly rather than explicitly: the conjunction of power, the execution of right and the perpetuation of tradition, which O'Donovan ostensibly derived from an exegetical analysis of Hebrew political terms associated with divine kingship, can only be seen in the Davidic monarchy and not in any other political circumstance in Israel's variegated history. The proposition thus seems to be that the essence of political authority was revealed *historically* in the Davidic monarchy and *textually* in the Old Testament's account of that monarchy.

Scripture's portrayal of the Davidic monarchy, however, is not propitious for the "essence of political authority thesis." For a start, there is the undeniable

---

48. O'Donovan, *The Desire of the Nations*, 20.

"ambivalence" surrounding the emergence of the monarchy in the narrative of the Old Testament.[49] O'Donovan accepts that "it is a textbook commonplace that we can distinguish two competing strands of thought about the monarchy within the Hebrew Scriptures."[50] "There are," he rightly notes, "texts of anti-monarchical provenance (e.g. 1 Sam. 8) and texts of pro-monarchical provenance (e.g. 1 Sam. 9, 10)."[51] But he maintains that the opposition was not to the "idea of human mediation of divine kingship," but rather the "erection of an image of Yhwh," that is, a form of idolatry whereby the king replaced God.[52] He concludes accordingly that ultimately "nobody opposed the monarchy."[53]

This may be true in the sense that there was no concerted or serious movement to depose the monarchy, according to Scripture. But can the opposition to the monarchy really be construed as opposition merely to the "erection of an image of Yhwh"? The "anti-monarchical" *locus classicus* of 1 Sam. 8:4–7 suggests otherwise:

> Then all the elders of Israel gathered together and came to Samuel at Ramah, and said to him, "You are old and your sons do not follow your ways; appoint for us, then, a king to govern us, like other nations." But the thing displeased Samuel when they said, "Give us a king to govern us." Samuel prayed to the Lord, and the Lord said to Samuel, "Listen to the voice of the people in all that they say to you; *for they have not rejected you, but they have rejected me from being king over them* [emphasis mine].

The text of verse 7b—"for they have not rejected you, but they have rejected me from being king over them"—suggests that God regarded his people's move to install a king to be a rejection of his own kingly rule over them. 1 Sam. 8:22 gives the impression that God acquiesces to the people's demand for a king as a concession to human need more than out of any imperative related to salvation-history, let alone out of any sense that he sought to establish or reveal in this monarchy the essence of political authority. Scripture further intimates that God had a hand in the downfall of the monarchy that is at the heart of O'Donovan's theological account of political authority. According to 2 Chron. 36: 16–17,

> the wrath of the Lord against his people became so great that there was no remedy. Therefore he brought up against them the king of the Chaldeans, who killed their youths with the sword in the house of their sanctuary, and had no compassion on young man or young woman, the aged or the feeble; he gave them all into his hand.

---

49. "Ambivalence" is O'Donovan's characterization of Scripture's portrayal of the origins of monarchy in Israel. See Oliver O'Donovan, *On the Thirty Nine Articles: A Conversation with Tudor Christianity* (Exeter: Paternoster Press, 1986), 59.
50. O'Donovan, *The Desire of the Nations*, 52.
51. Ibid., 52–3.
52. Ibid., 52.
53. Ibid., 53.

If Israel's monarchy is to be regarded as politically normative and revelatory of the divinely mandated essence of political authority, why does Scripture, the arbiter of "true political concepts," present God as ambivalent and reluctant about its creation in the first place? Moreover, why does God then bring about its downfall, if it is so integral to the mediation of his rule over Israel, not to mention the source of political norms regarding political authority?

Israel's Variegated Covenantal Political History

God's chosen nation experiences just about every political circumstance known to recorded history, all the while remaining in covenant with their God: patriarchal, slavery, tribal, charismatic leadership (judges), monarchy, exile, priestly (theocratic) rule, migration/diaspora, and colonial rule. There is disagreement about how to properly schematize and classify the different phases in Israel's political history. Norman Gottwald, for example, identifies three "horizons" in the political history of Israel presented in the Hebrew Bible, which include decentralized politics embedded throughout its social institutions (1250–1000 BCE), centralized autonomous politics (1000–586 BCE) and a colonial form of centralized politics dictated by foreign sovereignties within which a native/Judahite hierarchy was empowered to act in local matters (586–63 BCE).[54] Paul Hanson identifies five different "political models:" theocracy, monarchy, prophetic, sapiential, and apocalyptic.[55] What is not in dispute is that Israel's political history is diverse and involves multiple forms of constitutional arrangement (or circumstance). O'Donovan is patently aware of this fact, noting himself in *Desire* that political theologians must "deal ... with a disclosure [the Old Testament] which took form in a succession of political developments, each one of which has to be weighed and interpreted in the light of what preceded and followed it."[56] He too schematizes Israel's history into different periods: "tribe, monarchy, cultural-ethnic enclave, moment of world-renewal."[57]

One of the problems confronting O'Donovan's "essence of political authority thesis" is that the position and function of the Davidic monarchy in the narrative of the Old Testament is that of an *interregnum* rather than either a climax or denouement. This narrative position does not appear to accord with the theopolitical importance attributed to it by O'Donovan. According to the

---

54. Norman K. Gottwald, *The Politics of Ancient Israel* (Louisville: Westminster John Knox Press, 2001), 15–16.

55. Paul Hanson, "Prophetic and Apocalyptic Politics," in *The Last Things: Biblical & Theological Perspective on Eschatology*, ed. Carl E. Braaten and Robert W. Jensen (Grand Rapids: Eerdmans, 2002), 43–4, 51–2, 57. Hanson describes these models as "strictly epiphenomenal," by which he means that "they are human responses to faith as faith seeks appropriate application in the concreteness of human existence."

56. O'Donovan, *The Desire of the Nations*, 27.

57. Ibid., 29.

biblical narrative there were three kings who ruled what historians call the "united monarchy": Saul, David, and Solomon (*c*. 1050–930 BCE) Yet this period of united monarchy was soon followed by division in a period known to historians as the "divided monarchy," in which two kingdoms each ruled a part of the Promised Land—Israel in the north and Judah in the south.[58] The northern kingdom came to an end with its seizure by Assyria in 722 BCE (also at the hand of God—2 Kings: 17: 7, 18) and the southern kingdom met its similar fate in 587/6 BCE at the hands of Babylon.[59] The exile of the Judeans in 587/6 BCE marked the permanent end of the Davidic dynasty and of Israelite monarchy in the biblical narrative (sacred history). Israel's secular history, however, saw the re-establishment of a monarchy in Palestine in the form of the Hasmonean dynasty (110–63 BCE) before it eventually succumbed to Rome.

The Hasmonean dynasty in particular forms an interesting case in relation to O'Donovan's "essence of political authority thesis," and to his contention that "Israel" is normative for Christian political theology. O'Donovan does not consider it in *Desire*, presumably because it falls outside the scope of sacred history. Its significance rests in the fact that it was not only the first and only recrudescence of monarchy in Israel's secular history following the fall of Judah, but it was the first and only Israelite government (until the creation of the state of Israel in 1948) that exercised rule over Palestine unambiguously in "one coordinated agency."[60] In fact, it was the first and only regime between the fall of the Davidic monarchy and the establishment of the state of Israel that can be said to have unambiguously exercised political authority on O'Donovan's definition—the conjunction of power, right, and tradition in one coordinated agency. It also explicitly cast itself as heir to the Davidic dynasty.[61] The Hasmonean monarchy, therefore, although it falls outside

---

58. Provan, Long, and Longman put the period of Israel's united monarchy into the following historical perspective: "Although the period of David and Solomon has often grasped the imagination of Bible readers down through the ages, the period during which Israel had one king who ruled over both its parts (Israel in the north and Judah in the south) was brief when compared to the following period in which Israel and Judah were each ruled by their own kings" (*A Biblical History of Israel*, 259).

59. There is disagreement about the exact year that the temple in Jerusalem was destroyed by the Babylonians. William S. Morrow, *Introduction to Biblical Law* (Grand Rapids: Eerdmans, 207), 17.

60. Larry R. Helyer, "The Hasmoneans and the Hasmonean Era," in *The World of the New Testament: Cultural, Social, and Historical Contexts*, ed. Joel B. Green and Lee Martin McDonald (Grand Rapids: Baker International, 2013), 44. Helyer points out that the Hasmoneans rejected the "dyarchy" that had characterized political rule in the Seleucid colonial period.

61. Ibid., 46. Helyer notes that "the author of 1 Maccabees imparts to his work a Davidic typology fulfilled in the Hasmonean leaders." In spite of these efforts the fact remained that the leaders were not in fact from the line of David and, as some scholars have pointed out, they ruled more in the mold of Hellenistic kings. See Adam Kolman Marshak, *The Many Faces of Herod the Great* (Grand Rapids: Eerdmans, 2015), 56.

of sacred history, and thus lacks revelatory status for Christian theology, actually marks the one solitary instance in Israel's post-exilic history (prior to the modern state of Israel) in which the normative mediation of God's rule inaugurated by the Davidic monarchy appears to have been in effect, on O'Donovan's conception of political authority.

Putting Israel's sacred and secular political histories together, we can say the following: God's people were ruled briefly (by historical standards) in a united monarchy ("one coordinated agency"—Saul, David, and Solomon) that mediated God's rule through the conjunction of power, the execution of right, and the perpetuation of tradition before splitting into two rival kingdoms ("coordinated agencies"), both of which presumably mediated God's rule in some sense, before God brought both to an end on account of their persistent sin and breach of their covenantal responsibilities; The northern kingdom disappears from sacred history at this point and the people of the southern kingdom (or at least some of them) endure a period of exile living under the coordinated agency of a foreign power that rules according to an alien right and tradition; God's people are then released from exile and re-establish semi-autonomous rule within the context of an alien empire. This is followed by a period of Hellenistic rule and cultural colonization that eventually produces a backlash that leads to the re-establishment of an independent Jewish monarchy (Hasmonean dynasty) that not only conceived of itself as standing in the Davidic tradition, but also exhibited the marks of the "essence of political authority" revealed previously in the Davidic monarchy. The Hasmonean monarchy is replaced by Roman rule and then the Christ-event sets political authority on a new path altogether (according to O'Donovan). The question is: to what extent is it coherent to suppose that God would reveal a political norm through the Davidic monarchy and then remove, by his own hand, that norm permanently in the life of Israel?

It is certainly true that, although the Davidic monarchy did come to a permanent end, it nevertheless continued to serve as an ideal political type and political goal of Second Temple Judaism.[62] O'Donovan could potentially argue, on this basis, that the Davidic monarchy performed a normative function in the political imagination of post-exilic Israel, in spite of dual authority becoming the political norm in practice. While other periods in Israel's variegated political history occupied a significant place in the collective memory and identity of the Jewish people, as seen in the Passover celebration, for example, no other period

---

62. Brueggemann notes that "David is the dominant figure in Israel's narrative." Walter Brueggemann, *David's Truth: In Israel's Imagination and Memory*, 2nd ed. (Minneapolis: Fortress Press, 2002), 1. Blenkinsopp has noted that "the preservation of the genealogy of David's descendants by the author of Chronicles ... demonstrates that for some of Nehemiah's contemporaries hope for the restoration of the dynasty had not faded." Joseph Blenkinsopp, *David Remembered: Kingship and National Identity in Ancient Israel* (Grand Rapids: Eerdmans, 2013), 108. Walzer, however, describes this Davidic hope as an "impractical, apolitical, messianic fantasy" (*In God's Shadow*, 71).

served as a political archetype in the manner in which the Davidic monarchy did following its eclipse.

O'Donovan could further point to the consistent allusions in Scripture to Jesus being the fulfillment of the Davidic promise, something which again elevates the status and importance of the Davidic monarchy relative to other periods of Israel's political history *vis-à-vis* the Christ-event.[63] As O'Donovan correctly notes,

> Jesus laid claim to the legacy of Davidic expectation in his great entry into Jerusalem, a demonstration of popular support staged to evoke the memory of the king's coming in triumph to Zion in Deutero-Zechariah."

However, at the heart of O'Donovan's "re-authorization thesis" (discussed in the next chapter) is the idea that the Christ-event transforms the Davidide role into something new and different:

> The divine authority is irreplaceably immediate in the dying, rising and future disclosing of Jesus. The Davidides are not forgotten at this moment, but consciously recalled. Yet what we see there is *nothing like a revival*. It carries the role forward to a moment of revelation that is of *a different order entirely*.[64]

Prior to writing *Desire*, O'Donovan even went so far as to suggest that "the apostolic community was to see in the resurrection of Jesus God's decisive repudiation of the exclusive status of Israel's territory and institutions."[65]

Conclusion

The "essence of political authority thesis" is untenable in its present formulation and on the basis of the argumentation adduced in support of it. Its constituent concepts do not appear to be "authorized from ... Holy Scripture," in accord with the test O'Donovan sets for a sound political theology. Moreover, the thesis that those concepts formulate is extrapolated from an analysis of related, but in the end substantively different, biblical concepts, without sufficient and clear explanation as to the relationship between the biblical and extrapolated concepts. There is further evidence to suggest that the thesis has been brought to Scripture via Ramsey, rather than extrapolated from Scripture itself. And finally, the

---

63. For discussion of the Davidic promise, see Gary N. Knoppers, "David's Relation to Moses: The Contexts, Content and Condition of the Davidic Promises," in *King and Messiah in Israel and the Ancient Near East: Proceedings of the Oxford Old Testament Seminar*, ed. John Day (London: Bloomsbury, 2013).

64. O'Donovan, *The Desire of the Nations*, 124. Emphases mine.

65. Oliver O'Donovan, "The Loss of a Sense of Place," *The Irish Theological Quarterly* 55, no.1 (1989), 53.

circumstances in which the Davidic monarchy emerged, according to Scripture, its narrative position (interregnum in the context of the covenant), and the fact that in O'Donovan's own account the Christ-event represents a significant change from the way that political authority functioned in the Old Testament militate against the idea that Israel reveals the essence of political authority. In short, O'Donovan fails to substantiate the existence of a cogent biblical warrant for the "essence of political authority thesis." This has profound consequences for the tenability of his "re-authorization thesis" as I seek to show in the next chapter.

Chapter 4

ROMANS 13: 1–7 AND THE CHRISTOLOGICAL "RE-AUTHORIZATION" OF POLITICAL AUTHORITY

What I have characterized as O'Donovan's "re-authorization thesis" asserts that "the authority of secular government resides in the practice of judgment." In what follows, I question the tenability of the thesis on both exegetical and theoretical grounds.

The Problematic Biblical Evidence for the "Re-authorization Thesis"

O'Donovan maintains that the Christ-event "re-authorizes" political authority such that "judgment" (the execution of right) becomes the sole legitimate function of secular government in the wake of the Christ-event.[1] The "re-authorization thesis" ultimately hinges on a reading of Rom. 13: 1–7, "the most famous, and most disputed, discussion of political authority in the New Testament," which must be read with "fresh eyes," according to O'Donovan.[2] The exegetical path to the Rom. 13:1–7 warrant begins with Col. 2:15: "He [God] disarmed the principalities and powers and made a public show of them in Christ's triumphal procession."[3] This, O'Donovan argues, is "the primary eschatological assertion about the authorities, political and demonic, which govern the world: they have been made subject to God's sovereignty in the Exaltation of Christ."[4] The fact that the eschatological horizon awaits fulfillment is what "opens up an account of secular authority."[5] It is against this backdrop that O'Donovan contends that "the theme of Romans 13 is the authority which remains to secular government in the aftermath of Christ's triumph."[6]

O'Donovan insists that the "concern" of Rom. 13:1–7 is ecclesiological, but also indirectly Christological.[7] He argues that the description of political authority in

---

1. O'Donovan, *The Desire of the Nations*, 233.
2. Ibid., 147.
3. Ibid., 146. Although not stated, the biblical quotes in this section of *Desire* appear to be O'Donovan's own translations. Col. 2:15 in the NRSV is: "He disarmed the rulers and authorities and made a public example of them, triumphing over them in it."
4. Ibid., 146.
5. Ibid.
6. Ibid., 152.
7. Ibid., 152.

this section of Paul's letter to the church at Rome "follows from the understanding that the authority of the risen Christ is present in the church's mission," which raises the question: "To what extent is secular authority compatible with this mission and, so to speak, re-authorized by it?"[8] The answer rests in "judgment." As 1 Tim. 2:1–4 indicates, on O'Donovan's reading, secular political authority is "authorized" to provide and ensure the space required by the mission of the church to draw "men and women of every nation ... into the governed community of God's Kingdom."[9] Secular authorities, O'Donovan elaborates,

> are no longer in the fullest sense mediators of the rule of God. They mediate his judgments only. The power that they exercise in defeating their enemies, the national possessions they safeguard, these are now rendered irrelevant by Christ's triumph ... Such claims are overwhelmed by the immediate claim of the Kingdom. There remains simply the rump of political authority which cannot be dispensed with yet, the exercise of judgment.[10]

What O'Donovan means, then, by the notion of "re-authorization" is a diminution in the purpose and function of the political authority exercised by secular government. The Christ-event renders certain pre-Easter political functions redundant and, so to speak, un-authorized.[11] The residual need for, and ongoing relevance of, temporal judgment stems from the fact that the church's mission depends on a peaceable social and political environment in order to properly execute its mission. It is worth noting in this regard that in *Judgment* O'Donovan describes the church as "post-political," in the sense that it reveals "the final form of human society," that is, "complete and uncoerced fellowship with God."[12] In this light, the partial de-authorization of secular political authority coincides with and, to some extent, is a consequence of the partial (or proleptic) realization of the final form of human society.

Although O'Donovan offers ecclesiological and Christological rationales for the "re-authorization thesis," the cogency of the thesis, as foreshadowed, actually depends on a particular reading of Rom. 13:1–7, namely its revelation that "the whole rationale of government is seen to rest on its capacity to effect the judicial task."[13] In relation to Kelsey's schema introduced earlier, it is

---

8. Ibid., 146.

9. Ibid.

10. O'Donovan, *The Ways of Judgment*, 151. Note once again that O'Donovan appears to be working from two conceptual models here. This is a rare instance where we are given "power" in the sense of "salvation," that is, military victory.

11. O'Donovan has helpfully clarified that the term "re-authorization" could readily be replaced with "partial de-authorization." Oliver O'Donovan, "Response to Gerrit de Kruijf," in *A Royal Priesthood?* 239.

12. O'Donovan, *The Ways of Judgment*, 240.

13. O'Donovan, *The Desire of the Nations*, 148.

4. "Re-authorization" of Political Authority

difficult to discern whether O'Donovan actually understands Rom. 13:1-7 to constitute the data for the "re-authorization thesis" or its warrant. In *Judgment*, for instance, he argues that

> such an interpretation of authority [in Rom. 13:4] … *self-consciously dispenses* with other functions of political authority that must have suggested themselves to readers of the Hebrew Scriptures as well as observers of the Roman world; it *strips down* the role of government to the single task of judgment, and forbids human rule to pretend to sovereignty, the consummation of the community's identity in the power of its ruler.[14]

The active verbs in this articulation of the "re-authorization thesis"—*dispenses, strips down, forbids*—suggest that O'Donovan possibly regards his reading of the passage as expositional, more so than interpretive, which is to suggest that the "re-authorization thesis" is in fact one advanced by Paul himself in Rom. 13:1-7. There is a point in *Desire,* too, where O'Donovan indicates that he might understand the "re-authorization" thesis to be expositional rather than interpretive: "St Paul's new *assertion* is that the performance of judgment alone justifies government; and this reflects *his* new Christian understanding of the political situation."[15] At other points in *Desire,* however, O'Donovan leaves the impression that the thesis is actually inferred from the aforementioned ecclesiological and Christological background he reads in Rom. 13:1-7, which would see the text function more like a warrant (an "inference-license" in Kelsey's language).[16]

In any event, the central question is whether Rom. 13:1-7 can support the "re-authorization thesis," in either the role of data or warrant. In this regard, there are grounds for questioning the cogency of O'Donovan's particular reading of Rom. 13:1-7. The most immediate problem stems from the fact that the "re-authorization thesis" is simply not found in the *text* of Rom. 13:1-7. As Wolterstorff has correctly observed of the "re-authorization thesis," "no New Testament writer says, concerning the authority of government, that once it was thus, now it is so," and nor does Paul add "and this is the entire extent of which rulers are now authorized to do."[17] Wolterstorff describes the "re-authorization thesis" as "an inference from silence."[18] It is actually an inference from omission. We recall that by the time O'Donovan had come to examine the political impact of the Christ-event on salvation-history in *Desire,* he had already concluded that the Old Testament revealed the essence of political authority: "power, the execution of right and the perpetuation of tradition … assured in one coordinated agency."

---

14. O'Donovan, *The Ways of Judgment,* 4. Emphasis mine.
15. Ibid. Emphases mine.
16. Ibid., 152.
17. Wolterstorff, "A Discussion of Oliver O'Donovan's *The Desire of the Nations,*" 102.
18. Ibid.

When O'Donovan says that Paul "self-consciously *dispenses* with other functions of political authority" and "*strips down* the role of government to the single task of judgment," what he appears to be inferring is that Paul's *self-conscious* omission of "power" and "tradition" is indicative of the re-authorization of political authority. This is a stronger claim than an inference from silence. O'Donovan infers that Paul himself has articulated the "re-authorization thesis" by consciously omitting elements constitutive of the essence of political authority revealed in the Old Testament.

This argument by omission is revealing for two reasons. Firstly, it places beyond doubt what was implicit in O'Donovan's development of the "essence of political authority thesis": the essence of political authority *really* was revealed in the Old Testament and Paul knew this to be the case (how could Paul *self-consciously* omit concepts constitutive of political authority if he did not know this to be the case?). Secondly, it makes the cogency of the "re-authorization thesis" dependent on the validity of the "essence of political authority thesis," which I have already shown to be untenable in the previous chapter.

A problem for O'Donovan is that his particular reading of Rom. 13:1–7 is not demanded by the text at all. It does appear, on the other hand, to be a reading demanded by his own "essence of political authority thesis." If O'Donovan is correct that the Old Testament has shown the essence of political authority to be the conjunction of power, right, and tradition in one coordinated agency, then he is forced to account for the absence of "power" and "tradition" in Paul's account of political authority in Rom. 13:1–7. But accounting for this absence is a problem unique to O'Donovan, something which renders his particular interpretation of Rom. 13:1–7 highly idiosyncratic when set against the interpretations of New Testament scholars, none of whom are committed to O'Donovan's specific "essence of political authority thesis," and thus forced to reconcile Paul's teaching about government in Rom. 13:1–7 with the "essence of political authority thesis."

New Testament Scholarship and Rom. 13:1–7

That O'Donovan's reading of Rom. 13:1–7 is idiosyncratic can be demonstrated readily via a survey of New Testament commentaries. Not only do many New Testament commentaries eschew O'Donovan's Christological framework for interpreting the text, many also explicitly rule it out on the very basis of the text. Ernst Käsemann, for instance, writes that "we do not find any sign of any specifically eschatological or christological motivation of the section ... Instead reference is made to the will of the Creator."[19] Leander Keck, who notes that "the basic warrant for submission is ... theological," maintains that "what makes the silence about Christ noteworthy is not just the absence of the name itself but

---

19. Ernst Käsemann, *Commentary on Romans*, trans. Geoffrey W. Bromiley (Grand Rapids: Eerdmans, 1980), 351.

the fact that the passage takes no account of the significance of the Christ-event as a whole."[20] Arland Hultgren argues that "least of all can the passage be considered Paul's 'Christological grounding of the state,' for there is no mention at all of Christ in the entire passage."[21] Joseph Fitzmyer observes that "it is remarkable that Paul can discuss this topic in the absence of any christological consideration."[22] John Toews simply concludes: "there is no Christology here; it is all theology."[23] In contrast, O'Donovan's "re-authorization thesis" posits that Paul's articulation of the new circumscribed role for secular government set out in Rom. 13:1-7 is predicated on a Christological understanding of how the Christ-event has altered the role of government this side of Easter.

In addition, while the exhortations in Rom. 13:1-7 are obviously addressed to an ecclesial community in a specific location, Rome, there is actually nothing in the text itself to suggest that Paul is thinking about the relationship of the church to secular political authority. As Thomas Schreiner points out, the "every person" of verse 1a ("Let *every person* be subject to the governing authorities ... ") "suggests that this injunction applies to both unbelievers and believers."[24] The first verse thus makes the context a single political order under God to which all humans are subject. Moreover, verses 3b-4b, in which Paul utilizes the rhetoric of "diatribe,"[25] address the second person singular (you), thus reinforcing the individual context of "every person" in verse 1a:

> Do you wish to have no fear of the authority? Then do what is good, and you will receive its approval; for it is God's servant for your good. But if you do what is wrong, you should be afraid, for the authority does not bear the sword in vain! (13:3b-4b)

This makes an ecclesiological reading somewhat strained. It is not so much the existence of the church—at that time a politically insignificant and organizationally disparate community—and its relationship with political authority that seem to form the context for Rom. 13:1-7, but how the individual Christian is to behave toward the earthly Caesar who makes certain demands of the Christian, such as the levying of taxes.

---

20. Leander E. Keck, *Romans* (Nashville: Abingdon Press, 2005), 312, 321.
21. Arland J. Hultgren, *Paul's Letter to the Romans: A Commentary* (Grand Rapids: Eerdmans, 2011), 467.
22. Joseph A. Fitzmyer, *Romans: A New Translation with Introduction and Commentary* (New York: The Anchor Bible Doubleday, 1993), 663.
23. John E. Toews, *Believers Church Bible Commentary: Romans* (Scottdale, PA: Herald Press, 1989), 318.
24. Thomas R. Schreiner, *Romans* (Grand Rapids: Baker Books, 1998), 682.
25. Richard N. Soulen and R. Kendall Soulen, *Handbook of Biblical Criticism*, 4th ed. (Louisville: Westminster John Knox Press, 2011), s.v. "diatribe": "An imaginary or fictitious dialogue of moral paraenesis."

Rom. 13:1–7: Theoretical or Paraenetic?

There is a common view among commentators that Paul offers neither a theory of state nor a theory of the relationship between church and state in Rom. 13:1–7. This judgment largely turns on the view that the passage is paraenetic or exhortatory, rather than theoretical, with the emphasis being on the proper response and disposition of the Christian *vis-à-vis* human political authority, not the nature of political authority or government *per se*.[26] Käsemann, for example, contends that "Paul is not advancing any theoretical considerations," while Keck maintains that "the literary context itself shows that Paul is *not* outlining his view of 'the state.'"[27] Hultgren believes Paul does not provide any "theory of the state" and is instead "more concerned about the life of the believer within the civil sphere than about the nature of the state itself."[28] He further contends that "Paul is not discussing in exhaustive fashion the relation of Christians to governing authorities."[29] Robert Jewett thinks "Romans 13:1–7 was not intended to create the foundation of a political ethic for all times and places in succeeding generations."[30] Michael Gorman agrees, arguing that the passage does not "create a political theology, especially not one for all times and circumstances."[31] John Stott remarks that Paul's "emphasis is on personal citizenship rather than on any particular theory of church–state relations."[32] Ben Witherington sees "no full-blown theology of church and state" in the passage, and believes that "it is what Christians do in reaction to the state that Paul is concerned about."[33] In a similar vein, Schreiner writes that "the text is not intended as a full-blown treatise on the relationship of believers to the state."[34] Charles Talbert argues that Rom. 13:1–7 "is not a complete statement about the Christians and government."[35] Gerrit de Kruijf, writing specifically in response to O'Donovan's "re-authorization thesis," contends that O'Donovan erred in extending the Christological reading into verse 4, an exegesis, he contends, no

---

26. For example, see Hultgren, *Paul's Letter to the Romans*, 467. "Within its literary context, the passage belongs to a lengthy paraenetic section of the letter (Rom 12:1–15:13) ... Paul's concern here is not with the state or civil government per se, but with the life of the believer that takes place in the world and within the civic life."
27. Käsemann, *Commentary on Romans*, 354; Keck, *Romans*, 311. Emphasis original.
28. Hultgren, *Paul's Letter to the Romans*, 472.
29. Fitzmyer, *Romans*, 665.
30. Robert Jewett, *Romans: A Commentary* (Minneapolis: Fortress Press, 2007), 786.
31. Michael J. Gorman, *Apostle of the Crucified Lord: A Theological Introduction to Paul & His Letters* (Grand Rapids: Eerdmans, 2004), 396.
32. John R. W. Stott, *The Message of Romans: God's Good News for the World* (Leicester: InterVarsity Press, 1994), 339.
33. Ben Witherington III, with Darlene Hyatt, *Paul's Letter to the Romans: A Socio-Rhetorical Commentary* (Grand Rapids: Eerdmans, 2004), 307.
34. Schreiner, *Romans*, 687.
35. Charles H. Talbert, *Romans* (Georgia: Smyth & Helwys, 2002), 296.

one has ever supported.³⁶ He maintains that "it is impossible for this text to carry the weight necessary for it to function as a definition of the political act in the exclusive way O'Donovan claims."³⁷

In light of the above perspectives on Rom. 13:1–7, it is prudent to ask if O'Donovan does in fact presuppose that Paul is offering a *theory* of state? The language O'Donovan utilizes to articulate the view of government expounded by Paul in Rom. 13:1–7 is highly suggestive of theory. Recall the language he uses to describe what Paul is doing in this passage: "self-consciously dispenses," "strips down" and "forbids."³⁸ On O'Donovan's account, the view of government offered by Paul in Rom. 13:1–7 is generic (universal in scope and application), exhaustive (judgment is the sole function of government), normative (other functions are excluded), and to a certain extent conceptually abstract (there is a change in the function of government based on the triumph of Christ—from "power," "right," and "tradition" to "judgment" alone). O'Donovan has gone as far as characterizing this famous passage in Romans as contributing to a *"reconception* of political authority in the Gospel era."³⁹

O'Donovan is not unique in perceiving a theory of government in Rom. 13:1–7. E.P. Sanders, for example, maintains that verses 3–4 "describe government as Paul saw it," but then adds *contra* O'Donovan: "If anyone is looking for a passage in the Bible that can no longer be literally applied, he or she need look no further."⁴⁰ Sanders cautions that Paul did not "construct a systematic theology," the likes of which can be found in that of Calvin, and that Paul's theological discussions tended to derive from "events and issues" faced in his ministry to the gentiles.⁴¹ There is no agreement about the precise pastoral question that prompted the inclusion of this specific exhortation about the governing authorities in this letter to the Christians at Rome. There is, on the other hand, broad agreement amongst New Testament scholars that Paul was likely addressing a specific question that may have been the subject of controversy amongst the Christians in Rome involving the "governing authorities" and the duties and obligations of believers to them.

---

36. Gerrit de Kruijf, "The Function of Romans 13 in Christian Ethics," in *A Royal Priesthood?* 234.
37. Ibid., 234–5.
38. O'Donovan, *The Ways of Judgment*, 4.
39. O'Donovan, *The Desire of the Nations*, 147. Emphasis mine.
40. E. P. Sanders, *Paul: The Apostle's Life, Letters, and Thought* (London: SCM Press, 2016), 692–3. Sanders offers a highly politically charged reading of Rom. 13:1–7 that barely disguises his discomfort with what he describes as Paul's "enthusiastic and idealistic, or perhaps naïve, description" of government which is "over the top" (694). He thinks some ulterior motive must have been driving Paul's exhortation and that he could not possibly have "approved all governmental actions with the degree of enthusiastic approbation shown in Rom. 13:1–7" in good conscience (695).
41. Ibid., 707. The most popular view is that it had to do with the question of paying taxes.

Rom. 13: 1–7: Continuity or Discontinuity with the Old Testament?

Another issue militating against O'Donovan's interpretation of Rom. 13:1–7 is that many biblical commentators see deep continuity between the attitude toward government expressed in the passage and that found in the Old Testament, contra O'Donovan's view that the passage marks a "new development," a "novelty," an "iconoclastic" interpretation of authority.[42] Käsemann, by way of example, argues that "the statements of Paul … unmistakably derive from the tradition of Judaism and especially of the Diaspora synagogue."[43] Keck maintains that "in verse 1 … Paul formulates in universal, generic terms what was a commonplace, as well as what he learned from scripture and inherited from Judaism."[44] "Paul knew," he continues, "that scripture too said that kingship comes from God, not only Israel's kingship (as in 2 Sam 12:7–8) but also that of its conqueror, Babylon (Jer. 27:4–7)."[45] Frank Matera contends that "Paul is not breaking new ground but affirming what Israel's scriptures already teach … 'By me kings reign, and rulers decree what is just; by me rulers rule, and nobles, all who govern rightly (Prov. 8:15–16).'"[46] According to Hultgren, "the admonition is in fact so general, and so much in keeping with both Jewish and Gentile Hellenistic traditions, that it is not clear that Paul has any particular problem at Rome in view at all."[47] He points to Josephus as support: "no ruler attains his office save by the Will of God."[48] Stott writes that Paul "had inherited a long-standing tradition from the Old Testament that Yahweh is sovereign over human kingdoms."[49] Schreiner considers Paul's exhortations in Rom. 13:1–7 to be "in continuity with both the OT and Jewish tradition."[50] Talbert sees the passage as expressing "a Jewish conviction" which "Early Christians endorsed."[51] Dorothea Bertschmann, writing specifically in the context of engaging O'Donovan's theology of political authority, concludes that "for Paul political authority has not changed after Christ."[52]

The fact that New Testament commentators see continuity between Paul's attitude to government and that found in the Old Testament, where O'Donovan sees novelty and change, is revealing. It reinforces the sense that there is absolutely nothing in the text to suggest that Paul is *reconceptualizing* O'Donovan's "essence of political authority thesis." Moreover, in the absence of this particular exegetical commitment, far from indicating discontinuity, the passage indicates continuity of perspective.

---

42. O'Donovan, *The Desire of the Nations*, 148, 233; O'Donovan, *The Ways of Judgment*, 4.
43. Käsemann, *Commentary on Romans*, 354.
44. Keck, *Romans*, 314.
45. Ibid.
46. Frank J. Matera, *Romans* (Grand Rapids: Baker Academic, 2010), 294.
47. Hultgren, *Paul's Letter to the Romans*, 469.
48. Ibid., 467.
49. Stott, *The Message of Romans*, 340.
50. Schreiner, *Romans*, 682.
51. Talbert, *Romans*, 294.
52. Bertschmann, *Bowing Before Christ—Nodding to the State?* 179.

This is perhaps the point at which O'Donovan's interpretation of Rom. 13:1–7 departs most significantly from that commonly found amongst New Testament scholars, showing in the process the consequences of his prior commitment to the idea that the Old Testament, and in particular the Davidic monarchy, reveals the very essence of a type of political authority that mediates God's divine kingship.

Does Rom. 13:1–7 Promote a "government-as-judgment" View of Government?

To my knowledge, no scholar disputes that verses 4b and 4c—"for the authority does not bear the sword in vain! It is the servant of God to execute wrath on the wrongdoer"—indicates that judgment is *a* legitimate function of political authority in the divine economy. There is, then, nothing contentious about the claim that a proper purpose of government is to execute judgment. As Schreiner observes, in concord with O'Donovan, "the state," according to Rom. 13:4, "mediates God's judgment in history."[53] However, verses 4b and 4c must be read in conjunction with verses 3c and 4a, with which they are clearly connected thematically and linguistically (e.g., use of the term "servant" (διάκονος) in both 4a and 4c and use of the prepositional pair γὰρ and δὲ in 4a and 4c, respectively):

> 3c) Then do what is good, and you will receive its [the authority's] approval 4a) for [γάρ] it is God's servant [διάκονος] for your good. 4b) But [δὲ]if you do what is wrong, you should be afraid, for the authority does not bear the sword in vain! 4c) It is the servant [διάκονος] of God to execute wrath on the wrongdoer.

The critical linking concept in these verses is *diakonos*, translated as "servant" in the NRSV. Verses 3c–4c indicate that political authority, what the NRSV calls "the authority" (ἐξουσία), is a servant (διάκονος) for two purposes: (1) "for your good" and (2) "to execute wrath on the wrongdoer." This is why verse 5 explains that it is right to be subject to the governing authorities "because of wrath" (διὰ τὴν ὀργήν) and "because of conscience" (διὰ τὴν συνείδησιν). The "wrath" of verse 5—"therefore one must be subject, not only because of wrath but also because of conscience"—relates back to the wrath of verse 4c and the "conscience" to the "good" of 4a. It is a matter of conscience to do good and facilitating this appears to be one of the tasks of government, according to Rom. 13:1–7.

This is certainly how some scholars interpret verse 4a. Käsemann believes that the good (τὸ ἀγαθόν) in this context relates to "political good conduct."[54] On the basis of this verse, Matera argues that "Paul affirms that God employs those who rule as his servants to assure the social order necessary for people to attain the good that God wills for them."[55] Bernd Wannenwetsch, who believes this verse has

---

53. Schreiner, *Romans*, 684.
54. Käsemann, *Commentary on Romans*, 353.
55. Matera, *Romans*, 295.

suffered from misleading translations, contends that the Greek should be rendered "it is God's *diakonos* for you *towards* the good" and not, as in the NRSV above, "it is God's servant [*diakonos*] *for* your good."[56] He concludes that "political authority is established to help and to enable people to do good works and thus contribute to the common good."[57] James Skillen, who disagrees with O'Donovan's "re-authorization thesis," along with its accompanying interpretation of Rom. 13:1–7, understands Paul to be telling the Roman Christians "to recognise the authorities as servants of God for their good."[58] Moreover, verse 6, which begins with "for the same reason" (διὰ τοῦτο), links the paying of taxes by Christians to the "wrath" and "conscience" of verse 5, something picked up by John Chrysostom in his homilies. On the basis of these verses he identified "civil order, peace, public service, including those responsible for military and economic arrangements," as "benefits accruing to cities from their governments."[59] In fact, John Chrysostom's interpretation of Rom. 13:1–7 is important for our purposes precisely because it recognizes the dual *diakonos* functions of government in Rom. 13:1–7, demonstrating that such a view is a part of the Christian exegetical tradition on Rom. 13:1–7:

> "Therefore one must be subject, not only to avoid wrath but also for the sake of conscience." What does "not only to avoid wrath" mean? He means, not only that insubordination opposes God and brings great evils on one's head, both at God's hands and the government's, but that *government is highly beneficial, ensuring peace and good administration of society. Innumerable benefits accrue to cities from their governments, and if you removed them everything would disappear* ...[60]

Calvin represents another interesting historical case on the exegesis of Rom. 13:1–7. In his commentary on Romans, he took account of verse 4a, saying: "'For he is God's minister for good,' etc. Magistrates may hence learn what their vocation is, for they are not to rule for their own interest, but for the public good."[61] Calvin broadly shares O'Donovan's view that judgment is central to the legitimate purpose of government: "But if we understand that the magistrate, in inflicting punishment, acts not of himself, but executes the very judgments of God, we shall be disencumbered of every doubt."[62] But unlike O'Donovan, he also sees a more constructive role for government in promoting the social good: "For it [civil

---

56. Bernd Wannenwetsch, "Soul Citizens: How Christians Understand Their Political Role," *Political Theology* 9, no.3 (2008): 381. First emphasis original, second emphasis mine.
57. Ibid.
58. Skillen, "Acting Politically in Biblical Obedience?" 410.
59. John Chrysostom, "Twenty-fourth Homily on Romans," in *From Irenaeus to Grotius*, 94.
60. Ibid. Emphasis mine. It is perhaps instructive that O'Donovan has said that "it was Latin-speaking Western Christendom that adhered most radically to Paul's conception" of government ("Government as Judgment").
61. John Calvin, "Commentaries on Romans," in *Calvin: On God and Political Duty*, ed. and intro. John T. McNeil (Indianapolis: Bobbs-Merrill Educational Publishing, 1954), 86.
62. John Calvin, "On Civil Government," in *Calvin*, 57, (*Institutes* 20.10). "But if we understand that in the infliction of punishments the magistrate does not act at all from himself, but merely executes the *judgments* of God ... [emphasis mine]."

polity] not only tends to secure the accommodations arising from all these things, that men may breathe, eat, drink, and be sustained in life, though it comprehends all these things while it causes them to live together."[63] Recall that O'Donovan maintains in *Judgment* that governments *only* bear responsibility for reflexively defending the common good, not promoting it. In this regard, it is noteworthy that verse 4a is conspicuously absent in O'Donovan's entire discussion of Rom. 13:1–7 in *Desire*.[64]

Conclusion

O'Donovan's "re-authorization thesis" presupposes that Paul is articulating a normative theory of government in Rom. 13:1–7 and that his omission of "power" and "tradition" in that text supports the inference that judgment alone is the new "re-authorized" (or "partially de-authorized") function of government post-Easter. O'Donovan suggests that this is a valid inference on Christological and ecclesiological grounds. However, in reality it presupposes, implausibly, that Paul had *O'Donovan's* "essence of political authority thesis" in mind when he came to compose his letter to the church at Rome. As we saw in Chapter 3, there is good reason to question the tenability of this thesis. This prior commitment to the "essence of political authority thesis" appears to have forced O'Donovan to explain what no other theologian or exegete has felt compelled to explain: the absence of any reference to "power" and "tradition" in the text of Rom. 13:1–7. This leaves O'Donovan with an interpretation of this much debated passage that is highly idiosyncratic in relation to several apparent consensuses, or well-established views, within New Testament scholarship.

The idiosyncrasy of O'Donovan's interpretation does not, in and of itself, prove that it is unsound. Consensuses can be, and sometimes are, overturned. So there is nothing intrinsically wrong with challenging a consensus in respect of Rom. 13:1–7. It does, on the other hand, require a strong "rebuttal" on O'Donovan's part, to return once again to Kelsey's schema, to show either that an existing consensus is actually mistaken or that O'Donovan's reading is not in fact incompatible with it. O'Donovan does no such thing.

Finally, there is the counterargument based on Rom. 13:4a, which many contemporary exegetes, and some prominent theological voices from the past (Chrysostom and Calvin), have understood as articulating a positive function for government in promoting the common good alongside that of performing judgment. O'Donovan ostensibly ignores this aspect of Rom. 13:1–7 and offers

---

63. Ibid., 46–7, (*Institutes* 20.3).

64. O'Donovan was even more explicit in his essay "The Political Thought of the Book of Revelation" where he said that the "central paradigm for politics" is "the punishing of wrongdoing." Oliver O'Donovan, "The Political Thought of the Book of Revelation," *Tyndale Bulletin* 37 (1986): 73. Skillen was the first to point out that O'Donovan with "chooses to ignore the beginning of … verse [4]" ("Acting Politically in Biblical Obedience?" 410).

no rebuttal to the view that the verse authorizes secular government to promote the good.

This all leaves the "re-authorization thesis" without compelling Scriptural warrant, which alters significantly the epistemic weight of the thesis. Another Anglican evangelical theologian Graham Cole provides wise counsel that is relevant in this regard: "If a putative doctrinal proposal is textless—that is to say, it lacks biblical support—then it may be held as a speculative possibility but not as a candidate for a non-negotiable conviction expressing the Faith."[65] "Speculative possibility" sounds like an apt description of O'Donovan's "re-authorization thesis" in light of the problems identified and discussed in this chapter surrounding its purported biblical warrant. The "re-authorization thesis," then, much like the "essence of political authority thesis," does not appear to be "authorized from … Holy Scripture" in the way that O'Donovan argues they are.

---

65. Graham A. Cole, *God the Peacemaker: How Atonement Brings Shalom* (Downers Grove: InterVarsity Press, 2009), 27.

Chapter 5

SALVATION-HISTORY, BIBLICAL THEOLOGY, AND POLITICAL AUTHORITY

Introduction

The previous chapter concluded that the "re-authorization thesis" is without Scriptural warrant and therefore can only be held as a speculative possibility rather than doctrine. The same could be said of the "essence of political authority thesis." Lack of Scriptural warrant has thus emerged as a common theme in the critique of O'Donovan's theology of political authority to this point. This naturally directs attention to O'Donovan's hermeneutic as a possible source of the problems that attend his theology of political authority. This chapter critically examines O'Donovan's salvation-history hermeneutic against the backdrop of this question: does a salvation-history hermeneutic necessitate either the "re-authorization thesis" or the "essence of political authority thesis"?

To aid this endeavor, I will bring O'Donovan into critical dialogue with G. Ernest Wright, focusing on his book *God Who Acts: Biblical Theology as Recital*.[1] I have selected *God Who Acts* for the fact that it adopts a similar salvation-history biblical hermeneutic to O'Donovan, leading Wright to emphasize, like O'Donovan, the connection between Christ's kingship and the Davidic monarchy as the locus of unity between the two testaments. Yet Wright's salvation-history hermeneutic does not lead him to anything resembling O'Donovan's "essence of political authority thesis" or "re-authorization thesis."[2]

For the sake of clarification, the purpose of this chapter is not to question a salvation-history biblical hermeneutic per se, nor O'Donovan's commitment to it. Nor is it to pass judgement on Wright's biblical interpretation, nor even to adjudicate which reading of Scripture is the better. It is to merely question whether a commitment to a salvation-history biblical hermeneutic demands O'Donovan's theology of political authority as a way of establishing if the problems identifiable in O'Donovan's theology of political authority are a product of his salvation-history biblical hermeneutic.

1. G. Ernest Wright, *God Who Acts: Biblical Theology as Recital* (London: SCM Press, 1966). O'Donovan makes no reference to *God Who Acts* in either *Resurrection*, *Desire* or *Judgment*.

2. Kelsey used the term "salvation-history" to describe Wright's approach to the Bible (*The Uses of Scripture in Recent Theology*, 50).

O'Donovan's Salvation-History Biblical Hermeneutic

Before turning to Wright's *God Who Acts*, it is necessary to examine O'Donovan's salvation-history biblical hermeneutic in greater detail. O'Donovan describes "salvation-history" as a "matrix" for reading Scripture.[3] He does not, however, provide a concise definition of his salvation-history biblical hermeneutic and nor has he written substantively on the issue in any concentrated fashion. So the contours of this biblical hermeneutic must be gleaned and reconstructed from various references across his corpus. Edward Klink and Darian Lockett, in *Understanding Biblical Theology*, define a salvation-history biblical hermeneutic, or what they call "biblical theology as history of redemption," as:

> ... discern[ing] the historical progression of God's work of redemption through an inductive analysis of key themes developing through both discrete corpora and the whole of Scripture. Major themes such as covenant or kingdom constitute the theological connecting fibres between the Old and New Testaments, and these themes necessarily run along a historical trajectory, giving fundamental structure to the theology of the Bible.[4]

Klink and Lockett maintain that "the relationship between the OT and the NT stands as one, if not the, central issue in a 'whole Bible' biblical theology" and that "the very DNA of biblical theology requires representing the biblical material in a unified form."[5] O'Donovan can be located within Klink and Lockett's "biblical theology as history of redemption" paradigm insofar as he maintains that "Israel's history must be read as a *history of redemption*" and "the triumph of God in Christ ... imposes the shape of salvation-history upon politics" and, moreover, that it is the one unified history of salvation that spans both testaments that constitutes the fundamental unity of Scripture.[6] That said, O'Donovan has a nuanced understanding of the relationship between Israel and the Christ-event that recognizes elements of "discontinuity" amidst a fundamental unity.[7] As he put it in *On the Thirty Nine Articles,* "empirical investigation reveals points of diversity and

---

3. O'Donovan, "Deliberation, History and Reading," 140.
4. Edward W. Klink III and Darian R. Lockett, *Understanding Biblical Theology* (Grand Rapids: Zondervan, 2012), 61. Klink and Lockett identify and discuss a five-fold typology of biblical theology, one of which is "biblical theology as history of redemption." The other four are: "biblical theology as historical description," "biblical theology as worldview-story," "biblical theology as canonical approach," and "biblical theology as theological construction." Influential evangelical scholar Don Carson is identified as a representative example of the "biblical theology as historical description" type.
5. Ibid., 17–18.
6. O'Donovan, *The Desire of the Nations*, 29; O'Donovan, *The Ways of Judgment*, 6.
7. O'Donovan makes the pertinent observation that the very concept of "history" presupposes a "unity" of some kind (*On the Thirty Nine Articles,* 61).

points of harmony" in the scriptural testimony.[8] The "line of continuity," according to O'Donovan, consists in "relating Jesus and the Christian faith to the history of the Jewish people."[9] This makes it possible to read scripture as "communicat[ing] a unified outlook and perspective."[10]

The way that O'Donovan deals with the discontinuity between the two testaments is through a process he describes as "historical dialectic."[11] The problem with the notion of "contradiction" in scripture, he explains, is that it "bespeaks an ahistorical, two-dimensional understanding of the Scriptural texts that conceives of them all as synchronous and competing propositions, rather than dialectically successive and mutually implicating testimonies of God's unfolding self-disclosure."[12] Klink and Lockett capture this idea when they note that "biblical theology's claim that God's revelation is progressive assumes *historical* progression."[13] Israel thus represents "part of the historical dialectic through which the gospel of Christ was revealed."[14] The objective of "historical dialectic," however, is not to smooth over all difference. Rather it is to recognize that the historically progressive nature of revelation presupposes some elements of disunity. As such, "reading for contrast," O'Donovan argues, "rather than simply reading for harmony, can be wonderfully illuminating of the text."[15]

The notion of "historical dialectic" presupposes a distinction between "contingent" and "universal" (O'Donovan's terms) elements in Israel's history as recorded in the Old Testament. "The theologian's task in expounding the Old Testament," says O'Donovan, "is to allow the contingent and the universal to emerge distinctly."[16] He goes on to explain that, "if the *universal* does not shine through the contingent, then what is done is not theology, but only history."[17] Conversely, "if the universal does not shine *through the contingent*, then what is done is bad theology … ."[18]

In sum, then, O'Donovan's salvation-history biblical hermeneutic recognizes a primary unity between the Old and New Testaments predicated on the relationship between Christ and Israel that is mediated through a "historical dialectic" that distinguishes contingent from universal elements in Israel's history. It is on this basis that O'Donovan concludes that "not everything about ancient Israel is equally paradigmatic."[19] This, in itself, is a telling concession, particularly with respect to

---

8. Oliver O'Donovan, "The Possibility of a Biblical Ethic," *Theological Students Fellowship Bulletin* 67 (1973), 19.
9. Ibid., 21.
10. O'Donovan, *On the Thirty Nine Articles*, 56–7.
11. Ibid., 61.
12. Ibid., 60.
13. Klink and Lockett, *Understanding Biblical Theology*, 62. Emphasis original.
14. O'Donovan, *On the Thirty Nine Articles*, 64.
15. Ibid., 57.
16. Ibid., 64.
17. Ibid. Emphasis original.
18. Ibid. Emphasis original.
19. O'Donovan, "Deliberation, History and Reading," 140.

our preceding analysis of the "essence of political authority thesis." O'Donovan's own salvation-history biblical hermeneutic provides a rationale for dismissing some, if not many or all, aspects of Israel's historical political forms as contingent rather than normative. I will return to this issue in due course.

God Who Acts

In *God Who Acts*, Wright argues that the best and most faithful way to do "biblical theology" is to read Scripture as "recital." "Biblical theology," as he explains it, "is first and foremost a theology of recital, in which Biblical man confesses his faith by reciting the formative events of his history as the redemptive handiwork of God."[20] Via a process of recital, the Christian identifies with and "participates … in the original events."[21] Scripture is thus construed as "a reflection on the meaning of God's acts" rather than as a system of ideas.[22] Underlying this reflection is the notion of the "unity and meaningfulness of universal history from the beginning of time until the end of time."[23] The meaning of history, according to the reflection of Scripture, is that "God through it was revealed as in process [*sic*] of redeeming all history."[24] Theology, for Wright, is therefore a process of drawing inferences from God's redemptive acts in history, and their interpretation in Scripture.[25]

O'Donovan made the perspicacious observation in *Desire* that "epochs are characterized not by positions but by debates."[26] *God Who Acts* is no exception to this rule.[27] The biblical theology as recital that Wright sets out in the book is offered as an alternative and remedy to the "abstract" and "propositional" approach of the systematic biblical theology of his day (1950s American Protestantism).[28] *Desire* forms part of a very different debate. It offers a remedy and alternative to both the contractarianism of modern liberal political thought and contemporary political theologies which have lost sight of the relevance of Israel's history. It is important to be mindful of this difference when comparing and contrasting the two books, as they form part of two very different debates. This difference is reflected in the fact that one is cast as a work in biblical theology and the other in political theology.

Notwithstanding the different debates toward which the respective works are orientated, clear parallels between the way Wright and O'Donovan approach Scripture can be discerned. While O'Donovan does not adopt Wright's language of "recital," he does employ the related term "proclamation." Reading Scripture

20. Wright, *God Who Acts*, 38.
21. Ibid., 28.
22. Ibid., 32.
23. Ibid., 39.
24. Ibid., 42.
25. Ibid., 44.
26. O'Donovan, *The Desire of the Nations*, 9. He added: "it is the way they state their disagreements rather than their agreements that binds the thinkers of an age together."
27. Wright, *God Who Acts*, 9.
28. Ibid.

as "proclamation," according to O'Donovan, involves reading it as the history of God's saving acts: "If the Scriptures are to be read as a proclamation, not merely as a mine for random sociological analogies dug out from the ancient world, then a unifying conceptual structure is necessary that will connect political themes with the history of salvation as a whole."[29] Whether or not "recital" and "proclamation" function precisely as synonyms in Wright and O'Donovan is beyond the scope of the present focus. Their clear connection, however, helps validate the notion that these two biblical hermeneutics are sufficiently similar to make comparison legitimate and productive.

Like O'Donovan, Wright regards the notion of divine kingship as central to salvation-history: "God's revealed purpose was that the whole earth shall become his kingdom."[30] And just like O'Donovan, Wright believes God's kingship is mediated firstly through the nation of Israel and subsequently through the exaltation of Christ: God "exercised his rulership by mediate means; that is, by leaders like Moses" and "in his resurrection ... [Jesus] ... assumed the royal or messianic office of Israel, so that he reigns on God's right hand over the universal creation."[31] Wright too interprets the "advent of Jesus Christ" as the "historical event which was the climax of God's working since the creation."[32] Wright also similarly places great emphasis on the link between king David and Jesus. He argues that "the most notable saving acts of God in Israel were seen concluded in David, only to be renewed again in Jesus Christ, who is in truth the new David long awaited."[33]

Despite the evident parallels between the salvation-history biblical hermeneutic employed by Wright and O'Donovan, the former does not draw the conclusion that the latter does about the revelation of the essence of political authority in the Davidic monarchy, or its re-authorization following Christ's exaltation. This can be explained by several critical differences in the way these two theologians interpret the significance and function of the Davidic monarchy in salvation-history and the nature of political authority. The first is that, unlike O'Donovan, who sees the mediation of God's authority primarily through institutions and the somewhat abstract concept of political authority, Wright identifies "personality" as "God's mediate *agent* in history."[34] This marginalizes the importance of the institutions of the Davidic monarchy in Wright's account of the relationship between Jesus' kingdom and that of David. It might also help explain why it did not occur to him that the way political authority functioned during the Davidic monarchy revealed either its essence or its specific norms for a Christian understanding of politics. "Political authority" is ostensibly of little importance to Wright's salvation-history

---

29. O'Donovan, *The Desire of the Nations*, 22.
30. Wright, *God Who Acts*, 25.
31. Ibid., 52, 62.
32. Ibid., 52, 56.
33. Ibid., 80. In relation to *God Who Acts,* Kelsey observes that "David is the shifting point from Old Testament *kerygma* to New Testament *kerygma*" (*The Uses of Scripture in Recent Theology,* 35).
34. Ibid., 60–1. Emphasis original.

biblical hermeneutic, because God's saving purpose is advanced by raising up charismatic leaders.

The second difference relates to Wright's typological understanding of Scripture, which construes King David as one of several Old Testament types fulfilled by Jesus ("lawgiver," "prophet," "priest," and "Adam" are the others).[35] "Typology," according to Wright,

> points to the centre of the Bible in a divinely directed, unique history wherein as a result of the fulfilment one is enabled to see that events of the Old Testament were meant by God to be preparatory events ... only to be comprehended fully in Jesus Christ.[36]

However, while he deems it "impossible ... to discard New Testament typology without separating ourselves from Biblical faith," he is conscious that "there is a great danger in typology if it is used as the exclusive, or even central, guide to the unity of the Bible."[37] His concern is that typology can all too easily slip into "allegory" or a "static approach" to Scripture.[38] "King" therefore forms one of several roles (types) that Jesus adopts which *together* fulfil God's promises to Israel. Wright's typological reading of Jesus' fulfillment of Israel's history naturally lends itself to (perhaps it is a product of?) an emphasis on the role of individual figures in mediating God's rule in history rather than institutions.

The third difference revolves around the role of covenant. Covenant constitutes the controlling concept for understanding the function of the Davidic "type" in relation to Jesus. In fact, covenant is the controlling principle of salvation-history itself: "promise and fulfilment," Wright explains, are "the central Biblical themes."[39] Moreover, covenant is what binds the personalities of Israel into a common, unified history of salvation: "the person and the office of Jesus are seen in pure typological relation to the various offices of the Israelite covenant community, so that he fulfils them all in himself."[40] Thus, while O'Donovan connects the political leaders of Israel's history through their exercise of political authority and mediation of God's judgments, for Wright it is covenant that connects the charismatic leadership type of Israel's history fulfilled in Christ, who assumes and consumes all Israelite political offices and roles in his person.

In a further indication of how Wright's emphasis on covenant leads him to different conclusions from O'Donovan, witness the following comment he makes in relation to the "centralized government" of the monarchy, recalling that this constitutes a critical development in the revelation of the essence of political

---

35. Ibid., 62.
36. Ibid., 64–5.
37. Ibid., 65.
38. Ibid.
39. Ibid., 25.
40. Ibid., 62. The meaning of the term "office" in relation to Jesus is unclear in this context.

authority, and ultimately its re-authorization in O'Donovan's account: "centralized government, however, while a political necessity was nevertheless a theological problem, for it had to be fitted into the framework of the theocratic covenant."[41]

In contrast to Wright, the concept of covenant plays little substantive role in O'Donovan's political theology and in his interpretation of the role of the Davidic monarchy in salvation-history specifically, despite O'Donovan identifying "the unique covenant of Yhwh and Israel" as "the point of disclosure from which the nature of all political authority comes into view."[42] This lacuna has come to the attention of several critics. Gordon McConville, for example, notes that "covenant … plays a surprisingly small part in the argument in *DN*, in view of its prominence in the OT."[43] R. W. L. Moberly has observed that Moses and the Sinai covenant are "near-invisible" in *Desire*.[44] In response to such criticisms O'Donovan has conceded that he said too little about covenant in *Desire*.[45]

Because O'Donovan interprets Jesus' fulfillment of the Davidic covenant through the lens of God's sovereignty, that is, his kingly rule, he is led to search for concrete, tangible links between the *way* that God's rule was mediated in the Davidic monarchy and the way that secular governments today mediate Christ's rule. This makes the politics of the Davidic monarchy relevant to an understanding of Christ's rule: "Israel's knowledge of God's blessings was, from beginning to end, a *political* knowledge."[46] Wright, on the other hand, does not regard the *political order* of the Davidic monarchy as germane to understanding Christ's rule. Rather it is Jesus' fulfillment of the covenantal promise that illuminates political themes like "justice" and "security."[47] This provides us with two alternative readings of the political implications of history from within a similar salvation-history hermeneutic.

Covenant versus Political Authority

Wright's focus on covenant makes for an illuminating contrast with O'Donovan's focus on political authority. One important difference—to be added to those already canvassed—is that covenant is unambiguously a biblical concept with political connotations, and thus ostensibly a true political concept "authorized" from Scripture in O'Donovan's terms. "In the Torah," William Morrow explains, "Israel's covenant with God is expressed in literary structures similar to political

---

41. Ibid., 52.
42. O'Donovan, *The Desire of the Nations*, 45.
43. McConville, "Law and Monarchy in the Old Testament," 81.
44. Moberly, "The Use of Scripture in *The Desire of the Nations*," 55.
45. O'Donovan, "Response to Gordon McConville," 89. "I plead guilty, on the other hand, to saying too little about 'covenant.'"
46. O'Donovan, *The Desire of the Nations*, 23. Emphasis mine.
47. Wright, *God Who Acts*, 56.

agreements called vassal treaties and loyalty oaths."[48] I do not mean to suggest that covenant is incompatible with O'Donovan's controlling concept of authority. Rather, it is a question of proper emphasis. It is surely instructive that the word "covenant" occurs 293 times in the New Revised Standard Version (NRSV) translation of the Old Testament and "authority" a mere 18 times, in which case one might expect to see a greater role for covenant in a political theology that seeks to work from an account of God's saving acts in history grounded in the political vocabulary of Scripture.[49] Furthermore, covenant arguably does a much better job at connecting the phases of Israel's variegated political history within the context of a unifying salvation-history biblical hermeneutic than does political authority. Horst Dietrich Preuss argues, by way of example, that the concept of "divine election" connects the different "spheres" of Israel's history, including "the exodus, the ancestors, the king, Zion and the priesthood."[50] Greater emphasis by O'Donovan on covenant therefore might have provided him with a means of integrating Israel's diverse political history under a framework of divine kingship with far greater Scriptural authority than his singular focus on political authority.

It is conceivable that O'Donovan's preference for political theology stems, at least in part, from a valid concern of relevance and intelligibility. "Political authority" is a term of currency in both scholarly and popular discourse, whereas "covenant" has largely fallen into disuse.[51] O'Donovan's aversion to covenant as a *Christian* theopolitical concept also appears to relate to its negative association with "contract," bearing in mind that contractarianism serves as *Desire's* foil. This semantic connection between covenant and contract was quite explicit in the early modern period of political thought. Hobbes, for example, in a characteristic passage of *Leviathan* writes: "From hence it followeth, that when the Actor maketh a Covenant by Authority, he bindeth thereby the Author, no less than if he had made it himselfe."[52] In this regard, O'Donovan has warned of the "temptation to the modern mind, for which the slide from 'covenant' to 'contract' was a fatally easy one."[53] While this might be a valid concern on O'Donovan's part, it hardly

---

48. Morrow, *Introduction to Biblical Law*, 28–9. "A vassal treaty is an agreement between a king and a lesser ruler."

49. The tables turn once we move into the New Testament, however, with the word "authority" occurring more frequently in the NRSV translation than "covenant." The connection between these two terms and the possibility that the perspective shifts from an emphasis on covenant to "authority" is a question that warrants further study.

50. Preuss, *Old Testament Theology*, 37.

51. Paul D. Hanson, *Political Engagement as Biblical Mandate* (Eugene, OR: Cascade Books, 2010), 70. Hanson notes that the "meaning" and "significance" of covenant "remain quite foreign to the thought of most people today."

52. Thomas Hobbes, *Leviathan*, ed. with intro. C. B. Macpherson (London: Penguin, 1968), 218. "Covenant" in this context obviously has a different meaning from covenant in the Old Testament, but it is not unrelated and demonstrates that it was an important concept in political thought of the seventeenth century.

53. O'Donovan, "Response to Gordon McConville," 89.

seems to justify the exclusion of "covenant" from an analysis of leading Hebrew terms associated with divine kingship in the Old Testament.

As foreshadowed in the introduction to this chapter above, the significance of Wright's covenant-based interpretation of the Davidic monarchy and its preparatory relationship to Christ's kingship is not its relative merits, but rather its demonstration of the fact that a salvation-history hermeneutic does not demand either the "essence of political authority thesis" or "re-authorization thesis." Nor does it demand the construal of Israel as politically normative for post-Easter politics. It also reveals that O'Donovan has omitted from his theology of political authority one of the most important, unambiguous and central political concepts in Scripture: covenant. This just so happens to be a theopolitical concept that shaped and became associated with a school of political thought to which O'Donovan stands in opposition, and to which his theology of political authority is offered by way of remediation. Moreover, O'Donovan's notion of "historical dialectic," as a way of distinguishing continuity and discontinuity, provides him with a perfectly sound rationale for arguing that the specific political forms in which God's rule was mediated through the Davidic monarchy can be treated as historically contingent. On the basis of the comparative analysis conducted in this chapter, it is possible to conclude that there is nothing intrinsic to a salvation-history biblical hermeneutic per se, nor O'Donovan's specifically, that would seem to demand, or even warrant, either the "essence of political authority thesis" or the "re-authorization thesis."

Chapter 6

THE "PROVIDENCE THESIS" AND ITS THEODICY IMPLICATIONS

We now turn our attention to the third foundational thesis underpinning O'Donovan's theology of political authority: the "providence thesis." That thesis states the following: "That any regime should actually come to hold authority, and should continue to hold it, is a work of divine providence in history, not an accomplishment of the human task of political service" (theorem 2 in *Desire*). The definition of authority in this context is that laid out in Theorem 1, what I have been calling the "essence of political authority thesis": "Political authority arises where power, the execution of right and the perpetuation of tradition are assured together in one coordinated agency." Although these are presented as two separate "theorems" (albeit on the same page) in *Desire*, they really form one single theopolitical proposition: political authority arises where power, the execution of right and the perpetuation of tradition are assured together in one coordinated agency (Theorem 1) by the work of divine providence (Theorem 2).[1]

In this chapter, I will attempt to show, via the case study of North Korea, that this thesis creates undesirable theodicy problems on account of the fact that it implies that a regime such as North Korea's possibly exists as a result of the work of divine providence. My contention is not that O'Donovan supports the regime in North Korea, or even that he regards it as the work of divine providence. It is that the "providence thesis," when applied to actual regimes, appears to legitimate some that Christians might otherwise wish to condemn.

The rationale for the sudden appearance of the "providence thesis" immediately after arrival at the "essence of political authority thesis" following an exegetical analysis of Hebrew terms habitually grouped with the concept of divine kingship in the Hebrew Bible is opaque. This opacity is due to the fact that "providence" does not form part of the preceding exegetical discussion and makes its first sudden appearance in the discussion of political authority with little in the way of explanation or argumentation. The lack of reference to "providence" in the preceding exegetical discussion possibly has something to do with the fact that,

---

1. I first made this point in Jonathan Cole, "Towards a Christian Ontology of Political Authority: The Relationship between Created Order and Providence in Oliver O'Donovan's Theology of Political Authority," *Studies in Christian Ethics* 32, no.3 (2019): 310.

as Don Carson notes, "Hebrew has no root for 'providence.'"[2] Still, as Carson also notes, the concept of providence is "woven into all divisions of the Hebrew canon."[3] On such a basis, O'Donovan might claim that the concept of divine providence is implicit in the narrative of Scripture, if not its actual language *per se*, or indeed that it is implicit in the very notion of divine kingship.[4] But again, returning to O'Donovan's own standard for judging the validity of theopolitical proposals, it is difficult to see how he might validate the idea that "providence" is a "true political concept ... authorized from ... Holy Scripture" in light of Carson's first observation.[5]

Context suggests that the "providence thesis" is presented as a corollary, or perhaps an implication, of the "essence of political authority thesis." The former appears to be primarily driven by the explicit axiom that political authority cannot be considered a human "achievement." O'Donovan makes this claim several times in *Desire*, saying, for example, that "whatever the role of political agents ... in determining the shape and form that political authority shall take in any time and place, no one can pretend to have invented authority or to have devised it as an instrument to serve some pre-political purposes of his or her own."[6] "It does not lie within the power of political orders," O'Donovan adds, "to secure the social conditions for their own indefinite prolongation."[7] Claims such as these intimate that the "providence thesis" is predicated on the idea that it is beyond the capacity of either rulers or governments to create and maintain the complex social conditions necessary for stable rule, in which case the Christian can posit that divine providence is responsible for providing the conditions in which political authority can arise at all.[8]

There is subtlety in O'Donovan's argument here. He does not have in mind acts of "*special* intervention of the divine to appoint a particular ruler."[9] Nor does he mean to imply that there is no human element in the exercise of political authority—a leading idea of *Desire*, after all, is that human political acts are authorized by, and therefore analogous to, divine acts in history. While political authority cannot be regarded as a human achievement, in O'Donovan's view, it is still a thoroughly human activity—the fact that human political authority mediates God's authority, per Rom. 13:4, "does not remove political authority from the sphere of the human."[10]

---

2. D. A. Carson, *Divine Sovereignty and Human Responsibility: Biblical Perspectives in Tension* (London: Marshall, Morgan & Scott, 1981), 3–4. There is also no occurrence of "providence" in the New Testament, although there are several references in the Apocrypha, possibly on account of their Hellenistic provenance.

3. Ibid.

4. Ibid.

5. Recall the statement that "nothing assures us a priori that politico-theological concepts are to be found; the question of their existence must be put to Scripture itself" (*The Desire of the Nations*, 15).

6. O'Donovan, *The Desire of the Nations*, 46–7.

7. Ibid., 47.

8. Rist thinks this aspect of O'Donovan's account of political authority is tantamount to the idea that "problems are so complicated that only an omniscient God could get them right." John Rist, "Judgment, Reaction and the Common Good," *Political Theology* 9, no.3 (2008): 371.

9. O'Donovan, *The Ways of Judgment*, 129.

10. Ibid.

Rather, the role of divine providence in relation to stable human political rule (the enduring possession and exercise of political authority) is the creation and maintenance of "a *general* provision of non-reciprocal relations under which we may flourish."[11] "Non-reciprocal relations" describes the asymmetric relationship between rulers and subjects, namely the fact that the latter willingly and freely accede to the authority of the former out of a sense of obligation: "That the ruler we elect and the forms we devise should be able to assert and retain authority, *that* is something we cannot undertake. We can only entrust them and ourselves to God's providential authorization."[12]

Epistemically, then, the "providence thesis" is best characterized as a speculative inference drawn from the axiomatic belief that humans did not "invent" (O'Donovan's word), and could not have invented, political authority.[13] The intuition that political authority is not something "invented" by humankind is, in my view, sound; there simply is no moment in recorded history where humans sit down and invent political authority. In fact, political authority simply appears with the dawn of recorded human history, operative in our oldest known civilizations (Egypt and Sumer). But it is one thing to posit that political authority is "something we simply stumble upon" and another thing entirely to suggest that its existence is attributable to divine providence, and divine providence alone, particularly in the absence of any biblical warrant for such an argument.[14]

The Normative Implications for the Legitimacy of Regimes Arising from the "Providence Thesis"

The "providence thesis," by virtue of its dependence on the "essence of political authority thesis" for its definition of "authority," becomes normative in its implications. It implies that a legitimate government is one which assures power, the execution of right, and the perpetuation of tradition in one coordinated agency for the purposes of exercising judgment. O'Donovan purports to know what political authority is because what it is was revealed in the Old Testament (in reality through the Davidic monarchy) and he knows what the normative function of political authority is this side of Easter because Paul has indicated as much in Rom. 13:1–7. In other words, any extant regime that assures power, the execution of right, and the perpetuation of tradition in one coordinated agency appears to exhibit political authority according to a biblical model, and does so because divine providence has created the conditions in which this is possible. In fact, as early as *Resurrection*, O'Donovan was explicit about the normative implications of his conception of political authority (mirroring that later offered

---

11. Ibid. Emphasis original.
12. Ibid. Emphasis original. O'Donovan notes that to act out of obligation is to act "freely, not under compulsion."
13. O'Donovan, *The Desire of the Nations*, 47.
14. O'Donovan, *The Ways of Judgment*, 128.

in *Desire*): "When these three authorities [might, injured right and tradition] are exercised by one subject, then they are endorsed by a *moral authority* which requires that we defer to them."[15] The "providence thesis" implies the following test, then, for a morally legitimate regime: Does regime x hold power, execute right, and perpetuate tradition in one coordinated agency in an enduring manner? If the answer is "yes," then that regime would appear to possess a type of political authority in accordance with the biblical standard, thanks ultimately to the "work of divine providence." As I endeavor to show below, it is not clear that a regime like North Korea's would actually fail this test, raising genuine theodicy concerns in relation to O'Donovan's theology of political authority, given most, if not all Christians, would be inclined to condemn the North Korean regime precisely on the grounds of Christian morality.

The Theodicy Problem: The Case of North Korean

There are two limitations to using North Korea as a case study to test the implications of moral legitimacy evident in the "providence thesis." Firstly, space prohibits an extensive critical engagement with the literature on North Korean politics.[16] Secondly, North Korea is a notoriously difficult society to research because the regime is highly secretive and researchers have very limited access to the country and its people. Thus, although the literature on North Korea is too vast to comprehensively treat here, it is, nevertheless, also characterized by significant gaps in knowledge that do not exist in connection with other societies.

Fortunately, the generic content of "power," "execution of right," "perpetuation of tradition," and "one coordinated agency" substantially attenuates the impact of these limitations. There is sufficient scholarship on North Korea to enable a satisfactory exploration of the implications of O'Donovan's generic conception of political authority and ill-defined concept of providence.[17] Finally, it is worth noting that O'Donovan does not apply any of his theses to any case studies of actual regimes, with the arguable exception of Christendom, which is more properly construed as a civilization than a regime *per se*. This lack of applied political theology is a general weakness of the discipline, and in that regard O'Donovan is far from unique in not applying and testing his theories to actual regimes, past or present.

---

15. O'Donovan, *Resurrection and Moral Order*, 128. Emphasis mine.
16. This is a constraint on any case study in this context.
17. I do not wish to imply that O'Donovan's conception of providence is ill-defined in general, just that it is ill-defined as it pertains and operates in relation to political authority.

North Korea: Power, One Coordinated Agency, and Longevity

It is possible to dispense expeditiously and uncontroversially with two elements of the "essence of political authority thesis" as it applies to North Korea: power and one coordinated agency. The North Korean regime objectively holds power on any definition. In fact, the regime arguably has more power over more of its society than any other extant regime.[18] The regime also incontrovertibly exercises authority in one coordinated agency, again, possibly to a greater extent than any other extant regime. It is also possible to dispense expeditiously and uncontroversially with the longevity element in the "providence thesis," notwithstanding the open-endedness of its formulation. The Democratic People's Republic of Korea was formally established in 1948 and at the time of writing is seventy-two years old. The country has been ruled by a single party within the context of a single polity and has experienced only two leadership transitions since its foundation.[19]

O'Donovan's Generic Conception of Right and Tradition in the "Essence of Political Authority Thesis"

It is more challenging to evaluate the question of right and tradition in the case of North Korea, as this entails making complex qualitative judgments. There is no question that the regime executes *a* right and perpetuates *a* tradition. The question is *what type* of right must be executed and *what type* of tradition perpetuated in order for a regime to be deemed legitimate under O'Donovan's "providence thesis," and does the type of right and tradition found in North Korea qualify?

We saw in Chapter 2 that O'Donovan defines judgment as "an act of moral discrimination that pronounces upon a preceding act, or existing state of affairs to establish a new public context."[20] O'Donovan clarifies that the objective of political judgment is not "absolute justice itself," but rather "a *tradition* of judgment" that strives for justice "in the relative sense in which it is appropriate to speak of it in

---

18. According to the South Korean Ministry of Unification's "Understanding North Korea" document, "North Korea was the most highly centralized economy among socialist states in the 20th century." "Understanding North Korea," *Institute for Unification Education, Ministry of Unification*, 2014. http://eng.unikorea.go.kr/content.do?cmsid=1817. The Ministry of Unification produces an annual edition of "Understanding North Korea" in Korean. The May 2012 edition was translated into English and published in 2014.

19. Oh notes that, from the perspective of longevity, the North Korean "regime has been a great success, even though the country is a basket case." Kongdan Oh, "Understanding North Korea," *Brookings Institution*, April 1, 2013, https://www.brookings.edu/articles/understanding-north-korea/, 6. Kang observes that North Korea has long defied "outsiders' expectations about its survivability." David C. Kang, "They Think They're Normal: Enduring Questions and New Research on North Korea—A Review Essay," *International Security* 36, no.3 (2011/2012): 143.

20. O'Donovan, *The Ways of Judgment*, 7–8, 10.

human communities."²¹ Judgment, he says, "achieves its goal only if a public moral context is established by the judgment, and the public moral context is, in some respect, *more just as a result*."²² This provides us with an initial criterion that can help guide our evaluation of whether the North Korean regime "executes right": this is to ask whether the North Korean regime realizes a kind of relative justice.

In terms of the scope of judgment, O'Donovan clarifies that he does not have in mind a conception of government reduced purely to a judicial function, "as in some libertarian fantasy."²³ Rather, he construes moral discernment to entail the exercise of political authority "in all its forms," including activities such as lawmaking, warmaking, welfare provision, and education.²⁴ However, while all judicial activity consists of acts of judgment, not all legislative and executive activities constitute judgment. Many "public" acts performed by government today, according to O'Donovan, and as we noted in Chapter 2, do not qualify as moral discriminations between right and wrong, and hence do not constitute judgments on his definition (e.g., deciding the outcome of a tender process, the appointment of statutory office holders and warnings related to health and public safety). However, the activities that governments do legitimately pursue today are to be "re-conceived … and subject to the discipline of enacting right against wrong."²⁵ It is clear, then, that an assessment of North Korea in this context cannot be limited to the performance of its judiciary alone, but rather must also take into consideration its legislative and executive functions through the lens of judgment, as O'Donovan conceives it.

Although O'Donovan defines judgment as a political act that discriminates between right and wrong (creating in the process a new public context), the execution of right entails more than the exercise of mere judgments. Governments have a duty to defend the common good, and included within the common good is "right," which is to say "the good and the right *of a community*."²⁶ In order for political authority to successfully defend the common good, "it must command the authority of right."²⁷ It is difficult to comprehend exactly what O'Donovan means to suggest in saying that a government's defense of the common good "must command the authority of right." This is because it is not entirely clear what O'Donovan understands by the term "right" in this context. "Right," he explains, is simultaneously "the right of the community to its participants and the right of the participants to their community."²⁸ In this sense, "right" is the one and only "fundamental and inalienable human right" conceivable, in O'Donovan's view— "the right of each member of society to be social."²⁹ Tying this back to O'Donovan's notion of judgment, the suggestion seems to be this: in order for a political authority to execute right (enact judgments regarding the moral right and wrong of a given

---

21. Ibid., 144. Emphasis original; O'Donovan, *Resurrection and Moral Order*, 129.
22. O'Donovan, *The Ways of Judgment*, 8. Emphasis mine.
23. Ibid., 4.
24. Ibid., 5.
25. Ibid.
26. Ibid., 138–9.
27. Ibid., 139.
28. Ibid.
29. Ibid.

situation), it must do so on behalf of a community, which is to say that it must be an execution of the *community's* right, which is necessarily the common good. As such, when governments make moral discriminations and establish new contexts *on behalf of the community's right*, they are defending the common good (presumably a wrong against the community as a whole, not just an aggrieved individual).

O'Donovan makes it clear in *Judgment* that there is a point at which political authority ceases to exist, either because "injured right is systematically ignored by those holding power" or because "those holding power have no right of tradition" behind them.[30] O'Donovan describes such scenarios as moments of "de-politicization."[31] He provides several examples of failures to execute right that fall short of "de-politicization," or, in my preferred language, that do not *de-legitimize* political authority. These include the improper acquisition of authority, incompetence, the iniquities of individual officials (including malice or neglect where these are acknowledged as defects), administrative failures born of "human limitation" and even unjust laws—"as one swallow does not make a summer, so one bad law—even a handful—do not make a refusal of right."[32] The latter is illustrated by legalized abortion, the injustice of which does not invalidate the regimes that have enacted the legalization and which preside over its implementation.[33] Even a limited systematic refusal of right, in O'Donovan's view, such as in the case of an apartheid regime, does not invalidate that regime's claim to legitimately exercise political authority. In such a scenario, the persecuted group owes the state no obedience, but "those whom it [i.e., the government] treats as citizens by enacting justice for them … may owe it the ordinary duties of citizens, though they do not owe it cooperation in its policy of planned injustice."[34]

Conversely, citizens have an obligation to "sustain" the bearers of authority that are in place in their context for the purposes of achieving "continuity of regime"—"interruption of authority," O'Donovan says, "is an evil to be avoided."[35] Moreover, wherever political authority does not exist, an obligation arises "to facilitate the emergence" of a bearer of authority in order to avoid social chaos.[36] However, the obligations that generally attend political authority have qualified limits. Not everything the bearer of political authority demands of citizens activates an obligation. A ruler "may make demands that do not pretend to political authority: he may urge us, for example, to buy something from him like a government bond or a state-owned railway, or he may press upon us the need to vote for his party in elections."[37] Similarly, a ruler "may lay claim to an authority that he does not have."[38] In other words, the proper sphere

30. Ibid., 143.
31. Ibid.
32. Ibid., 135, 144–5.
33. Ibid., 145.
34. Ibid.
35. Ibid., 135.
36. Ibid.
37. Ibid., 136.
38. Ibid.

of political authority is circumscribed: not everything the bearer of political authority can demand of citizens either commands obligation or comes within the scope of their legitimate authority. Citizens are to use their discretion to discern when the demands of political authority command their obedience and when they do not.[39]

It is clear from these examples that O'Donovan sets the threshold for de-legitimization ("de-politicization") rather high, at least by the standards exhibited in our current moment of liberal malaise. That said, he does recognize that there comes a point short of "de-legitimization" in which we are entitled or forced to ask whether a deficient, though ultimately legitimate, political authority might not be replaced by something better. In such a scenario, according to O'Donovan, the proper response is constituted by "acts of political reform"—a "justified revolution" that is "governed by constitutional law."[40] O'Donovan here draws a distinction between lawful political reform (or revolutionary reform) that is done constitutionally, perhaps in response to public opinion or outcry, and public or popular agitations for change that are unwilling or unable to utilize constitutional means to implement their desired reforms. The "cause of the oppressed," O'Donovan argues, can generate "the appearance of informal authority" and even command a type of "moral authority," but it does not amount itself to political authority (the convergence of power, execution of right, and perpetuation of tradition in one coordinated agency), and therefore cannot command obedience.[41]

In sum, O'Donovan sets a very conservative threshold at which a government's failure to execute right ends in de-legitimation of its political authority. It is possible for a government to exercise political authority and still be guilty of "grave faults," because a government's execution of right can only aspire to a relative justice in a fallen world and a defective political authority is a lesser evil than no political authority at all.[42] Moreover, constitutional reform is the only valid response to the injustices and failures invariably committed by legitimate governing authorities. It is instructive that the examples given by O'Donovan of states that crossed the threshold to de-politicization are Bosnia, Rwanda, and Somalia (in the 1990s).[43] If that is the threshold at which a government's failure (or inability) to execute its community's right translates into illegitimacy, then it would seem to make virtually any state that functions short of civil war or genocide legitimate, including, in our case, North Korea.

(The reason I think the language of "de-legitimization" is preferable to "de-politicization" is that even in the cases of Bosnia, Rwanda, and Somalia an internationally recognized government continued to operate and exercise at least some authority, albeit greatly diminished and impaired. What O'Donovan is really pointing to is the fact that in each of these cases the governments in question

---

39. Ibid., 137.
40. Ibid., 145.
41. Ibid.
42. Ibid.
43. Ibid., 146.

reached a threshold at which their authority no longer *legitimately* commanded the obedience of all, perhaps even most, of its citizens, even if in practice it did command the obedience of some citizens to some extent in the moment of their crisis).

In *Judgment,* O'Donovan provides the following succinct definition of tradition: "Tradition is 'what is established'; and 'what is established' is not the past, but the present as determined by the past."[44] "The authority of tradition," he adds, "is that of its *continuity with immediate history*" and "its claim is the claim of what has proved its worth by survival."[45] The latter contention illuminates the longevity component of the "providence thesis": the tradition within which a regime rules must enjoy some degree of historical continuity. O'Donovan provides two important qualifications to this conception of tradition. First, the goods produced by tradition are "limited" and "corruptible."[46] Second, tradition must be "representative" if right is to be enacted on a community's behalf: "An unrepresentative power might do all kinds of good, but it would do it from the outside; it would not be a good done *by* that community."[47] "Representative" in this context does not necessarily imply democratic representation; it denotes the embodiment of a community's identity, something that can be achieved via different constitutional arrangements, such as monarchy in the case of Biblical Israel.[48] As with the execution of right, O'Donovan sets the threshold for the de-legitimation of tradition at regime failure. This is evident from his citation of the Soviet Union and Yugoslavia as examples of regimes that lost political authority by virtue of being deserted by their tradition "overnight."[49] O'Donovan attributes the collapse of both regimes to the "sudden relocation of the community's identity."[50] The argument effectively runs as follows: any enduring tradition that is broadly representative of a people's identity is legitimate until it isn't.[51]

44. Ibid., 140.
45. Ibid.; O'Donovan, *The Desire of the Nations,* 194. Emphasis original.
46. O'Donovan, *The Ways of Judgment,* xiv–xv.
47. Ibid., 140, 160. Emphasis original. O'Donovan would later come to describe representation as "one of the essential elements of political authority" ("Representation," 135).
48. O'Donovan, *The Ways of Judgment,* 140. Note that in *Common Objects of Love* O'Donovan appears to attribute a people's identity to providence: " ... but to have a political identity means accepting the contingent determination of one's society by the decrees of God's historical providence, which allows no justification or criticism." Oliver O'Donovan, *Common Objects of Love: Moral Reflection and the Shaping of Community* (Grand Rapids: Eerdmans, 2002), 43.
49. O'Donovan, *The Ways of Judgment,* 147.
50. Ibid.
51. O'Donovan is cognizant that traditions, let alone the community identity of which they are said to represent, are never homogeneous. They are, in his characteristically evocative prose, "the confluence of a multitude of streams" (*The Ways of Judgment,* 147) "Social controversy," he notes elsewhere, is of "the very essence of tradition." The very fact that there is a "hegemonic tradition to be contended for" testifies to the important role that tradition plays in community identity ("Judgment, Tradition and Reason," 405–6).

Two clear criteria regarding the legitimacy of tradition emerge from this discussion: first, a tradition needs to be in continuity with the immediate past (to have proved its worth by its survival); and second it must be representative of the community's identity.

The Non-prescriptive Nature of Right and Tradition in "The Essence of Political Authority Thesis"

The analysis above concerning the meaning of right and tradition in relation to the "essence of political authority thesis" reveals that they are relative and non-prescriptive. What constitutes legitimate political authority is the execution of *a* right within *a* tradition. There is no sense that the right and tradition in question must be this right and this tradition, and not that right and that tradition. This is exactly as it ought to be given what is in view is the essence of political authority, and by definition the essence must be able to accommodate all instances, whether the Islamic right and tradition through which the Saudi monarchy rules or the liberal right and tradition through which the democratically elected government of the United States rules. O'Donovan is even explicit in this regard with respect to tradition: "recognizing the right of tradition … is an amoral business, depending on *post hoc* judgments about how things have actually gone."[52] It is important to keep the relative and non-prescriptive character of right and tradition in mind as we assess the extent to which the North Korean regime can be said to execute right and perpetuate tradition in such a way that would make it qualify as one of the regimes that holds the biblically revealed essence of political authority thanks to the work of divine providence.

Perpetuation of Tradition in North Korea

Given tradition intrinsically involves questions of continuity with the past, any assessment of the legitimacy of North Korea's political tradition must contend with the historical context in which it emerged. From 1392 until 1910, the Korean peninsula was ruled by the Choson dynasty (also known as Joseon). As Michael Robinson explains, the political order of the Choson dynasty consisted of a "monarch rul[ing] through a centralized bureaucratic system that was staffed by the *yangban* elite," which functioned much like an aristocracy.[53] The *yangban* elite "maintained itself through the legal and de facto inherited status privileges,

---

52. O'Donovan, *The Ways of Judgment*, 147.
53. Michael Edson Robinson, *Cultural Nationalism in Colonial Korea, 1920–1925* (Seattle: University of Washington Press, 1988), 15.

landholding, officeholding and utilization of Confucian orthodoxy."[54] Choson monarchs ruled through what Robinson describes as a "Confucian political ideology," which, among other things, "support[ed] a stratified social structure."[55]

The traditional Korean legal system in the Choson era was heavily influenced by Confucianism and Chinese legal norms and did not recognize a separation of powers between the judiciary and the executive.[56] In 1876, Korea entered the international system through a series of treaties with Western powers, embarking, in the process, on a program of modernization.[57] The modernization process involved the introduction of Western legal concepts and Korea's first modern written constitution in 1894.[58]

Japan annexed Korea in 1910 and ruled it as a colony until its defeat in 1945. During the colonial period, the Japanese legal system was enforced throughout Korea, replete with Japanese judges and a Japanese governor-general who held "absolute administrative and legislative powers."[59] Kipyo Kim points out that, at the time Japanese colonial rule began, "there was no written law in Korea to govern civil law matters, except for a few provisions included in criminal codes," so the colonial administration established a system of "customary law" that "reworked old Korean laws and popular practices."[60] One of the tensions the Japanese colonial administration encountered was how to deal with "customs based on Confucian rituals" that the Japanese, whose legal code had been heavily influenced by the German legal code, regarded as "irrational and impractical."[61] They found a solution in codifying and reworking Korean customs and Confucian rituals into a body of law.[62]

Following the liberation of Korea in 1945, the peninsula was divided into two administrative zones: a Soviet zone in the North and an American zone in the South. These zones were run by the Soviet and American militaries, respectively, until the establishment of the Democratic People's Republic of Korea in the North and the Republic of Korea in the South in 1948. North and South Korea were established under Soviet and American supervision, respectively. As a consequence, North Korea was established as a socialist state along Soviet lines. However, it was never a Soviet clone and quickly developed its own distinctively Korean socialist culture and political norms.[63]

---

54. Ibid.
55. Ibid., 15–16.
56. Kipyo Kim, "Overview," in *Introduction to Korean Law*, ed. Korea Legislation Research Institute (New York: Springer, 2013), 2.
57. Robinson, *Cultural Nationalism in Colonial Korea*, 19.
58. Kim, "Overview," 3–5.
59. Ibid., 5.
60. Marie Seong-Hak Kim, "Law and Custom under the Choson Dynasty and Colonial Korea: A Comparative Perspective," *The Journal of Asian Studies* 66, no.4 (2007): 1069.
61. Ibid., 1082.
62. Ibid.
63. Institute for Unification Education, "Understanding North Korea," 11.

Important aspects of North Korean socialism that are peculiar to North Korea include hereditary rule, *suryong* ("monolithic one-man control"), *juche* ("self-reliance"), and *songun* ("military-first")—the latter two are formally recognized in the constitution.[64] Of these, *juche* is the most important, but also the most difficult to define. It is the creation of North Korean founder Kim Il-sung and is claimed to date back to his guerrilla days fighting Japanese occupation.[65] Juche is "a nationalist ideology" resting on three pillars: "political sovereignty," "independent economy," and "military self-defence."[66] "*Juche* philosophy," says Patricia Goedde, "pervades all aspects of North Korean society" and could be regarded as a "spiritual creed that requires putting North Korea first in every respect."[67]

O'Donovan has given us two criteria by which to judge the legitimacy of a tradition: continuity with the past and representation of a community's identity. The case of North Korea demonstrates just how difficult it is to make objective judgments about an actual political tradition on the basis of these criteria. On the face of it, the establishment of the socialist state in North Korea represents a radical break with Korea's past. But on closer inspection, it is not clear that it marks radical discontinuity with either the Choson or colonial political orders that preceded it. All three, for example, were authoritarian, with absolute power vested in a single ruler. All three recognized no functional separation between executive and judicial authority. In all three regimes, the people had no say in the running of their government. This authoritarian tradition is also in evidence when one considers the parallel history of South Korea. Kongdan Oh notes that South Korea differed little from North Korea in the 1950s, observing that "both countries were dictatorships and both were poor."[68] In this regard, it is worth noting that democracy was not established on the Korean Peninsula until the 1990s (in the South), in which case North Korean *juche*-socialism arguably has a better claim to immediate continuity with the Korean past than South Korean democracy, and a credible claim, at the very least, to being representative of the Korean people's *traditional* identity.

The North Korean regime's claim to continuity with Korean history and identity does not end with monarchical rule alone. Scholars identify strong traditional Confucian currents in North Korean political culture and institutions. As South Korea's Institute of Unification Education notes, "Confucian norms and traditions are relatively strong in North Korean society."[69] Changyang Choi identifies "honor" (face saving) and the "culture of collectivism" as "traditional

---

64. Ibid., 1; Institute for Unification Education, "Understanding North Korea," 12, 32.

65. Patricia Goedde, "Law 'Of Our Own Style': The Evolution and Challenges of the North Korean Legal System," *Fordham International Law Journal* 27, no.4 (2003): 1265–6.

66. Ibid., 1273.

67. Ibid.

68. Oh, "Understanding North Korea," 6.

69. Institute for Unification Education, "Understanding North Korea," 17. Such norms include "Grand Socialist Family," which requires North Koreans to give their "trust, love [and] respect" to the leader figure.

characteristics of Korean society" still extant in North Korea.⁷⁰ Goedde notes that "strands of traditional Korean legal history underlie the North Korean legal system in subtle but enduring ways."⁷¹ She argues that concepts from the Choson "Neo-Confucian ideology," such as "ancestral lineage and worship, as defined by patrilineal descent," are evident in North Korea "in terms of dynastic succession and inheritance of family class status."⁷² She even suggests that the Workers' Party of Korea (WPK) has replaced the traditional *yangban* as the "elite core of society."⁷³ This is not to suggest that the establishment of a socialist state in North Korea does not also mark substantive change from Korea's past. Rather, it is to suggest that there are important aspects of continuity between the North Korean regime and Korean history and identity that are perhaps obscured by the language of "communism," which have tended to produce Western interpretations of North Korea that see it as little more than Soviet replica. It also brings into focus the fact that the more recently established democratic regime in South Korea is no more obviously in continuity with the Korean past and identity than the Korean-style communist regime in the North. In fact, it is arguably a greater departure than *juche*-socialism.

On the other hand, O'Donovan's insight that tradition must be in continuity with the immediate past and representative of a community's identity does make it possible to conclude that the Japanese colonial administration was illegitimate. It was not representative of any Korean tradition or identity. Indeed, Korean political identity was usurped by the imposition of foreign rulers who introduced and governed according to alien laws, institutions, and traditions. Moreover, given Japanese colonial rule began abruptly following military conquest, its rule looks very much like the kind of "interruption" to political authority that O'Donovan regards as an "evil."⁷⁴ Armed resistance and the birth of modern Korean nationalism are testament to the unrepresentative nature of this rule. Moreover, it was out of this resistance and nationalism that the Democratic People's Republic of Korea was established, as articulated in the preamble to its Socialist Constitution: "Comrade Kim Il Sung authored the immortal Juche idea and, by organising and leading the anti-Japanese revolutionary struggle under its banner, created the glorious revolutionary traditions and achieved the historic cause of national restoration."⁷⁵

---

70. Changyang Choi, "'Everyday Politics' in North Korea," *The Journal of Asian Studies* 72, no.3 (2013): 667.

71. Goedde, "Law 'Of Our Own Style,'" 1274.

72. Ibid. Haggard and Noland point out that North Korea administratively classifies its people into three classes: "reliable supports, the basic masses and the 'impure class.'" They add that "family background is a key determinant of life in North Korea." Stephan Haggard and Marcus Noland, "Economic Crime and Punishment in North Korea," *Political Science Quarterly* 127, no.4 (2012): 671.

73. Ibid.

74. O'Donovan, *The Ways of Judgment*, 135.

75. "Socialist Constitution of the Democratic People's Republic of Korea," in *Foreign Languages Publishing House* (Pyongyang: North Korea, 2014), 1.

Thus, restoring Korean rule and identity, albeit in new form, is at the heart of the establishment of North Korea, and certainly at the heart of its own self-conscious tradition today, as reflected in its constitution.

Whether viewed through the prism of the longevity of the North Korean regime (seventy-two years), its restoration of Korean self-determination, the popularity of the implementation of socialism (at least in the early years), the legitimacy and popularity of its founding leader Kim Il-sung, or the Choson-Confucian roots of North Korea's unique brand of socialism, the regime in Pyongyang can lay claim to rule within a broadly representative tradition. At any rate, it is difficult to show otherwise, recalling the generic, non-prescriptive content of "tradition" in O'Donovan's "essence of political authority thesis." If *Juche*-socialism is not representative of the North Korean people's identity, then it is difficult to say what is: Neo-Confucianism, Choson monarchy, Western liberal democracy?

Execution of Right in North Korea

That North Korea is a serious and serial human rights abuser is beyond dispute.[76] However, establishing that the regime fails in its responsibility to execute right to such an extent and in such a manner that it rises to O'Donovan's threshold of illegitimacy is not so straightforward. Given unjust laws, partial systemic injustice and administrative failings do not, in and of themselves, constitute illegitimacy, according to O'Donovan, we must take a more wholistic view of the relative justice achieved, or not achieved, by the North Korean regime. Doing so requires consideration of several factors: the formal legal-institutional arrangements that reflect the intention of how society is supposed to be run and administered; the de facto system of how things operate in practice; and popular perceptions about whether the regime enacts the community's right. I will restrict my focus to North Korea's judicial system, which I take to be indicative of the regime more broadly. I take this approach on the basis that North Korea is a one-party state and in

---

76. Human Rights Watch describes North Korea as "one of the most repressive authoritarian states in the world" responsible for "systematic, widespread and gross human rights violations committed by the government include[ing] murder, enslavement, torture, imprisonment, rape, forced abortion and other sexual violence." "Human Rights Watch World Report 2017," *Human Rights Watch,* https://www.hrw.org/sites/default/files/world_report_download/wr2017-web.pdf, 457. A study of 1,300 North Korean refugees conducted between 2004 and 2005 found that, of the 10 percent who had been incarcerated in detention facilities, "90 percent reported witnessing forced starvation, 60 percent deaths due to beating or torture and 27 percent executions." In another example, a great famine in North Korea in the years 1995 to 1998, brought about in part by maladministration (weather was another factor), is thought to have killed between 600,000 and 1,000,000. Haggard and Noland, "Economic Crime and Punishment in North Korea," 660; and Kang, "They Think They're Normal," 153.

practice there is no functional separation between the executive, the legislature and the judiciary.

The first thing to acknowledge is that North Korea's legal and institutional arrangements aspire to achieve justice. It is easy to be cynical in this regard, but the reality is that these legal and institutional arrangements have not been consciously constructed to oppress the North Korean people.[77] North Korea has a "tri-level court system" consisting of a Central Court, twelve provincial courts and approximately 100 people's courts.[78] These courts usually deal with criminal and divorce cases.[79] A Central Procuracy, in conjunction with provincial and county procuracies, investigates and prosecutes crimes and audits state organs.[80] Unlike in Western legal systems, all North Korean lawyers work for the state. Judges and "public prosecutors" (the English translation used in North Korea's official translation of the Socialist Constitution) are appointed by and accountable to the Supreme People's Assembly, North Korea's legislative body.[81] The constitution stipulates that "court cases are heard in public and the accused is guaranteed the right of defence" (Article 164) and "in administering justice, the Court is independent, and judicial proceedings are carried out in strict accordance with the law" (Article 166).[82] At the constitutional and institutional level North Korea has a justice system that is organized, coherent, and ostensibly capable of administering justice.

In reality, however, the judiciary functions as an extension of the WPK and is therefore not independent in the way suggested by the constitution.[83] Judges, prosecutors, and lawyers are party members and are appointed by the People's Assembly, which is again made up exclusively of party members. Cho explains that "North Korean courts and judges appear to lack any independence whatsoever and are wholly subservient to the dictates of the Worker's Party, constitutional provisions notwithstanding."[84] The role of the WPK in the North Korean judicial system reflects the very different philosophical assumptions that govern socialist jurisprudence. Goedde helpfully clarifies that in North Korea "law is derivative of … party policy, a means to implement State objectives, a party code that citizens should follow, and a ruthless mechanism by which to punish those [who] do not."[85]

77. The constitution's framers ostensibly believed that they were instituting a just society, particularly in the context of Japanese colonial rule, and there is, it seems to me, no reason to doubt that a just regime, no matter how tragically misguided this turned out to be in practice, was the genuine goal and aspiration.
78. Goedde, "Law 'Of Our Own Style,'" 1277. There is also a separate military court, just as there is in Western countries.
79. Ibid.
80. Ibid.
81. "Socialist Constitution of the Democratic Republic of Korea," 32–4.
82. Ibid., 34.
83. WPK = Workers' Party of Korea.
84. Sung Yoon Cho, "Judicial System in North Korea," *Asian Survey* 11, no.12 (1971): 1181.
85. Goedde, "Law 'Of Our Own Style,'" 1267.

The North Korean judicial system has some additional characteristics that are germane to an assessment of whether the North Korean regime can be said to execute right to a standard that meets the threshold of legitimacy (in accord with standards indicated by O'Donovan). These relate to the degree of arbitrariness in the way the judicial system functions in practice and the regime's expansive conception of crime, such that it includes a category of "political crimes" unrecognized in Western judicial systems (North Korea has "political prison camps"—*kwan-li-so*, for example).[86] Political crimes in particular are an area of serious human rights abuse in North Korea under the terms of Western legal norms. Haggard and Noland explain that "a distinctive feature of the management of political crimes is that there is little pretense of due process," as "political crimes appear to fall outside of criminal statute altogether and are managed ... by the NSA [National Security Agency]" rather than the judiciary proper.[87] A 2008 study of 102 refugees who had been incarcerated found that just 13 reported receiving any trial at all.[88] North Korea also utilizes collective punishment that includes incarcerating extended family members.[89]

The category of "political crimes" is reflective of a different philosophical approach to administering justice. Goedde attributes this to the fact that the rights accorded citizens in the constitution "are unavailable to those located outside its ideal socialist society."[90] Such people include those deemed guilty of giving offense to the state, whether intentionally or not.[91] North Korea's official class system is also a contributing factor to this state of affairs, with the descendants of reactionaries, pro-Japanese and former landowners being subject to constant scrutiny from peers and the state alike, often for the smallest of offenses.[92]

As far as popular opinion in the West is concerned, the authoritarian nature of the North Korean regime, the lack of personal freedoms afforded its citizens, the widespread poverty of its people and, above all, the systematic human rights abuses evident in its justice system are more than enough to condemn the regime. But one of the virtues of O'Donovan's generic and non-prescriptive conception of execution of right and perpetuation of tradition is that only a relative justice need be achieved for a regime to hold and maintain political authority.

O'Donovan's realist insight is that a regime need only exercise *enough* power, enact *enough* right, and perpetuate a *sufficiently* representative tradition for political

---

86. Haggard and Noland, "Economic Crime and Punishment in North Korea," 662.

87. Ibid., 663. Interestingly, the arbitrariness of judicial authority works both ways, with many refugees reporting arbitrary release well before completing statutory sentences (673).

88. Ibid., 673. Haggard and Noland do not indicate whether these respondents were incarcerated for breaching the criminal or civil code, or for political crimes, or indeed a mixture thereof.

89. Ibid., 663.

90. Goedde, "Law 'Of Our Own Style,'" 1278.

91. Ibid. One should not assume that all those found guilty of "political crimes" are innocent of the charges thereof, irrespective of what one thinks about the justice of the criminalization of such activity.

92. Ibid.

authority to exist and be efficacious. Prevalent Western caricatures of North Korea as "hell-on-earth" fail to appreciate this seminal insight. Such caricatures fail to recognize that it is possible for a regime like North Korea's to still enact genuine right *even while* it commits systemic injustices of the type that seem to be akin to O'Donovan's "apartheid" example in *Judgment*.[93]

The confronting truth is that even repressive and authoritarian regimes are capable of genuinely enacting right and of ruling within the bounds of a legitimate tradition, at least to a minimum extent that facilitates regime longevity. North Korea's human rights abuses must be weighed (for our purposes) against the fact that its judiciary prosecutes and convicts offenders for many crimes uncontroversially regarded as such in the West, whether it be theft, rape or murder. If the punishment of offenders for such crimes is just in Western legal systems, then it follows that it is similarly just in the case of North Korea, even if the procedures used to prosecute and convict, along with the system itself, are deemed deficient. When the North Korean judicial system convicts offenders for crimes such as these it makes a moral discrimination between right and wrong and creates a new public context (of some sort) that is conceivably more just than would otherwise be the case if heinous crimes went unpunished. The paradox here, as it so often is even in less egregious case studies, is that a regime can simultaneously perpetrate injustices in one or more areas while effectively enacting justice in others, or at least in specific cases. Once we arrive at the realization that the North Korean regime both violates human rights *and* enacts right, we are in a position to frame the question properly: does the injustice perpetrated by the regime undermine the justice it realizes to such an extent that the regime crosses O'Donovan's threshold of illegitimacy? In reality, this is something best judged by the North Korean people, and for reasons that hardly need explaining, it is impossible to resolve this question because of our inability to survey public opinion in North Korea. The assumptions of Westerners and the views of North Korean defectors and refugees (of whom there are relatively few) are not necessarily reliable guides in this regard.

The US Department of State estimates that there are between 80,000 and 120,000 political prisoners in North Korean prison camps.[94] Accurate figures are not available, so the real number is conceivably higher. It is reasonable to assume that a significant, and likely much higher, proportion of North Koreans have never been incarcerated. Notwithstanding the challenges of accurately estimating the

---

93. North Korea scholars warn against prejudiced Western judgments made according to unrealistic standards. Goedde, for example, counsels that North Korea's "multifaceted legal system ... warrants more than ritual dismissal for not conveniently falling under a rule-of-law heading." Goedde, "Law 'Of Our Own Style,'" 1287. Kang similarly cautions that "there is a potential danger in evaluating North Korea based on outside standards," observing that "the North Korean system works for a reason; it is often dysfunctional, but still functional enough to sustain itself like many other nation-states around the world" ("They Think They're Normal," 169).

94. "Prison Camps of North Korea," US Department of State, Humanrights.gov, https://www.humanrights.gov/dyn/news/features/prison-camps-of-north-korea/.

total current and former prisoner population in North Korea, it is important to recognize that the figure of 120,000 does not actually place it amongst the ranks of nations with high incarceration rates, especially when one factors in its total population of over 24 million (The US prison population at the end of 2019 was 1,430,800, according to the US Department of Justice).[95] Commonsense dictates that a much higher percentage of North Koreans has never been incarcerated. We must further assume that a percentage of those who are incarcerated are guilty of the crimes charged (it is inconceivable that all prisoners are innocent political prisoners and that none is guilty of actually committing a crime on Western conceptions of criminality). The point I'm driving at is that one cannot assume that even a majority of North Koreans has been subjected to the more egregious human rights violations that have rightly led to the regime's global notoriety. This is relevant to the question of the perception of North Koreans about the legitimacy of the regime in Pyongyang and the relative justice it enacts.

It is impossible to say what North Korean perceptions of the legitimacy of the regime in Pyongyang and the relative justice of its political order are.[96] It is conventional wisdom in the West to assume that North Koreans are either "brainwashed robots," as Kang puts it, or would-be liberal democrats stoically suffering in silence.[97] But both these views are indicative of "the fears and hopes" that Westerners "project" onto North Koreans, to borrow from Kang.[98] Kang argues that North Koreans regard themselves as normal "and take the circumstances of their lives for granted."[99] It is easy to overlook the social good provided by a "bureaucracy [that] is routinised and stable."[100] For all its dysfunction, North Korea is not a failed state, like Syria (at the time of writing), and certainly not like Bosnia, Rwanda, or Somalia in the 1990s. O'Donovan's conception of political authority is able to recognize that there is a genuine good in political order, no matter how inadequate and even unjust, in specific respects, it may be, especially when contrasted with civil conflict, disorder, and war. This is no doubt an unpopular and unpalatable view for a Westerner to hear and absorb. But the truth is that North Korea is an ordered state and there is an objective "good" in an ordered state, even one of the ilk of North Korea.

We can take it for granted that no human being desires to be imprisoned and tortured, or to starve. But can the Western observer really assume that, because

---

95. Thomas Spoorenberg and Daniel Schwekendiek, "Demographic Changes in North Korea: 1993–2008," *Population and Development Review* 38, no.1 (2012): 140. The last census, in 2008, recorded a population of 24,052 million; E. Ann Carson, "Prisoners in 2019," *U.S. Department of Justice*, October 2020, 1, https://www.bjs.gov/content/pub/pdf/p19.pdf.

96. Choi, "'Everyday Politics' in North Korea," 657.

97. Kang, "They Think They're Normal," 146. Kang is describing the common view of Westerners toward North Koreans, not his own view of them.

98. Ibid., 169.

99. Ibid.

100. Ibid., 147.

some North Koreans have suffered such a fate, all North Koreans regard the state as illegitimate, or even that they regard torture and political crimes as in principle illegitimate? Ken Gause highlights that some of the human rights abuses (by Western standards) are grounded in traditional Korean culture, and therefore might not strike the North Korean as particularly unusual, foreign or perhaps even illegitimate: "*Yeon-jwa-je*—guilt by association—imprisonment in political prisoner camps of up to three generations ... and *Songbun*, North Korea's discriminatory social classification system, both originate in the Chosun Dynasty's feudal practices."[101]

Citizens also have a tendency to attribute their problems to external causes rather than to their own government, traditions, or cultural practices. One cannot assume that North Koreans blame their government for famines, as opposed to the weather, or the Western "imperialism" that forces them to maintain an enormous army, labor under sanctions, and so forth. Charles Armstrong notes some interesting results from refugee studies in this regard, including that "most North Koreans leave their country for economic reasons, not out of political dissatisfaction"; that "defectors maintain an overall positive view of ... DPRK founder Kim Il Sung"; and "33% say they would return to the North if they could."[102] Political psychology is relevant in this regard. "Systems justification theory," for example, as van der Toorn and Jost explain, "proposes that people actively defend and bolster existing social arrangements, often by denying or rationalising injustices and other problems."[103]

Then there is the difficult question of propaganda. One cannot underestimate the impact of state propaganda in shaping the attitudes of North Koreans. It is far from clear, however, that regime propaganda imposes on North Koreans an utterly alien *weltanschauung* which, in the absence of coercion, would otherwise have no meaning, resonance or relevance to their history, traditions, culture, and sense of identity. Kang argues that "the North Korean state's effectiveness at embedding its rule within Korean cultural and social foundations" is at least in part attributable to "casting 'long-standing Confucian family traditions ... as the basis of a universal structure.'"[104]

On the basis of the preceding discussion, I conclude that it is very difficult to conclusively show that North Korea so abjectly fails to execute right, or executes right within a tradition that is so unrepresentative of the people's identity, that the regime can be construed as *not* holding political authority on O'Donovan's definition. The "providence thesis" says: *that any regime should actually come to*

---

101. Ken E. Gause, "Coercion, Control, Surveillance, and Punishment: An Examination of the North Korean Police State," *The Committee for Human Rights in North Korea*, 2012, 5.

102. Charles K. Armstrong, "Trends in the Study of North Korea," *The Journal of Asian Studies* 70, no.2 (2011): 359.

103. Jojanneke van der Toorn and John T. Jost, "Twenty Years of System Justification Theory: Introduction to the Special Issue on 'Ideology and System Justification Processes,'" *Group Processes & Intergroup Relations* 17, no.14 (2014): 414.

104. Kang, "They Think They're Normal," 163.

hold authority, and should continue to hold it, is a work of divine providence in history ... And as O'Donovan suggested in *Resurrection*, when might (power), injured right, and tradition are exercised together by one subject, they command a certain deference.[105] By linking the mere existence of political authority to providence, and with political authority construed non-prescriptively and relatively, O'Donovan's theology of political authority appears to legitimize the North Korean regime. Indeed, it appears to make God responsible, or at least complicit, in the regime's existence—a conclusion that many Christians will find jarring.

In Search of an Objective Normative Definition of Tradition and Right

The North Korea case study examined above reveals two things about O'Donovan's theology of political authority: the very real explanatory power of the "essence of political authority thesis," on the one hand, and the theodicy problem created by the "providence thesis," on the other. The case study reveals the real virtue of the "essence of political authority thesis," notwithstanding its tenuous biblical basis raised in Chapter 3. It does exactly what it promises to do: it explains the essence of political authority, that is, what constitutes and sustains political authority in *actual* regimes.

The application of O'Donovan's theology of political authority to the case study of North Korea suggests the need for an important refinement to the "essence of political authority thesis" that has the potential to enhance its explanatory power:

> Political authority arises and *endures* where *sufficient* power, the execution of *sufficient* (relative and non-prescriptive) right and the perpetuation of a tradition that is in *sufficient* continuity with the immediate past and is *sufficiently* representative of the community's identity are assured in one coordinated agency.

This formula can help explain the North Korean regime's impressive and surprising longevity. Bashar al-Assad's regime in Syria, in contrast, clearly failed to maintain this kind of effective political authority (effective sufficiency) when a significant proportion of Syria's populace took up armed rebellion in 2011, clearly having concluded that the regime no longer executed sufficient right within a sufficiently representative tradition to command either their obedience or quiescence. O'Donovan's insight about the nature and function of political authority is not, paradoxically, prima facie *theological*. It ostensibly requires no theological commitment and thus could be efficaciously employed by atheists in the kind of empirical research routinely done in political science. Indeed, it could make a very serious contribution to our understanding of regime stability.

This, however, still leaves unresolved the theodicy question. According to O'Donovan's theology of political authority, any regime that assures power, the

---

105. O'Donovan, *Resurrection and Moral Order*, 128.

execution of right, and perpetuation of tradition in one coordinated agency and falls short of a failed state enjoys a kind of divine legitimacy. For the political authority that it holds, and continues to hold, is a work of divine providence *and* reflects the essence of political authority revealed in the Davidic monarchy (as recorded in Scripture), which is to say that it mirrors to some extent the kind of political authority that mediates God's judgments. According to this standard, the North Korean regime arguably enjoys a kind of implicit divine legitimacy, and yet, not only is it a contender for one the world's worst human rights abusers, it is also one of the worst state persecutors of the Christian church.[106]

There are several options open to O'Donovan to avoid the undesirable theodicy implications of the "providence thesis." One is to clarify the nature and scope of the contribution made to political authority by divine providence. I recommend a way that this can be done in Chapter 9. Another is to make the constitutive parts of the definition of political authority (power, right, and tradition), upon which the "providence thesis" is dependent, specific and normative rather than relative and non-prescriptive. There is an irony in regard to this second option because O'Donovan does propound "a *normative political culture* broadly in continuity with the Western liberal tradition" in *Desire*, founded on four key political principles that emerged from Christendom: "freedom," "merciful judgment," "natural right" (natural equality, affinity, and reciprocity), and "openness of speech" (including access to public deliberations and responsible government).[107] A cogent case for North Korean failure on all four counts is eminently possible. However, these marks of "Christian liberalism," as O'Donovan terms it, are not constitutive of the essence of political authority revealed in the Old Testament. They are the historical fruits of Christian reflection on the political import of the Christ-event.[108] Another option would be to adopt a rather absolute view of divine providence, one which might view the North Korean regime as having been raised up by God as a "public avenger," in the language of Calvin, who took such an approach.[109]

---

106. Open Doors, "About North Korea," opendoorsusa.org, https://www.opendoorsusa.org/christian-persecution/world-watch-list/north-korea/.
107. Ibid., 254–70.
108. The relative and non-prescriptive *esse* of political authority in contrast to its specific and normative Christian *bene esse* can be seen in the following sentiment: "To demand that ["societies outside the European sphere of influence, which do not have the historical experience of Christendom behind them"] conform to the practices normative in the West deserves, perhaps, the over-used epithet 'cultural imperialism' as clearly as anything does" (*The Desire of the Nations*, 230).
109. Calvin, "On Civil Government," (*Institutes* 4.20.30).

O'Donovan's Davidic Problem

The dependence of the "essence of political authority thesis" on the Davidic monarchy might explain the relative and non-prescriptive nature of that thesis in contrast to the specific and normative *historical* expression of O'Donovan's Christian liberalism. The fundamental problem presented by the Davidic monarchy vis-à-vis the *bene esse* of political authority is that it does not conform to the normative liberal political culture that O'Donovan believes the Christian theologian ought to embrace and affirm. While "merciful judgment" does have some claim to Old Testament roots, "freedom," "natural right," and "openness to speech" are not leading Hebrew concepts associated with divine kingship, nor ostensibly marks of Israel's political order, at least not in the liberal sense that O'Donovan construes them. Indeed, it goes without saying that "liberal" and "liberalism" are not Hebrew concepts either. In short, while it is possible to identify these concepts in the course of Christian history, it is difficult to exegete them from the Bible. As such, it is "power," "execution of right," and "perpetuation of tradition" (in reality "salvation," "judgment," and "possession") that O'Donovan is able to extract from the Old Testament, and given the *bene esse* of the political authority that will emerge from the Christ-event has the marks of "freedom," "merciful judgment," "natural right," and "openness of speech," the Old Testament can only yield the *esse* of political authority, and in a rather generic fashion at that. If the Davidic monarchy (or any other phase in Israel's constitutional history) were truly normative for Christian political authority, then Western liberalism, and to a lesser extent Christian liberalism, would ostensibly mark a deviation from that norm.

Chapter 7

O'DONOVAN'S (CONSERVATIVE) CHRISTIAN LIBERALISM

Christian Liberalism

The previous chapter raised the issue of Christian liberalism, which per O'Donovan, represents the actualized historical fruits of Christ's triumph over the nations' rulers, that is, the re-authorization of political authority in the paradigm of "government-as-judgment."[1] This, as we saw, led O'Donovan to the avowal that "a Christian theologian can venture to characterise a *normative political culture* broadly in continuity with the Western liberal tradition."[2] However, in order "to display the liberal achievement correctly," he added, "we have to show it as the victory won by Christ over the nations' rulers."[3] Christian liberalism is a normative proposal grounded in a particular reading of history. It emerged as a historical reality, in O'Donovan's telling, in late-medieval Christendom, specifically the period 1100–1650—O'Donovan's "High Tradition" of Christian political thought.[4] The political order of Christendom arose as a response to the church's mission,

---

1. A version of this chapter was originally published as Jonathan Cole, "Political Theology and Political Authority: Evaluating Oliver O'Donovan's Christian Liberalism," *ABC Religion & Ethics*, June 21, 2021, https://www.abc.net.au/religion/political-theology-oliver-odonovans-christian-liberalism/13401594. The term "Christian liberalism" only appears once in *Desire*, albeit accompanied by the cognate "Christian liberal tradition" (229). Nevertheless, it is an apt description of the type of liberalism O'Donovan affirms and similarly makes an apt contrast with contemporary secular liberalism (my term), what O'Donovan at one point describes as "ex-Christian liberalism" (278). Chaplin has also used the term in relation to O'Donovan's political theology ("Political Eschatology and Responsible Government").
2. O'Donovan, *The Desire of the Nations*, 230. Emphasis original.
3. Ibid., 229.
4. O'Donovan, *The Desire of the Nations*, 4. In reality, this period traverses what are deemed in much scholarship to be two distinct conventional historical periods: late-medieval and early modern. I use the single term "late-medieval Christendom" in recognition that O'Donovan regards this period as a unified period of thought and political praxis. He has explained that he uses the term "Christendom" to refer to the "historical idea" of "a professedly Christian secular [here with the sense of temporal] political order, and the history of that idea in practice" (*The Desire of the Nations*, 195).

and the Church (at least in Western Europe), reflecting on the significance of Christ's exaltation, accordingly developed a set of political ideas which together came to define Christian liberalism.

Christian liberalism denotes a form of liberalism that is genealogically and genetically connected to what I will henceforth refer to as "secular liberalism." These two forms of liberalism can be contrasted and differentiated on the basis of the former's theological content and warrant. Definitions of liberalism are legion and, like virtually all political concepts, essentially contested. For present purposes, I point to the succinct definition of liberalism offered in the *Oxford Concise Dictionary of Politics* as an indicative secular definition lacking any theological content or warrant: "the belief that it is the aim of politics to preserve individual rights and maximise freedom of choice."[5]

The four defining principles of Christian liberalism raised in the previous chapter were: freedom, merciful judgment, natural right, and openness to speech.[6] Some of these principles are obviously cognate to well-known secular liberal principles, such as individual rights and freedom of speech. However, O'Donovan's principles of Christian liberalism contain or convey theological content absent in standard secular construals.

The Christian liberal idea of freedom, for instance, is conceived by O'Donovan as the "recognition of a superior authority which renders all authorities beneath it relative and provisional."[7] This conception of freedom denotes neither a pure assertion of individuality or creative impulse, nor a constellation of individual rights, but rather "a new disposition of society around its supreme Lord which sets it loose from its traditional lords."[8] In other words, Christian freedom constitutes freedom from idolatrous human tyranny. It secures this freedom through Christ's triumph over the nations' rulers, which has forced secular political authorities into retreat under the shadow of the church. It is worth contrasting O'Donovan's conception of the Christian liberal idea of freedom with the indicative definition provided in the *Oxford Concise Dictionary of Politics*: "absence of interference or impediment."[9]

Merciful judgment conveys the idea that secular judgment is "under the judgment which God made upon the cross, a judgment that was at the same time a redemption."[10] Secular judges now stand under the ultimate judgment of God, according to O'Donovan, and are thus under an obligation to show humility and mercy in dealing with the consequences of sin. Moreover, judges, like the

---

5. McLean and McMillan, *Oxford Concise Dictionary of Politics*, s.v. "liberalism."

6. Chaplin has questioned the extent to which the Christian liberal principles identified can be construed as connected to the "core of the gospel message" and "authentic manifestations of Christian faith" ("Political Eschatology and Responsible Government," 273).

7. O'Donovan, *The Desire of the Nations*, 252.

8. Ibid., 254.

9. McLean and McMillan, *Oxford Concise Dictionary of Politics*, s.v. "freedom."

10. O'Donovan, *The Desire of Nations*, 256.

community writ large, are to work toward the ultimate aim of reconciliation in instances of injustice, not merely punishment. The suggestion is that the concept of merciful judgment, flowing from the Christological re-authorization of political authority, allows for a more effective, if still relative, justice in the context of human associations. Interestingly, this is the one principle of O'Donovan's Christian liberalism for which there appears to be no cognate in contemporary secular liberal theory.

O'Donovan's Christian liberal principle of natural right does, on the other hand, have a secular liberal cognate in the form of natural rights (plural), now more commonly known as either individual or human rights.[11] The concept of natural right (singular) comprises three elements: natural equality, affinity, and reciprocity. Natural equality represents the idea that "each human being may encounter any other as a partner in humanity, neither slave nor lord."[12] Affinity relates to the bonds that constitute national, local, and cultural communities, such as family, language, tradition, culture, and law. And reciprocity denotes that mode of human fellowship which transcends local and national boundaries. O'Donovan contrasts his Christian liberal principle of natural right with subjective natural rights (plural), what Greek philosopher Christos Yannaras has described, in a way likely to meet with O'Donovan's approval, as legally enforceable private interests.[13] Indeed, the *Oxford Concise Dictionary of Politics* defines rights as "legal or moral recognition of choices or interests to which particular weight is attached."[14]

The final principle of Christian liberalism articulated by O'Donovan is "openness to speech." As with the preceding principles, "openness of speech" is given a theological interpretation: "the church created by the act of God at Pentecost was characterised by freedom of address—to God in its prayer, and from God in its prophecy."[15] "The church's openness of mutual address," O'Donovan writes, "constituted an address to society, summoning society to admit the free passage of the word of God and to respond to it in its turn in speech."[16] Needless to say, this is a far cry from the contemporary conceptualization of "free speech" which centers on the scope for the unsanctionable expression of a sovereign will.

---

11. For a more extended discussion of human rights, see Oliver O'Donovan, "The Language of Rights and Conceptual History," *Journal of Religious Ethics* 37, no.2 (2009): 193–207. O'Donovan's preference for "unitary right" over a plurality of rights turns on the question of moral ontology: "multiple rights express a plural ontology of difference, the differences between the right-bearer and every other, instead of a unitary ontology of human likeness" (202).

12. O'Donovan, *The Desire of the Nations*, 262.

13. Christos Yannaras, Ἡ ἀπανθρωπία τοῦ δικαιώματος [The Inhumanity of Rights] (Athens: Domos, 1998), 174.

14. McLean and McMillan, *Oxford Concise Dictionary of Politics*, s.v. "rights."

15. O'Donovan, *The Desire of the Nations*, 268.

16. Ibid.

The Ambiguous Place of Secular Liberalism in Salvation-History

We recall that the Christian liberalism that emerged from the "High Tradition" of Christian political thought, culminating in the principles of freedom, merciful judgment, natural right, and openness to speech, led O'Donovan to the twin affirmations: "A Christian theologian can venture to characterize a normative political culture broadly in continuity with the Western liberal tradition" and "to display the liberal achievement correctly, we have to show it as the victory won by Christ over the nations' rulers."[17] There is a perceptible tentativeness in O'Donovan's qualified affirmation of the Western liberal tradition in these quotations. Why "broadly" in continuity with the Western liberal tradition rather than fully, or at all? Moreover, the current state and prevailing understanding of liberal culture and political order today do *not* appear to display the liberal achievement correctly, per O'Donovan. The source of this ambiguity can be traced back to the all-important year 1650. This year marks the end of the "High Tradition" of Christian political thought, as O'Donovan defines it, which is to say the era in which the liberal achievement *was* displayed as the victory won by Christ over the nations' rulers and which consequently now figures as something of a normative political paradigm by which to judge subsequent historical expressions of liberalism.[18]

The year 1650 marks the beginning of the protracted process by which Christian liberal principles became secularized, which is to say set adrift from their theological foundation.[19] The severance of liberalism from its theological mooring has left its governing ideas and principles in a state of unintelligibility, according to O'Donovan. The incoherent pretensions of contractarianism—the idea that individual wills voluntarily enter into comprehensive social contracts—is, for O'Donovan, the epitome of liberal incoherence. As he has evocatively put it, "modernity is the child of Christianity, and at the same time … has left its father's house and followed the way of the prodigal."[20] Secular liberalism, for O'Donovan, represents what Aristotle might have called a παρέκβασις—a deviation from a sound political paradigm. Much as Aristotle regarded tyranny to be a deviant form of kingship, secular liberalism stands as a deviant form of Christian liberalism. This helps to illuminate both the equivocal adverb "broadly," which qualifies O'Donovan's affirmation of secular liberalism, and the normatively pregnant caveat that the Christ-event is integral to liberal coherence.

The principles of secular liberalism still reflect, to some extent, their Christian genetic ancestry, which is why a Christian can venture, albeit cautiously, to

---

17. Ibid., 229–30.
18. Ibid., 195. "Christendom is … an era in which the truth of Christianity was taken to be the truth of secular politics … it is the idea of a confessionally Christian government, at once 'secular' (… confined to the present age) and obedient to Christ, a promise of the age of his unhindered rule."
19. Ibid., xi.
20. Ibid., 275.

support secular liberal political order—secular liberalism, in light of competing political visions, whether Marxist, fascist, anarchist, or authoritarian capitalist, still bears the closest likeness to normative Christian political order. However, secular liberalism's progressive deviation from its parentage in Christian liberalism ultimately risks descent into outright perversion, prompting O'Donovan to countenance the idea that modernity might in fact be conceived as Antichrist—"a parodic and corrupt development of Christian social order."[21]

This provocative Antichrist reference is revealing. Because salvation-history—in practice the Bible in O'Donovan's case—serves as the hermeneutic cipher for unlocking both political norms and the meaning of political history, his political theology winds up hostage to historical developments. Whatever happens historically after Christ's triumph over the nations' rulers is, by definition, necessary in the flow of redemptive history, bringing history closer to its eschatological fulfillment. Once late medieval Christian political thought and order are identified as the culmination and climax of Christ's triumph over the nations' rulers within the framework of salvation-history, the decline into secular liberalism arguably can only point to an impending apocalypse—God's final judgment and the true dawn of humankind's post-political future.

It is my contention, however, that O'Donovan's salvation-history political theology leaves Christian citizens of contemporary Western liberal democracies in a place of profound uncertainty vis-à-vis how they are to respond to a de-theologized liberalism in the throes of Milbank and Pabst's "metacrises." For they find themselves, on O'Donovan's account, in a veritable salvation-history no man's land. While O'Donovan's political theology offers an account of the political past and has a vision of humankind's post-political destiny, it struggles to cogently locate the present moment of liberal tumult within the flow of redemptive history. How is the church to act in the context of a political order which emerged as a response to its mission, still bears the vestiges of that missiological order, but no longer recognizes, let alone supports, the mission from which it was born? Today it is the church which is in retreat, not secular political authority, and the post-political kingdom to which the church witnesses now lies further beyond the horizon than it once did. In short, Christ's triumph over the nations' rulers looks to have reverted to the rulers' triumph over Christ.

O'Donovan's Christian liberalism, along with its theopolitical scaffolding and undergirding historical narrative, produces what appears to be a profound tension: qualified Christian support for a political order that might represent the Antichrist. It is not clear whether the Christian political task is to salvage the liberal achievement by restoring Christ (and the church) to the apex of liberal order, or if it is to abandon liberalism to its apocalyptic fate, vesting all hope in the consummation of God's post-political kingdom. The sense of ambiguity is heightened by O'Donovan's clarification, in the face of criticism, that he does *not* call for a return to Christendom.

21. Ibid.

The sense of ambiguity would evaporate, of course, if O'Donovan did in fact wish to see a reversion to a political order akin to Christendom. In such a scenario, the Christian political task would be rather straightforward, if exceedingly difficult. The ambiguity arises because O'Donovan is clear, on the one hand, that Christendom is relevant and instructive for contemporary liberal political order, yet equally clear, on the other, that a return to Christendom is not feasible. This creates a degree of uncertainty regarding what shape a contemporary liberal order that profits from the politico-theological gains of Christendom ought to take, particularly when there is a secular consensus that Christendom is neither relevant to, nor instructive for, contemporary liberalism.

O'Donovan's Conservative Christian Liberalism

In Chapter 1, I provided an embryonic intellectual history of O'Donovan. The many names that emerged, from Augustine to Barth and beyond, are predominantly theological or Christian figures. It is perhaps no surprise, then, that his readers, for the most part themselves theologians, have struggled to classify his political theology within the conventional categories of secular political thought. His sympathetic view of Christendom, what Hauerwas and Fodor have dubbed his "Christendom project," in conjunction with his strong emphasis on political authority as a means of mediating divine rule, would seem to position him somewhere on the conservative right-hand side of the conventional secular political spectrum, at least by the standards of contemporary political orthodoxies.[22] Indeed, Gorringe has suggested that "O'Donovan's sympathies seem to be with the kind of conservatism we associate with Roger Scruton."[23] Yet Christopher Rowland has perhaps spoken for many, when, commenting on *Desire*, he made this remark:

> When I reached the end of the book, I found it difficult to understand how Oliver could be neatly categorised as an apologist for a conservative political theology, when the thesis is in many ways an apology for a consciously theological, though much chastened, liberal polity.[24]

An undoubted source of confusion is O'Donovan's choice of language—Christian liberalism unavoidably, and in fact quite consciously, evokes secular

22. Hauerwas and Fodor, "Remaining in Babylon," 48–9, 51. It is increasingly becoming *de rigueur* for intellectuals to dismiss the left-right distinction in favor of some new and often more sophisticated schema. This overlooks, in my view, the fact that political protagonists, by and large, still use the language of left and right making the terms meaningful, at least sociologically.
23. Gorringe, "Anglican Political Thought," 108.
24. Christopher Rowland, "Response to *The Desire of the Nations*," *Studies in Christian Ethics* 11, no.2 (1998): 77.

liberalism rather than conservativism. In fact, O'Donovan has explicitly distanced his Christian liberalism from contemporary conservative movements by describing conservatism as "the name of a quite precise heresy to do with the status of tradition."[25] In O'Donovan's self-conception, his Christian liberalism stands above and beyond the fray of partisan left-right polarity on account of its foundational dependence on *both* freedom and authority, concepts respectively championed by the left and the right in his view.[26]

Nevertheless, it is difficult to overlook the fact that O'Donovan's Christian liberalism, notwithstanding what it seeks to evoke, points to a type of pre-Burkean conservatism, particularly if we take historical pedigree to be a defining characteristic of conservativism. It is interesting to juxtapose, for example, the title of conservative doyen Russell Kirk's best-selling classic, *The Conservative Mind: From Burke to Eliot*, with the title of O'Donovan's book (with wife Joan) *From Irenaeus to Grotius: A Sourcebook in Christian Political Thought, 100–1625*.[27] We recall that for O'Donovan the point at which Christian liberalism begins its long descent into corruption is 1650, while for Kirk "conscious conservatism" begins in 1790 with the publication of Burke's *Reflections on the Revolution in France*.[28] If the holy book for contemporary conservatives is Burke's *Reflections* and the political paradigm eighteenth-century Britain, what does it say about O'Donovan's political inclinations that his holy book is the Bible, his political paradigms ancient Israel and Christendom, and the summit of normative political thought the medieval period 1100–1650?[29] The fact of the matter is that O'Donovan's Christian liberalism sets a reference point much further in the past than is typical for contemporary conservatism, and well outside the scope of any contemporary secular liberalism. Moreover, O'Donovan is conscious of this difference. In *Judgment*, he describes conservatism as a "modern doctrinal option" of "purely modern provenance," suggesting colorfully that, "though the lyre it [conservatism]

25. O'Donovan, "Response to the Respondents," 99.
26. Ibid., 100–1.
27. Russell Kirk, *The Conservative Mind: From Burke to Eliot* 7th rev. ed. with an introduction by Henry Regnery (Washington, DC: Gateway Editions, 1985).
28. It is worth noting that Kirk, a Catholic who regarded government as "a contrivance of human wisdom, under Providence, to provide for human wants," thought the roots of America's constitutional order could be traced all the way back to Jerusalem (via London, Rome, and Athens). With O'Donovan, he thought Israel's seminal contribution to the Western tradition was the notion and contours of an objective moral order. However, contra O'Donovan, Kirk maintained that Israel left no lasting legacy in relation to the West's institutional order: "of practical political establishments in Israel or Juda or the later Jewish principalities, nothing remains." Russel Kirk, *Russel Kirk's Concise Guide to Conservatism*, with an introduction by Wilfred M. McClay (Washington, DC: Gateway Editions, 2019), iBooks, chapter IV, "Conservatives and Individuality." Russell Kirk, *The Roots of American Order*, 4th ed., with a foreword by Forrest McDonald (Wilmington, DE: ISI Books, 2003), 6.
29. Edmund Burke, "Reflections on the Revolution," in *Burke: Revolutionary Writings*, ed. Iain Hampsher-Monk (Cambridge: Cambridge University Press, 2014).

plays is a state-of-the-art electronic instrument, its appeal rests on its ability to sound in an antique mode."[30]

It is true that O'Donovan is not alone in pointing to a classical liberal tradition that pre-dates the emergence of conservatism. But the question in view is how to classify O'Donovan's Christian liberalism using conventional contemporary political categories. In that vein, it is difficult to envisage a classification that locates him to the left of conservatism in light of his sympathy for Christendom, the normative role of ancient Israel, the political authority of the Bible and the notion that the role of secular government is to secure the church's mission, to the extent of warranting an established church. In fact, notwithstanding the comment regarding conservative heresy above, O'Donovan has, on occasion, sounded a more nuanced tone on conservatism and its relationship to his own political theology. In *Judgment*, for instance, he notes that conservatism is characterized by both a virtue and a vice: "the virtue is a sensibility for traditional practice in practical decision-making, the vice a reluctance to question it."[31] As a "political principle," he adds, conservatism entails "making the continuity of tradition foundational to the political task."[32] This is precisely what O'Donovan does in making "perpetuation of tradition" constitutive of political authority (along with power and execution of right), and thus integral to the legitimate exercise of judgment, the exclusive post-Easter political end of secular government. Hence, while O'Donovan distinguishes his Christian liberalism from conservatism, he does, on the other hand, accord the "political principle" of conservatism a place of prominence at its foundation.

One could further point to O'Donovan's intimation in the essay "Government as Judgment" that the British constitution lost its way in the sixteenth century when parliament began transitioning from "a body that existed to represent popular concerns *to* government [the monarch in parliament], to become a *branch* of government."[33] As with his sympathetic account of Christendom, there is no suggestion here that O'Donovan seeks to turn back the constitutional clock. Rather, he questions the prevailing assumption that Britain's contemporary constitutional order is an unambiguous improvement on the past. In fact, in keeping with his own liberal narrative, the suggestion is that Britain's contemporary constitutional order is a deviation from a sounder footing in the past. This sympathetic reading of Britain's sixteenth-century constitutional order, much like that of Christendom, no doubt would strike many contemporary political thinkers and actors, both left and right, as quixotically conservative.

There is yet another, perhaps far simpler, way of establishing the conservative credentials of O'Donovan's Christian liberalism, which is to note the patent lack of

30. O'Donovan, *The Ways of Judgment*, 183.
31. Ibid., 180.
32. Ibid., 181. Apropos Gorringe's comment above, O'Donovan draws on Scruton's *The Meaning of Conservatism* in his brief exposition of the "political principle" of conservatism. See Roger Scruton, *The Meaning of Conservatism*, 3rd ed. (Basingstoke: Palgrave Macmillan, 2001).
33. O'Donovan, "Government as Judgment." Emphases original.

appetite on the center-left, again judging by the standards of prevailing orthodoxies, to countenance the idea that the Bible, ancient Israel, or Christendom have any relevance to or legitimacy in contemporary political thought. Indeed, the narrative now routinely touted by secular liberals, in both the British and American senses of the term, is that liberalism emerged in spite of O'Donovan's favored historical paradigms and now stands in condemnation of them. Suffice to say, O'Donovan's affirmation of a normative Western liberal tradition grounded in Christendom is anathema to contemporary progressives for whom that tradition is now a byword for oppression and injustice.[34] From the vantage point of those situated on the left of the conventional left-right divide, O'Donovan's Christian liberalism not only looks conservative, but perhaps *ultra*-conservative.

These observations all add up to the conclusion that O'Donovan's Christian liberalism is rather idiosyncratic within the context of secular political discourse and the conventional typologies used to describe it. It is idiosyncratic because, while it identifies itself with the liberal tradition, it contains theological and conservative elements which locate it firmly outside the taxonomy of contemporary liberalism. Moreover, its conservative strains are similarly idiosyncratic by the standards of contemporary conservative orthodoxy. I therefore propose that O'Donovan's political theology is best thought of as a type of idiosyncratic conservative Christian liberalism, where "conservative" refers to the Christendom genealogy of liberal ideas, "Christian" refers to the theological content and warrant of those ideas and "liberalism" refers to a tradition that encompasses their secular evolution.[35]

Identifying O'Donovan's political theology as an idiosyncratic form of conservative Christian liberalism might help to shed light on why O'Donovan's political theology has had such a significant impact in Christian political theology, yet a negligible impact on secular political theory. Amongst theologians, for whom conventional secular political categories are less important, if at all, O'Donovan's political theology has elicited plaudits and a critical engagement rivalled by few others, even if admirers and critics alike have tended to cast him in the mold of Scrutonesque conservative.[36] O'Donovan's political theology has proven to be particularly influential with Anglican evangelicals in Great Britain and Australia,

---

34. The author had occasion to outline O'Donovan's Christian liberalism to a prominent atheist progressive public intellectual in Australia, who described it as "reactionary."

35. The idea of "conservative liberalism" is not unknown in Christian political theology. VanDrunen, for example, in *Politics after Christendom*, makes a case for what he calls "conservative liberalism," although his "conservative liberalism" is really a Christian via media between liberal (Democratic) and conservative (Republican) ideas (VanDrunen draws on O'Donovan's work for the development of his underlying political theology, centered on the Noahic covenant, but not in relation to his "conservative liberalism"). David VanDrunen, *Politics After Christendom: Political Theology in a Fractured World* (Grand Rapids: Zondervan Academic, 2020).

36. McEvoy has noted that "even O'Donovan's strongest critics acknowledge the significance of his contribution to political theology." McEvoy, "A Dialogue with Oliver O'Donovan about Church and Government," 953.

and, to a lesser extent, evangelicals (in all their variety) in the United States.[37] Its idiosyncrasy, however, in the context of secular political categories—dissociated as it is from conservatism by virtue of its evocation of liberalism, yet too conservative for liberals and anyone to the left of them—possibly explains its marginalization in secular political discourse, notwithstanding the fact that it directly addresses the central question of our age: the provenance, nature, and future of liberalism.[38]

---

37. For a British and Australian influence respectively, see Luke Bretherton and Andrew Errington. Luke Bretherton, *Christianity & Contemporary Politics* (Oxford: Wiley-Blackwell, 2010); Errington, "Authority and Reality in the Work of Oliver O'Donovan,"; and Errington, "Between Justice and Tradition." For an American example, see Matthew Lee Anderson, "O'Donovan Contra Liberalism," *Mere Orthodoxy*, August 3, 2009, https://mereorthodoxy.com/odonovan-contra-liberalism/. O'Donovan has also found a sympathetic and critical engagement amongs Catholic theologians. See, for example, Neuhaus, "Commentary on *The Desire of the Nations*"; Robert A. Markus, "Political Order as Response to the Church's Mission," *Political Theology* 9, no.3 (2008); Rist, "Judgment, Reaction and the Common Good"; Cavanaugh, *Migrations of the Holy*.

38. Rowan Williams has noted the conspicuous absence of O'Donovan in John Milbank and Adrian Pabst's book *The Politics of Virtue*. Rowan Williams, "Liberalism and Capitalism Have Hollowed Out Society—So Where Do We Turn Now?" *New Stateman America*, October 18, 2016, https://www.newstatesman.com/culture/books/2016/10/liberalism-and-capitalism-have-hollowed-out-society-so-where-do-we-turn-now.

Chapter 8

PROVIDENCE AND THE CREATED ORDER:
THE ONTOLOGICAL TENSION IN THE
ACCOUNTS OF POLITICAL AUTHORITY IN
RESURRECTION AND *DESIRE*

The Tension in O'Donovan's Account of the Ontology of Political Authority in Resurrection *and* Desire

There are two final problematics in relation to O'Donovan's theology of political authority that need to be canvassed and discussed before proceeding to the constructive final chapter in the study. We noted in Chapter 3 that Chaplin was the first to observe the similarity between O'Donovan's formulation of political authority in both *Desire* and *Resurrection*, what I have characterized throughout this study as the "essence of political authority thesis." While the two formulations of the thesis are formally similar, there is a subtle difference of consequence that has gone largely unnoticed and unremarked in the secondary literature.[1] The all-important adjective "natural," which qualifies the constitutive concepts that form political authority in *Resurrection*, namely "might," "tradition," and "right" (the latter cast as *relatively* natural), disappears in the formulation in *Desire*.[2]

As I argue below, the disappearance of this adjective presages a significant and substantive shift in the ontological grounding of political authority, placing the

---

1. Skillen is a notable exception, observing that in *Resurrection* political authority is "political from the beginning to the end of creation, and human government, just as family life, friendship, agricultural and animal husbandry and much more, reveals or images the Creator," whereas in *Desire* "O'Donovan has nearly, if not entirely, lost from view the meaning of creation and creation redeemed" ("Acting Politically in Biblical Obedience?" 404).

2. The respective definitions are: "Political authority arises where power, the execution of right and the perpetuation of tradition are assured together in one coordinated agency" (*Desire*) and "The distinctive form of authority which we call 'political' is, then, at its simplest, a concurrence of the *natural* authorities of might and tradition with that other 'relatively *natural*' authority, the authority of injured right" (*Resurrection*—emphases mine).

two accounts in tension.³ By tension, I mean to suggest that the two accounts, in the form in which they are articulated, cannot both be right.⁴ Clarifying statements regarding the ontology of political authority provided in both *Resurrection* and *Desire*, along with some made after the publication of *Desire*, reinforce this sense of tension.

The entire premise of O'Donovan's account of authority in *Resurrection* (not to be confused with *political* authority in this context) is that it is an intrinsic part of the created order. Indeed, the section immediately preceding the "digression" on political authority is aptly titled "Natural Authority and the Authority of Truth." We saw in Chapter 3 that O'Donovan's account of authority begins with the notion that "created beings can evoke free action" and that "many characteristic features of human society arise because some human beings have this power over others."⁵ We further saw that O'Donovan identified four primary kinds of natural authorities found within the created order which "command" and "compel" human action: beauty, age, community, and strength, respectively (the last is said to include "the whole range of natural virtue, from might to wisdom").⁶ "To account for authority," according to O'Donovan, "is to describe a borderland between culture and *nature*, where culture draws upon, and is shaped by, *natural* forces."⁷ "Injured right," which in this context denotes "the authority which shapes our structures of justice and governance," is said to be *relatively natural* in the sense that "it belongs to the natural order as it is encountered under the conditions brought about by Adam's sin."⁸

The fact that authorities are natural does not mean humans are to respond to them uncritically. They are not "unconditional" by virtue of their sheer existence within the created order. "Natural authority," O'Donovan writes, "is subject to the review of a higher authority" in the form of "truth," although truth too is said to be a form of natural authority given it is "inherent in the created order."⁹ What is distinctive about the authority of truth is that it is not experienced immediately

---

3. Segments of this chapter have been taken from Cole, "Towards an Ontology of Political Authority." The final, definitive version of this paper has been published in *Studies in Christian Ethics*, 32, 3/2018 by SAGE Publications Ltd, All rights reserved. © https://journals.sagepub.com/doi/full/10.1177/0953946818775559.

4. Errington, contra my view that this tension is problematic, describes what he refers to as O'Donovan's "dialectical tension between created order and the triumph of Christ" as a "virtue" of O'Donovan's political thought (*Every Good Path*, 190, footnote 371).

5. O'Donovan, *Resurrection and Moral Order*, 124.

6. Ibid. Emphasis mine. In *Self, World, and Time*, O'Donovan reiterates that beauty is an authority, while naming several authorities "implied" in various "social phenomena," such as teaching, learning, questioning, admiring, loving, and "practical effectiveness" (*Self, world, and Time*, 55).

7. O'Donovan, *Resurrection and Moral Order*, 125. Emphases mine.

8. Ibid., 124.

9. Ibid. The relationship between truth and authority is taken up again in *Self, World, and Time* (55–6).

like other authorities (self-explanatory grounds for action). Truth, rather, relates to a comprehension of the world "as an ordered whole," in contrast to other authorities which "belong to differing elements within it."[10] In *Resurrection*, then, O'Donovan's understanding of authority is explicitly and inextricably intertwined with his notion of a natural created order of ends and kinds that make human action intelligible.[11] In fact, O'Donovan's insights regarding political authority specifically emerge out of his reflection on the authorities that are embedded in the created order. As such, political authority is ontologically grounded in the created order in *Resurrection*: it is constituted by a conjunction of natural authorities existing in the created order, even if one of those authorities, judgment, is only *relatively* natural, that is, part of the created order as encountered, not as intended. As O'Donovan notes in *Resurrection*, "political authority ... owes something both to the immediacy of *natural authorities* and to the critical reflectiveness of moral authority."[12]

When O'Donovan came to pen *Desire* ten years later, however, the adjective "natural" disappeared entirely from both the definition of political authority (the "essence of political authority thesis") and the discussion of political authority in general. Power and tradition are nowhere described as natural in *Desire*, as they were in *Resurrection*. Nor is right described as relatively natural. The same situation characterizes *Judgment*. There is a reference in *Desire* to "natural ... structures of human community" and a similar reference in *Judgment* to the natural sociality of human beings: "mankind is communal by virtue of God's creation, not by political invention."[13] But there is no sense in either work that there is anything natural about political authority, or that it is connected in any substantial way to the created order.[14] Instead, *Desire* ties political authority to the providential order of history. Indeed, there are statements in *Desire* that imply that political authority is wholly distinct and separate from the created order: "political structures are

---

10. Ibid.
11. Ibid., 127.
12. Ibid. Emphasis mine.
13. O'Donovan, *The Desire of the Nations*, 279; O'Donovan, *The Ways of Judgment*, 156.
14. There is one intriguing exception in *Desire*, where O'Donovan writes the following:

Christian ethics ... respects the *natural structures of life in the world*, while looking forward to their transformation. This can be seen ... in the First Epistle of Peter, which starts with a general characterisation of the Christian life in terms of "hope," which is set "fully upon the grace that is coming to you at the revelation of Jesus Christ," and then a special ethics in terms of respectful submission "for the Lord's sake" to every institution of human life, especially the *institutions of government*, labour and marriage (1 Pet. 1:13; 2:13ff.) ... A hope which envisages the transformation of existing *natural structures* cannot consistently attack or repudiate those structures (*The Desire of the Nations*, 58, emphases mine).

This appears to locate "government" in the same category as "labour" and "marriage," which is to say the category of "natural structures."

historically fluid, not, as some other structures are, given in nature."[15] Thus, although *Resurrection* and *Desire* offer formally similar conceptions of political authority, they appear to assume different ontologies of political authority: nature versus providence (or history). It is this ontological variance that creates the aforementioned tension.

It is possible that this tension might be attributable, at least in part, to the different contexts in which the respective discussions of political authority occur, and the very different methods adopted in each case. As noted above, the discussion in *Resurrection* is portrayed as a "digression" that emerges in the context of O'Donovan's reflections on the natural authorities embedded in the created order of ends and kinds that make human action immediately intelligible. Accordingly, the digression involved no biblical exegesis.[16] *Desire* (and *Judgment*), on the other hand, proceeds from the premise that human political acts are authorized by, and to some extent analogous to, God's providential acts in history. The purpose of human political acts (political authority) is to mediate God's judgments in the secular age (secular in the temporal sense of the term). Given Scripture, according to theology (or at least the Evangelical tradition that has shaped O'Donovan's theology), is the one reliable and authoritative account of God's divine acts in history, it follows that a *theological* account of political authority ought to begin with exegesis. Thus, whereas the starting point for the discussion of political authority in *Resurrection* is the created order, in *Desire* it is the biblical refrain *Yhwh mālak*.

O'Donovan subsequently reiterated the distinction between the natural order and providential history as it pertains to politics in response to criticisms of *Desire*: "politics belongs within the category of history, not of nature" and "political order is a *providential* ordering."[17] This apparent dichotomy was again reinforced in *Judgment*, where O'Donovan distinguished political authority from certain "social authorities" on the basis that the latter are natural: "When every allowance has been made for the lines of connection between political authority and *natural* social authorities such as parents and teachers … ."[18] O'Donovan has also clarified that he regards politics and government as *post lapsum* developments, observing in *Judgment* that "the earliest Christian reflections on the origins of civil government, led by the Yahwist primeval history, located the origin of government *post lapsum*, a doctrine that prevailed throughout the patristic period."[19] The location of

---

15. Ibid., 14.
16. Chaplin was also the first to make this observation ("Political Eschatology and Responsible Government," 298).
17. O'Donovan, "Deliberation, History and Reading," 137. Emphasis original.
18. O'Donovan, *The Ways of Judgment*, 134.
19. Oliver O'Donovan, "Response to Craig Bartholomew," in *A Royal Priesthood?* 115; O'Donovan, *The Ways of Judgment*, 59.

political authority within the providential order of history is made most forcefully in the "providence thesis" examined in Chapter 6:

> That any regime should actually come to hold authority, and should continue to hold it, is a work of divine providence in history, not a mere accomplishment of the human task of political service.

Tellingly, there is no suggestion in *Resurrection* that providence plays anything like the central role it would come to play in the theology of political authority propounded in *Desire*.[20]

In *Resurrection,* O'Donovan makes an interesting distinction between the regularity of the created order and the *sui generis* character of God's providential intervention in history:

> Moral authority is the authority of order, the created order of kinds and ends in which all created beings participate. It is "universal" ... that is, it supposes a universe of meaning which created beings inhabit in common. The authority of divine transcendence, on the other hand, is beyond world-order, and can only appear to us as an unaccountable and mysterious breach in the world-order. *Encounter with divine authority must be a unique event, irreducibly particular, incapable of comparison with any other.*[21]

"History," O'Donovan contends, "must be shaped by the unique, by that which cannot be guessed from the scrutiny of natural repetitions."[22]

Yet the "irreducibly particular" and "unique" character of history seems to be at odds with the idea that there is an essence of political authority—that there are some universal and unchanging forms that constitute political authority, synchronically and diachronically. Moreover, if political authority substantively exists in and emerges from the natural authorities in the created order, as *Resurrection* suggests, then one is entitled to question why there is any need at all to posit that divine providence is necessary to explain, foster, and maintain the social conditions in which political authority can emerge and endure.

The primary implication of the subtle shift away from grounding political authority in the natural authorities of the created order to locating it exclusively in the realm of providential history is that it leaves the latter account (*Desire/ Judgment*) without an explanation for how political authority can evoke

---

20. There is one solitary mention of providence in *Resurrection*'s digression on political authority, which is to the perfunctory statement that Christian thought traditionally "attribute[es] the origin of authority to divine providence." However, there is nothing approaching the "providence thesis" in this first discussion of political authority (*Resurrection and Moral Order*, 130).
21. Ibid., 143.
22. Ibid., 83.

meaningful, intelligible, and free human action, recalling that this is precisely the function of natural authorities in the created order per *Resurrection*. O'Donovan makes a cogent case in *Resurrection* that without the "generic intelligibility" of natural authorities there would be "nothing in the world which invited our action," thus making the very notion of freedom "problematic," something more akin to "an irruption into a system that was closed against it."[23] This idea even found its way into *Desire*, where O'Donovan again maintained that authority "evokes free action, and makes free action intelligible."[24] O'Donovan also noted in *Desire* that political authority "needs a background in the ontology of human freedom."[25]

By attributing the existence of political authority exclusively to the work of divine providence in *Desire*'s "providence thesis," epitomized in the *unique and paradigmatic* way that God ruled Israel *historically*, O'Donovan loses the explanatory power of his insight about the way that natural authorities in the created order evoke free and intelligible human action. If political authority ultimately owes its existence to divine providence rather than the created order, then it is not clear how it could evoke the free and intelligible collective human response that it so clearly does, thus establishing stable political order, unless we assume that all stable political order is directly the work of providence, bringing us once again face to face with a theodicy problem.[26] It is the ability of political authority to evoke *free* action, after all, that distinguishes it, in O'Donovan's own account, from force—the all-important distinction between power and authority.[27]

Contrary to the anarchist maxim that political authority can never have legitimate "binding moral force," the weight of history suggests that most people find nothing morally objectionable at all about obeying political authority.[28] The widespread historical and contemporary propensity to recognize the legitimacy of political authority and to accede to its demands, even when patently unjust, appears to provide empirical vindication for the ontological account of political authority provided in *Resurrection*: political authority provides immediate and self-evident grounds for action by virtue of being embedded in the network of created authorities that make human action both free and intelligible. As O'Donovan observed in *Judgment*, "our situation in the face of political authority, far from being out of the ordinary like an encounter with an angel or a divine revelation, is simply a special case of a situation deeply woven into our experience as human agents: finding ourselves under obligation to do something."[29]

23. O'Donovan, *Resurrection and Moral Order*, 122.
24. O'Donovan, *The Desire of the Nations*, 30.
25. Ibid.
26. O'Donovan, *The Ways of Judgment*, 132. O'Donovan notes that, in relation to political authority, "an end of action must be intelligible, not only from the actor's point of view but from the observer's point of view."
27. O'Donovan, *The Desire of the Nations*, 30.
28. Robert P. Wolff, "The Conflict between Authority and Autonomy," in *Authority*, ed. Joseph Raz (Oxford: Basil Blackwell, 1990), 29.
29. O'Donovan, *The Ways of Judgment*, 129. This is a fine example of the potential contribution O'Donovan's insights about the nature of political authority could make to secular discourse in political theory.

O'Donovan revisited the issue of authority, albeit briefly, in the more recent work, *Self, World, and Time*. There, he suggests that "divine authority begins with God's self-disclosure in creation and providence," elaborating that

> the divine in its sheer absoluteness has no 'authority,' only control ... But the divine ... has shaped a world to ground our being, a covenanted sphere of communication between himself and ourselves, evoking agency and practical reason among us.[30]

On Rom. 13:1, he notes that while "all authority is from God," all authority is also "of the world."[31] He even admonishes P.T. Forsyth for adopting a model of authority in *The Principle of Authority* based on the miracle, with the attendant consequence that he fails to pay due attention to "the purpose and moral order of the world *as creation*."[32] Yet the "world-order," as O'Donovan calls it here, is not only created, but also "*sustained* by the constant activity of God," with "the event of 'authoritative' disclosure" belonging to God's sustaining work.[33]

It is difficult to know what to make of the short discussion of authority (just seven pages) in *Self, World, and Time*, containing only occasional references to political authority specifically. On the one hand, it tantalizingly indicates that O'Donovan recognizes that *both* providence and created order are integral to a theology of political authority. On the other hand, it is only suggestive, not conclusive, with the potential of integration raised, but not pursued. Consequently, *Self, World, and Time* does not resolve the tension in the ontology of political authority created by the differing accounts given in *Resurrection* and *Desire/Judgment*.

In the next chapter, which marks the transition to the promised constructive phase in this study, I will suggest that O'Donovan's instinct in *Resurrection* was sound and that it was a mistake to abandon (or lose sight of) the idea that political authority is substantively embedded in the natural created order. I will argue that recapturing and integrating this insight into the account of political authority provided in *Desire/Judgment* could avoid the criticisms I have made regarding the "essence of political authority thesis," the "providence thesis" and the "re-authorization thesis." Before doing so, however, there is one final problem to note in regard to O'Donovan's theology of political authority, one that is germane to the resolution I will propose in the next chapter. This relates to the definition of "political."

---

30. O'Donovan, *Self, World, and Time*, 57.
31. Ibid.
32. Ibid., 58. Emphasis original. P. T. Forsyth, *The Principle of Authority in Relation to Certainty, Sanctity and Society* (London: Independent Press, 1913).
33. O'Donovan, *Self, World, and Time*, 58. Emphasis original.

O'Donovan's Extra-biblical Conception of "Politics" and "Political"

Michael Kessler, in his introduction to *Political Theology for a Plural Age*, notes that "different definitions of political theology abound."[34] One central, yet by no means exclusive, reason for this definitional proliferation stems from the semantic variability of the constitutive concept *political*. It is not uncommon for those writing on *political* theology to provide no definition of the concept at all. When a definition is provided, it is often done so in a way that accords "political" such unwieldy and expansive scope as to encompass just about any and every aspect of human social behavior.[35] When "political" is defined in more precise and circumscribed ways, great variability in meaning is still in evidence. (A similar problem attends the concept of *theology*, but its variability is not relevant to the discussion here.)

In reality, the conceptual instability attending the term "political theology" simply reflects the truism that the concept "politics," as Iain McLean and Alistair McMillan note, "is highly, perhaps essentially, contested."[36] Secular political thought, whether in the guise of political science or political philosophy, is thus similarly beset by definitional pluralism. However, as Keith Dowding notes in *The Philosophy and Methods of Political Science*, this definitional pluralism is not particularly problematic in political science because scholars are accustomed to defining the concept "politics" in the context of the specific research being conducted.[37] It is the consistent failure on the part of those writing on political theology to define the constitutive term "political" at all, or to define it too opaquely when they do, that is problematic in the context of Christian political theology.

O'Donovan fell prey to this tendency in *Desire*, failing to ever clarify precisely what he understands and means by the term *political* in the context of his political theology, the subject of the book. This omission was addressed in *Judgment*, where

---

34. Michael Jon Kessler, introduction to *Political Theology for a Plural Age* (Oxford: Oxford University Press, 2013), 1. Not everyone sees this as a negative. See, for example, Luke Bretherton, *Christ and the Common Life: Political Theology and the Case for Democracy* (Grand Rapids: Eerdmans, 2019), 25.

35. See, for example, Hovey and Phillips' definition in *The Cambridge Companion to Political Theology*: "An inquiry carried out by Christian theologians in relation to the political, where the political is defined broadly to include the various ways in which humans order common life" (*The Cambridge Companion to Political Theology*, xi–xii). The same phenomenon is also in evidence in secular political thought. See, for example, this definition from Shepsle: "For the purposes of our discussion, I will take politics to be utterly indistinguishable from the phenomena of group life generally." Kenneth A. Shepsle, *Analyzing Politics: Rationality, Behavior, and Institutions*, 2nd ed. (New York: W. W. Norton, 2010), 11.

36. McLean and McMillan, *Oxford Concise Dictionary of Politics*, s.v. "politics." One could say the same of "theology" too, of course.

37. Keith Dowding, *The Philosophy and Methods of Political Science* (London: Palgrave, 2016), 243.

he did come to provide a definition of "political." Given the close connection between the two books, it is reasonable to assume that the definition provided in *Judgment* also applies to *Desire*.[38] Noting the disputed nature of the term—"a jungle of incompatible conventions"—O'Donovan makes a distinction between the semantic fields of the noun "politics" and the adjective "political."[39] The former has to do with "government," whereas the latter can include "any kind of socially aware activity ... from writing poetry to organizing a drop-in shelter."[40] Seeking something of a "mean" between the widest and narrowest definitions of "politics" and "political," O'Donovan settled on the following definition: "those activities with a direct relation to government, but not only those activities with a direct relation to elected office."[41] This is a rather conventional definition of "politics" and "political," albeit at the narrower end of the definitional spectrum—note that, although O'Donovan identifies a difference between the semantic fields of "politics" and "political," he actually collapses both terms into this single definition.[42]

Although O'Donovan does not offer a definition of "political" per se in *Desire*, he does offer something approaching a definition of political theology in that book: "proposals ... which draw out an earthly political discourse from the political language of religious discourse."[43] That discourse, as we have seen throughout this study, ultimately finds its basis in Scripture. O'Donovan elaborates that such proposals do not proceed on the basis of a "literal synonymity between the political vocabulary of salvation and the secular use of the same political terms," but rather on the basis of "an analogy grounded in reality."[44] That analogy, as we have noted previously, is "between the acts of God and human acts," both of which take place within the context of "the one public history."[45] Combining the conception of "political theology" provided in *Desire* with the definition of "political" provided in *Judgment* permits the reproduction of what might be termed a more fulsome definition of political theology: "proposals ... which draw out an earthly ... discourse [regarding 'those activities with a direct relation to government'] from the political language of religious discourse."

I mentioned above that it is not unusual for political theologians to avoid defining the term "politics" in works that profess to be in, on or about political theology. But in O'Donovan's case one does wonder if the omission might stem from his restrictive methodology: the pursuit of true *political* concepts authorized from Holy Scripture. Neither the term "politics," nor the term "political," occurs

---

38. O'Donovan, *The Desire of the Nations*, ix.
39. O'Donovan, *The Ways of Judgment*, 55.
40. Ibid., 55.
41. Ibid., 56.
42. Ibid. Emphasis mine. This is not atypical. While O'Donovan is not alone in seeing a distinction between the noun and adjective in this case, many scholars treat "political" simply as an adjective of "politics," however defined, and thus with identical semantic fields.
43. O'Donovan, *The Desire of the Nations*, 2.
44. Ibid.
45. Ibid.

anywhere in Scripture.[46] As a consequence, neither is strictly speaking a biblical term. The problem is obvious: O'Donovan's entire political theology proceeds from the premise that true *political* concepts must be authorized from Scripture. But in the absence of any explicit definition of the concept "political" in Scripture, on what basis can O'Donovan use Scripture to verify the veracity of true *political* concepts? The answer is what all biblically minded political theologians do, which is to introduce their own extra-biblical definition of "political" to their analysis and exegesis of Scripture.[47] The non-occurrence in Scripture of any Hebrew, Aramaic, or Greek word(s) that could be translated by the English term "political" (or "politics") does not prevent O'Donovan from defining "political" in the context of political theology—something he did in *Judgment*. And as I indicated above, this definition is entirely conventional, which is to say that it is a definition one routinely encounters in secular discourse, and therefore is shared by scholars who hold no theological convictions whatsoever.[48]

The fact that O'Donovan's conception of "political" is extra-biblical, and as a consequence theologically arbitrary, brings into question the methodological wisdom of searching for true *political* concepts in Scripture. Aside from the problem that the Bible offers no definition of the very thing it is supposed to serve as a criterion for judging, there is the additional problem alluded to above: the essential contestability of the term and its consequent definitional variability, a contestability and variability to which Christian theology is not immune. Prominent Orthodox theologian Christos Yannaras, to take but one example, approaches the question of *political* theology with a very different conception of "politics" to O'Donovan. He construes politics as relating to the pursuit of

---

46. Several cognate terms do occur, such as "*politeuma*" (Phil. 3:20), "*politeia*" (Acts 22:28, Eph. 2:12), "*politis*" (Luke 15:15, 19:4, 21:39), and "*politarches*" (Acts 19:14, 17:6, 17:8). But the adjective "*politikos-i-o*" (political) does not occur. I acknowledge that a limitation of this work is that the author does not have biblical Hebrew. An electronic search of the NRSV translation of the Hebrew Bible reveals that it does not include either the English term "politics" or "political." That said, there are terms used in the Scriptures which would uncontroversially be regarded today as "political" terms, such as ἀρχή (arche)—rule, for example, Luke 20:20 and ἡγεμών (hegemon)—governor, for example, Matt 2:6.

47. This appears to be an example of what Biggar was driving at when he admonished O'Donovan for not being clearer about what "pre-understandings" and "pre-biblical convictions" he brought to *Desire*. Nigel Biggar, "On Defining Political Authority as an Act of Judgment: A Discussion of Oliver O'Donovan's *The Ways of Judgment* (Part I)," *Political Theology* 9, no.3 (2008): 278.

48. For a similar conventional definition, see Bertrand de Jouvenel, *Sovereignty: An Inquiry into the Political Good*, trans. J. F. Huntington (Cambridge: Cambridge University Press, 1957), 15: "The use of the word 'politic' designates not a thing, but the relations of anything to government."

"truth" and "authentic existence."[49] Politics, he says, is "the organic consequence of the participation of the citizen in the common struggle of a communion of relationships."[50] Because authentic existence has its origin and telos in the Trinitarian Christian God, authentic politics becomes about living in communion with all creation in the image of and in direct relationship with what Yannaras calls "the personal otherness of a creative loving communion of persons which forms the trinitarian first principle of the existent."[51] Yannaras, like O'Donovan, cannot claim that his conception of "politics" can simply be expounded in Scripture (and he makes no such claim). Yet it is a distinctively *Christian* conception of politics, unlike O'Donovan's rather conventional secular definition. This is not an argument in favor of Yannaras' definition *per se*, nor is it to question either the validity or utility of O'Donovan's particular definition of "political" in the context of *political* authority. It is merely to highlight its *theological* arbitrariness and the way that this arbitrariness undermines O'Donovan's normative method for political theology.

The absence of explicit reference to the concepts "politics" and "political" in Scripture is not, of course, evidence that the biblical authors had no concept of what we now understand (or stipulate) by those terms. Nor does it suggest that contemporary construals of such terms cannot serve as useful categories for analyzing the text of the Bible. One can hardly argue with any seriousness that the Davidic monarchy had no politics, or that Paul, when he wrote his famous exhortation to the Christians at Rome, had no concept of what we mean by the term "political," including "activities with a direct relation to government" (O'Donovan's definition). It is simply to question the viability of O'Donovan's methodological axiom that true political concepts must be authorized from Scripture, and to suggest that this might be a source, perhaps *the* source, of the problems that undermine the tenability of his foundational theses regarding the *theology* of political authority. In light of the untenability of these theses, as I have argued is the case, one is entitled to ask whether O'Donovan's core problem is that he is simply looking for something in Scripture that is not there: a theory of political authority. Again, to be clear, as I endeavored to show in Chapter 6, I maintain that O'Donovan actually has a powerful and efficacious conception of political authority with great explanatory potential in the context of political science. But the conclusion I draw here obviously has profound implications for the very project of Christian political theology, particularly for the theologian who regards the Bible as essential for theology (as I do). I explore these implications in the coming chapter.

---

49. Jonathan Cole, "The Communo-centric Political Theology of Christos Yannaras in Conversation with Oliver O'Donovan," in *Mustard Seeds: Between and Beyond Theology, Philosophy, and Society*, ed. Sotiris Mitralexis (Wilmington, DE: Vernon Press, 2017), 71.
50. Ibid.
51. Jonathan Cole, "Personhood, Relational Ontology, and the Trinitarian Politics of Eastern Orthodox Thinker Christos Yannaras," *Political Theology* 20, no.4 (2019): 9.

O'Donovan's extra-biblical conception of "political" also appears to be an impetus behind the distinct shape of the particular theses of political authority examined in previous chapters. If, for example, politics relates to "those activities with a direct relation to government," then it is perhaps not difficult to see why O'Donovan might think that the Christ-event re-authorizes the legitimate scope of politics to the effect that it is restricted to the moral judgments made by governments. The question is whether such a view is possible without O'Donovan's apparent pre-commitment to a conception of politics that orbits around the sun of government. It is certainly plausible that much of O'Donovan's theology of political authority is driven by his pre-conceived extra-biblical conception of politics/political, which has been imported to his exegesis and analysis of Scripture through a salvation-history hermeneutic.

Chapter 9

THE REDEMPTION OF POLITICAL AUTHORITY AND ITS NEW HISTORICAL *BENE ESSE* AS THE WORK OF DIVINE PROVIDENCE

This final constructive chapter seeks to reconcile the tension raised and discussed in the previous chapter and, in the process, resolve the problems identified in relation to the "essence of political authority thesis," the "re-authorization thesis" and the "providence thesis." It is important to be clear that I do not offer below an alternative theology of political authority. What I propose is a refinement of O'Donovan's own theology of political authority. The goal is to make O'Donovan's theological account of political authority more cogent than it is in its existing formulation, mostly by utilizing and integrating insights from his own work, namely *Resurrection*.

Differentiating the Need for Judgment from The Task of Executing Judgment

O'Donovan's postlapsarian understanding of politics is founded on the coherent notion that there could not have been any injured right to redress in the good creation. Given O'Donovan's conclusion in *Desire* that the normative function of secular government following the Christ-event is judgment, it is not difficult to discern a motive for locating political authority in the realm of history and theologically attributing its existence to divine providence.[1] The question, however, is whether the conviction that government serves the function of "restraining and remedying sin," as O'Donovan's mentor Ramsey once put it, demands a providentialist account of political authority.[2] I think O'Donovan's account of political authority in *Desire/Judgment* fails to adequately differentiate between the *need* for public moral discriminations, on the one hand, and what is *practically* involved in the human task of *executing* judgment, on the other.

---

1. O'Donovan, *The Ways of Judgment*, 7.
2. Ramsey, *Basic Christian Ethics*, 330. I have borrowed the description of O'Donovan's theology of political authority as "providentialist" from Chaplin. See Jonathan Chaplin, review of "*The Ways of Judgment*," by Oliver O'Donovan, *Scottish Journal of Theology* 61, no.4 (2008): 482.

Whether viewed from the perspective of legislative, executive, or judicial judgments, the act of making public moral discriminations between right and wrong ostensibly consists, perhaps entirely, of the utilization of faculties and resources properly understood as belonging to the natural ends and kinds of the created order, as O'Donovan defines them in *Resurrection*. These include reason, communication, speech, writing, consultation, coordination, organization, collaboration, deliberation, labor, and the human ingenuity to put all these together into laws and institutions capable of exercising consistent judgment. Even if one assumes that it is divine providence that directs all these natural authorities toward the end of justice, there is nothing *prima facie* ontologically supernatural about the *human* activity of executing right. As O'Donovan observed in *Judgment*, "no human act can be *radically* creative in the sense of giving existence to things that had no existence before."[3]

There is a sense, then, in which the execution of right is not even "relatively" natural, but rather wholly natural. Moreover, one could argue that it is the utilization of natural authorities in the *act* of executing judgment that makes that act meaningful, intelligible and, ultimately, capable of gaining acceptance by the community concerned (the "community's right," in O'Donovan's language). What is unnatural is the need to execute right in the first place. That need emerges historically as a consequence of the fall. The failure to clearly differentiate between the unnatural end of executing right and the natural "authorities" (in O'Donovan's sense) involved in *executing* right might provide a possible explanation for why O'Donovan felt compelled to look to providence rather than creation to explain the origin and nature of political authority when he came to write *Desire*. It might also help to explain his decision to begin with the enthronement psalms in *Desire* rather than the doctrine of creation, as he did in his initial discussion of political authority in *Resurrection*.

The argument I seek to make here is more subtle than a mere Thomist critique of O'Donovan's postlapsarian definition of politics. While I do think Aquinas' intuition was sound that human sociality necessitates some degree of authority for the purposes of realizing the common good, I still think the fall introduces a new political function that is alien to the good creation: the enactment of justice (remedying wrong).[4] I think there is actually a great deal of synergy between Aquinas' conception of the function of authority in the prelapsarian "state of innocence" and the role O'Donovan sees for natural authorities in the created order. But this synergy is obscured by O'Donovan's very narrow definition of "politics," restricted to governments exercising the solitary task of making moral

---

3. O'Donovan, *The Ways of Judgment*, 9. Emphasis original.
4. Saint Thomas Aquinas, *Summa Theologiae Prima Pars*, 50–119, trans. Fr. Laurence Shapcote, ed. John Mortensen and Enrique Alarcón (Lander, WY: The Aquinas Institute for the Study of the Works of St. Thomas Aquinas, 2012), 1a.96.a4ad. "Man is naturally a social being, and so in the state of innocence he would have led a social life. Now a social life cannot exist among a number of people unless under the presidency of one to look after the common good."

discriminations between right and wrong.⁵ Such a definition necessarily makes politics utterly alien to the good creation. But, as I argued in the previous chapter, O'Donovan's definition of politics is brought to his analysis of Scripture, not derived from it. Given the Bible does not provide a definition of politics, rendering any definition for the purposes of political theology unavoidably stipulative, there is no obstacle, in principle, to broadening the definition of politics to include both judgment, in O'Donovan's sense, and the pursuit of the common good. This, as I canvassed in Chapter 4, is a viable reading of Rom. 13:1-7 with some traditional pedigree (Chrysostom and Calvin). Indeed, it is my contention that O'Donovan, by expanding his conception of politics to include *dominium*, in the Thomist sense, could better explain how it is that political authority can efficaciously deal with what is alien to creation, "injured right," that is, by drawing on the natural (political) authorities found in the created order that make collective human action possible and capable of commanding obedience.

The Christological Redemption of Political Authority

In *Resurrection*, O'Donovan argues that "morality is man's participation in the created order."⁶ The ability of humans to participate morally in the created order, however, is hampered by sin, which has resulted in humankind's "persistent rejection of the created order" and "an inescapable confusion in [its] perceptions of it."⁷ The Christ-event "redeems" or "vindicates" the created order, thus restoring humankind's ability to participate morally in it, in accordance with the proper ends and kinds for which humans were created.⁸ In practical terms, it is the Holy Spirit who "makes the reality of redemption *present* to us" and who "evokes our *free* response as moral agents to the reality of redemption."⁹ The spirit restores humans "as moral agents" and its "redemptive work ... restor[es] ... our access to reality."¹⁰

I think O'Donovan's insight about the way that Christ redeems humankind's ability to participate morally in the created order offers a way to resolve the tension, or remove the appearance of tension, in his account of the ontology of political authority. This is to locate the *esse* of political authority in the created order, as he did in *Resurrection*, and to locate its *bene esse* in Christ's redemption of the whole created order, which is to say in the providential realm of history—part of

---

5. Interestingly, O'Donovan has indicated that he does not regard the dichotomy between the Thomist and Augustinian views of the place of politics in the divine economy as irreconcilable (*The Ways of Judgment*, 60).

6. O'Donovan, *Resurrection and Moral Order*, 76.

7. Ibid., 19.

8. Ibid., 76. "Christian morality is his glad response to the deed of God which has restored, proved and fulfilled that order, making man free to conform to it."

9. Ibid., 102, 106; emphases original.

10. Ibid., 106, 112.

humankind's restored access to reality. This distinction between the *esse* and *bene esse* of political authority is present in *Desire*. Furthermore, it is clear in *Desire* that O'Donovan understands the meaning of "Christ's triumph" to be "the restoration of creation."[11] The problem is that in *Desire* the *esse* and *bene esse* are both located in the realm of providential history and political authority does not appear to be among the natural authorities redeemed by Christ's triumph. O'Donovan's initial instinct in *Resurrection* to locate the *esse* of political authority in the created order, and therefore among the ends and kinds redeemed in Christ, offers a more compelling basis for a theology of political authority.

Under such a refinement, the role of providence becomes more specific and definite in contrast to the generic and opaque role it assumes in the "providence thesis." The catalytic act of providential intervention in history is the Christ-event, which redeems the possibility of a morally right exercise of political authority, consisting of a conjunction of specific natural authorities in creation. There are passages in *Resurrection* that appear to support such an idea. For instance, O'Donovan maintains that Christ's vindication of creation redeems "mankind in his context as the ruler of the ordered creation that God has made," and "in Christ man was able for the first time to assume his proper place within it, the place of dominion which God assigned to Adam."[12] The Holy Spirit, which is more or less absent in O'Donovan's theology of political authority, could be integrated at this point as the agent that facilitates the movement of individuals and communities toward a redeemed exercise of political authority, or, with respect to political judgments, that helps rulers and communities to make just moral discriminations. This notion of the Christological redemption of political authority is also perfectly compatible with a salvation-history biblical hermeneutic, that is, the idea that the Christ-event moves forward redemptive history in ways that have profound ramifications for the human exercise of politics.

Chaplin interprets O'Donovan's position in *Desire* "to be that salvation *restores and vindicates* the created orders of *society*, but *restrains and disciplines* the providential order of *government*."[13] This interpretation appears to reconcile or explain the differing accounts of political authority provided in *Resurrection* and *Desire/Judgment* by relying on a distinction between society and government.[14] I confess to not finding this distinction so clearly articulated and maintained in *Desire* as Chaplin apparently does. Moreover, militating against Chaplin's interpretation is the absence of the created order in O'Donovan's account of the essence of political authority. We are told, it is true, at the beginning of *Desire* that "the history of divine rule safeguards and redeems the goods of creation."[15] But political authority does not appear to be one of those goods. Instead, we have to

---

11. O'Donovan, *The Desire of the Nations*, 143.
12. O'Donovan, *Resurrection and Moral Order*, 24, 54–5.
13. Chaplin, "Political Eschatology and Responsible Government," 296. Emphasis original.
14. I must confess that I do not find this view clearly articulated in *Desire*.
15. O'Donovan, *The Desire of the Nations*, 19.

9. The Redemption of Political Authority

turn to Scripture's account of Israel in order to learn what the essence of political authority is. Indeed, in *Desire* it is Israel that appears to form the locus for the redemption of political authority, right down to the language of vindication and restoration: " ... Israel's history must be read as a *history of redemption*, which is to say, as the story of how certain principles of social and political life were vindicated by the action of God in the judgment and restoration of the people."[16] The Christ-event, for its part, redefines and restricts the *historical* function of political authority, but does not appear to redeem it—"the recovery of something given and lost."[17] In any event, it is not clear how a distinction between the redemption of society and the taming of political authority can resolve the question of how O'Donovan's providentialist account of political authority can explain its ability to evoke a free and intelligible human response if it is not grounded in the regularity of the created order like other authorities.

O'Donovan made some important refinements to his understanding of authority (as distinct from *political* authority) in *Self, World, and Time*. Describing the account of moral authority that he had offered in *Resurrection* as "flat and this-worldly," he confessed that he had come to appreciate that "authority is not simply vested in the world, self, and time as soon as we awake to them."[18] Rather, authority is mediated in the form of an "*event in which a reality is communicated to practical reason by a social communication*" in a process described by O'Donovan as "focused disclosure."[19] "Focused disclosure" is a somewhat abstruse concept. It is said to "filter" a "perception of reality demanding action" through a particular demonstration, personality, theory, or command.[20] It seems to be a way of signifying the mediatory nature of authority: "Without disclosure there is no authority; there is only unaided understanding on one side, brute exercise of power on the other."[21] The notion of "focused disclosure" does not, however, imply complete perspicuousness, as "we do not have the luxury of perfecting our knowledge before we set our foot upon the path of action."[22] Thus, while authority provides us with reasons for acting, and while the reasons for acting are grounded in truth, the reasons and truth are "implicit, and only partially disclosed."[23]

The idea that authority is mediated and communicated through a focused disclosure is not only compatible with my proposal that we ground political authority in the ontology of creation, the created order of ends and kinds, it is positively conducive. Political authority could be construed as the primary mediatory mechanism by which natural authorities in creation command obedience, that is, the vehicle of the kind of focused disclosure of which O'Donovan speaks. If all authority is mediated in this way, then political authority is no exception. If, on

16. Ibid., 29. Emphasis original.
17. O'Donovan, *Resurrection and Moral Order*, 54.
18. O'Donovan, *Self, World, and Time*, 53.
19. Ibid. Emphasis original.
20. Ibid., 54.
21. Ibid.
22. Ibid., 56.
23. Ibid.

the other hand, political authority is mediated through divine providence alone, as opposed to every other authority in the created order, then what we have in view arguably is not a species of authority at all, but something of a different kind altogether.

Israel's Role in Political Authority

By making the distinction between the natural ontology of political authority and the unnatural ends toward which it is providentially directed in history, O'Donovan could abandon the problematic notion that Israel, or Scripture, *reveals* the essence of political authority. Such a move would negate my criticism of the unacknowledged and unwarranted conceptual move that O'Donovan makes between the "divine kingship as salvation, judgment and possession paradigm" and the "essence of political authority thesis" analyzed in Chapter 3. It would also obviate other problems raised and discussed in my critical engagement with O'Donovan's theology of political authority: the lack of explicit Scriptural warrant for regarding the Davidic monarchy as politically normative; the Old Testament's ostensible lack of interest in political authority at the theoretical level; the ambivalence about the rise and status of the monarchy evident in Scripture; the fact that Israel is not the first regime in history to combine power, right, and tradition in one coordinated agency; the need to explain why God raises then ends the Davidic monarchy; and the paradox that Jesus did not reinstate the monarchy, but rather "re-authorized" it on a new footing. It also nullifies the Ramsey question: if Ramsey is an influence in O'Donovan's "essence of political authority thesis" then this is no problem.

All O'Donovan need do is show that Scripture confirms, accords with, or, perhaps more minimally, is not incompatible with, what can be empirically observed through a study of human political history. He could go further than this, however, and credibly claim that *he* arrived at his highly incisive conception of political authority through his study of the way Israel mediated God's rule, thus making Israel *relevant*, if not *normative*, to discourse about the *essence* of political authority, including to secular political philosophy and political science. In and of itself this represents a significant and valuable contribution and goes a long way to addressing O'Donovan's well-founded concern to demonstrate and restore the relevance of Israel (and the Old Testament) to Christian political theology.[24]

There are also other ways to retain the significance of Israel in the flow of salvation-history that do not require positing the Davidic monarchy's political forms as normative for Christian political theology today. One could view Israel's history primarily through the lens of covenant, as other theologians have done, such as Wright. As we discussed in Chapter 5, "covenant" occurs far more frequently in Scripture than "authority" and is unambiguously a political concept. It better

---

24. He claimed in *Desire*, for instance, that "failure to attend to Israel is what left Christian political thought oscillating between idealist and realist poles" (*The Desire of the Nations*, 27).

accounts for the *whole* of Israel's variegated political history as the people of God, including those periods when Israel was subject to an alien political authority that was neither in continuity with, nor representative of, its tradition. The covenant with God never ceased throughout Israel's tumultuous history and arguably constitutes the more obvious and biblically grounded framework for a coherent understanding of Israel's highly variable sacred politico-historical experience.[25] Covenant is also central to the Bible's account of Jesus, the inaugurator of new covenant, and a primary bridge between Old and New Testaments (covenants).

I am not suggesting that O'Donovan erred in focusing on political authority; Only that it was a mistake to underplay covenant in the context of a political theology in pursuit of political concepts authorized from Scripture. The remedy is not to exchange political authority for covenant but to integrate both concepts into a more holistic biblical and historical account of the way that God reigned over Israel. An account that focuses on political authority to the exclusion of covenant, and which purports to be biblical, is incomplete.

Replacing "Re-authorize" with "Redeem"

If the Old Testament does not *reveal* the essence of political authority, then there is no need to posit that Paul expounds its "re-authorization" by omitting constitutive elements of the "essence of political authority thesis" in Rom. 13:1–7. This releases O'Donovan from the implausible view that Rom. 13:1–7 argues that judgment is the sole legitimate function of political authority following Christ's triumph. It also allows a more expansive conception of the role of government that retains, on the one hand, the undisputed role for judgment, but adds, on the other, a constructive role for promoting the common good. This more expansive view of the function of government is more compatible with Rom. 13:1–7, and in particular verse 4a "For it is God's servant for your good."

Instead of the "re-authorization thesis," O'Donovan, drawing on his insights in *Resurrection*, could re-term and re-conceive the thesis as the "redemption of political authority thesis," which is to say the restoration of humankind's capacity to participate fully and efficaciously in the created moral order, including those natural authorities that constitute political authority (political here in the Thomist sense discussed above). The redemptive view of political authority preserves O'Donovan's belief that the Christ-event fundamentally changes the function and role of political authority in salvation-history. O'Donovan can still claim—perhaps with even more conviction—that "much has changed in history, and much of that change may derive one way or another from the events of Bethlehem and Calvary."[26] The seminal historical development in the history of God's reign is the

---

25. Preuss argues, by way of example, that the concept of "divine election" connects the different "spheres" of Israel's history, including "the exodus, the ancestors, the king, Zion and the priesthood" (*Old Testament Theology*, 37).

26. O'Donovan, "Deliberation, History and Reading," 138.

restoration of Adamic rule made possible through Christ's exaltation and triumph over the nations' rulers.

"Christian Liberalism" as the Bene Esse *of Political Authority*

As a historical achievement, the Christian could regard the emergence of Western (Christian) liberalism as "a work of divine providence in history, not a mere accomplishment of the human task of political service" (the "providence thesis"). We recall that O'Donovan argues that a form of "Christian liberalism" emerged out of the "high tradition" (1100–1650) of Christian political thought marked by "freedom," "merciful judgment," "natural right," and "openness of speech."[27] This Christian liberalism formed the basis, as I indicated in Chapter 7, for the conclusion that a political theologian can propound a "normative political culture" in broad continuity with the Western liberal tradition. Instead of divine providence being responsible for the existence of the essence of political authority, it could be reconceived as redeeming the created good of political authority in the Christ-event, thereby facilitating the *historical* realization of its redeemed *bene esse* in the form of Christian liberalism.[28] This is, in effect, what O'Donovan argues in *Desire*:

> To display the liberal achievement correctly, we have to show it as the victory won by Christ over the nations' rulers. It presupposes original political authority, on the one hand, and proclaims the transformation of it wrought by Christ's Spirit on the other. Apart from this salvation-historical background, liberal expectations lose their meaning, which is to point to a *bene esse* of political society which presumes an *esse*. They represent a (provisional) perfection and fulfilment of *political* order which derives its political character from the rule of divine providence.[29]

However, this argument does not imply the "providence thesis." In fact, it would be more cogent if we assumed, with O'Donovan in *Resurrection*, that what is redeemed by the Christ-event is the natural authorities that constitute political authority, and that it is Christian liberalism, rather than political authority *per se*, that is the "work of divine providence" in history.

It is important to note that, while the conjunction of power, right, and tradition in one coordinated agency is a prerequisite for realizing the fruits of Christian liberalism—"freedom," "merciful judgment," "natural right," and "openness of speech"—there is no suggestion in *Desire* that they are, in and of themselves, constitutive of political authority, nor necessary products thereof. Political

---

27. O'Donovan, *The Desire of the Nations*, 4, 275, 278; emphasis original.
28. Wolterstorff has asked why the "re-authorization of governmental regimes ... would not instead imply the healing of their malformation" ("A Discussion of Oliver O'Donovan's *The Desire of the Nations*," 102).
29. O'Donovan, *The Desire of the Nations*, 229. Emphasis original.

authority has not only an *esse* and *bene esse*, but also a *male esse*, that is, a perverted form. By making the ontological distinction between an *esse* of political authority grounded in the created order and a *bene esse* of political authority that is the product of divine providence in history, O'Donovan possesses a powerful theological explanation for the existence of oppressive and unjust regimes, such as that of North Korea's, which does not make God complicit in their existence, as implied by the "providence thesis." As a conjunction of natural authorities in the created order, political authority is there to be discovered and used, or manipulated and abused, as the case may be, by all humans.[30] God is no more morally responsible for the misuse of political authority than he is for the misuse of any other natural authority in creation. Human sin is culpable in this respect. Moreover, this distinction provides O'Donovan with a constructive normative Christian liberal political manifesto that is distinct from contemporary secular Western liberal offerings. O'Donovan's Christian liberalism can argue that the only viable way for non-liberal regimes to realize the liberal achievement is to recognize and participate in Christ's redemption of the created order, the *sine qua non* of (Christian) liberalism.[31] This would liberate Christians from being hostage to history, along with the ambivalence and uncertainty this creates regarding the present actuality of liberalism. History can be recast as an enduring struggle between the *bene esse* of Christian liberalism wrought by Christ's triumph over the nations and its *male esse* in political forms which reject Christ's exaltation. In other words, the Christian, with O'Donovan, can still proclaim that Christ really is the desire of the nations and work toward making that proclamation a reality, including in erstwhile Christian liberal polities that now fail to acknowledge this. To that end, O'Donovan's Christian liberalism is not just a potentially constructive roadmap for non-liberal regimes to realize the liberal achievement, but also, crucially, a vital reform agenda for tired Western liberal polities struggling to retain a firm grip on the fruits of the Christian liberal achievement.

Is There Biblical Support for a Creation Ontology of Political Authority?

In deference to O'Donovan's concern for a biblically informed, if not exactly a biblically formed, account of political authority, I note two passages in Scripture that appear to lend some support to my proposal to ground the essence of political authority in the created order. These are Col.1:16 and 1 Peter 2:13–14.[32] Col.1:16 says:

---

30. O'Donovan, *Resurrection and Moral Order*, 88. O'Donovan observes that "the universe, though fractured and broken ... remains accessible to knowledge in part."
31. O'Donovan, *The Desire of the Nations*, 229.
32. O'Donovan does not explicitly refer to Col. 1:16 in either *Desire* or *Judgment*, although there is a reference in the former to Col. 1:15 & 18 (*The Desire of the Nations*, 181).

> For in him [Jesus] all things in heaven and on earth were created, things visible and invisible, whether thrones [θρόνοι] or dominions [κυριότητες] or rulers [ἀρχαί] or powers [ἐξουσίαι]—all things have been created through him and for him.[33]

Exousiai (ἐξουσίαι), commonly translated as "authorities," is the all-important term (also in the plural) found in Rom. 13:1: "Let every person be subject to the governing authorities [ἐξουσίαις ὑπερεχούσαις—*exousiais hyperechousais*] ... " The term powers in this context, therefore, likely had connotations for Greek speakers of that era which included something akin to what today might be called "political authority," although it must be recognized that its semantic field also included angelic and demonic authorities. One of the real curiosities of *Desire* is that, having undertaken some linguistic analysis of Hebrew terms associated with divine kingship in the Old Testament, O'Donovan conducts no substantive or systematic analysis of the Greek political vocabulary of the New Testament. This is especially surprising given the frequency of the Greek term *exousia* (ἐξουσία) in the New Testament, the closest we get to a concept of "political authority" in the language of Scripture itself, including in Rom. 13:1–7, where something akin to *political* authority is clearly in view.

That said, in the case of Col. 1:16 many commentators favor an interpretation of "thrones," "dominions," "rulers," and "powers" that relates specifically to the angelic and/or demonic realm—there is dispute about which of the two provides the correct context—even while admitting that a reading that views the referents as both mundane and supermundane is possible.[34] Even so, Douglas Moo helpfully reminds that the introduction to the hymn in verse 15—"He is the image of the invisible God, the firstborn of all creation"—evokes the creation story in Genesis.[35]

It is important to consider the term *exousia* and its occurrence (in the plural) in Col. 1:16 in a wider perspective, given it is a frequently occurring term in the New Testament with a complex semantic field requiring multiple English words for effective translation. *The Theological Dictionary of the New Testament*, for instance, explains how *exousia* can "express the invisible power of God whose Word is *creative* power," as well as denote "the power of decision ... active

---

33. Col. 1:16 forms part of a poem or hymn which runs from verses 15–20. As N. T. Wright explains, "most scholars agree that the passage is skillfully worded and rhythmically balanced, deserving to be called a poem," and that "some have ... suggested that it is, or contains, a hymn already well known before being quoted" by Paul. N. T. Wright, *Colossians and Philemon: Tyndale New Testament Commentaries Volume 12* (Downers Grove, IL: InterVarsity Press, 1986), 68.

34. See, for example, Markus Barth and Helmut Blanke, *Colossians: A New Translation*, trans. Astrid B. Beck (New York: The Anchor Bible, 1994), 201; Peter T. O'Brien, *Colossians, Philemon: World Biblical Commentary Volume 44* (Waco, TX: Word Books, 1982), 46; and Douglas J. Moo, *The Letters to the Colossians and to Philemon* (Grand Rapids: Eerdmans, 2008), 113.

35. Moo, *The Letters to the Colossians and to Philemon*, 122.

in a legally ordered whole, especially in the state and in all the authoritarian relationships supported by it."³⁶ *The Theological Dictionary of the New Testament* further indicates that *exousia* "can also denote the fact that His will prevails in the sphere of *nature* as an ordered totality" and, moreover, that "the frequent use of the term in this context shows that nature is regarded as an ordered totality."³⁷

It is essential to understand the connection between these different senses in which *exousia* is used in the New Testament. "Governing authorities," or perhaps "political authority," appears to have been understood as a species of "authority" in a hierarchy that begins with God, pervades the angelic and demonic realm and then infuses the natural order and human social life—an "ordered totality." Consequently, even if *exousiai* has a strictly supermundane sense in Col. 1:16, it is likely that the original audience would have understood the term in the context of an "ordered totality" that included earthly political *exousiai*. The notion that God could create such authorities through Christ opens the door to countenancing the possibility that *all* authority, including what we have come to know as *political* authority, was created in and for Christ. N. T. Wright's interpretation of Col. 1:16 accords with this "ordered totality" sense of *exousia*: "No power structures are, however, independent of Christ: for *all things were created by and for him*."³⁸

1 Peter 2:13-14 uniquely connects the noun *ktisis* (κτίσις)—"creation" (translated as "institution" in the NRSV)—to positions of human political authority such as "emperors" and "governors":

> 13. For the Lord's sake accept the authority of every human institution [*ktisis*], whether of the emperor as supreme, 14. or of governors, as sent by him to punish those who do wrong and to praise those who do right.

Some commentators regard the NRSV translation of *ktisis* as "human institution" to be misleading.³⁹ As Boring explains, "since elsewhere in the Bible 'creation' [*ktisis*] always refers to God's act ... it is better to see the phrase as referring to the structures of society as part of God's creation."⁴⁰ There are other interpretations, of course, such as that of Michaels, which sees the focus of the passage center on "humanity as God's creation."⁴¹ But it is possible to interpret this passage in such a way that connects what we now recognize as political institutions of authority,

---

36. Gerhard Friedrich, ed., *The Theological Dictionary of the New Testament, Volume II*, trans. and ed. Geoffrey W. Bromiley (Grand Rapids: Eerdmans, 1964), s.v. ἐξουσία, 566. Emphasis mine.

37. Ibid., 566-7.

38. Wright, *Colossians and Philemon*, 77. Emphasis original.

39. See, for example, Lewis Donelson, *I & II Peter and Jude: A Commentary* (Louisville: Westminster John Knox Press, 2010), 71; and Edmund P. Clowney, *The Message of 1 Peter: The Way of the Cross* (Leicester: InterVarsity Press, 1988), 105.

40. Eugene M. Boring, *1 Peter* (Nashville: Abingdon Press, 1999), 115.

41. J. Ramsey Michaels, *1 Peter: World Biblical Commentary Volume 49*, (Waco, TX: Word Books, 1988), 124.

such as emperors and governors, ontologically to creation *without* contorting the text.

This all-too brief discussion of Col.1:16 and 1 Peter 2:13–14—two passages that play a negligible role in the exegetical discussion of political authority in *Desire*—indicates that there is, prima facie, some biblical support for a refinement of O'Donovan's theology of political authority along the lines that I propose. That said, the two passages cited here and discussed only briefly can only be regarded as suggestive, falling well short of the standard of biblical warrant. It goes without saying that detailed and systematic analysis of the entirety of Scripture is required before anything stronger can be said in this regard. The point I make is merely to note that the refinement I propose has some prospects of biblical support, or, more minimally, biblical compatibility (i.e., non-contradiction).

True Political Concepts Authorized from Holy Scripture?

J. Budziszewski, in *Evangelicals in the Public Square*, identifies and analyzes several "fallacies" of evangelical political theory.[42] Two are particularly apposite to O'Donovan's theology of political theology: "projective accommodation" and "inflationary strategies." "Projective accommodation" consists of "accommodating Scripture to one's own political views by reading those views into the biblical text."[43] This might apply to O'Donovan's importation of an extra-biblical definition of "political" that appears to predispose him to a government-centric political theology (government-as-judgment). "Inflationary strategies" denote the tendency of Evangelicals to find more political content, which is to say more political theology, in the Bible than can be objectively supported.[44] This might apply to O'Donovan's entire project to the extent that he is looking for a clear, unambiguous, and coherent *theoretical* account of political authority in a text that shows little preoccupation with such questions. As an interesting aside, one of the specific inflationary strategies identified by Budziszewski is the assumption that "the biblical pattern of covenant represents the divine blueprint for all political authority," which is more applicable to Wright than to O'Donovan.[45] Still, O'Donovan arguably falls into a related version of this fallacy in that he quite clearly assumes that the biblical pattern of divine kingship represents the divine blueprint for all political authority. In any event, the crux of the problem, as Budziszewski rightly observes, is not the Evangelical instinct to "ground their political reflection in revelation"; it is the demands placed on Scripture to answer

---

42. J. Budziszewski, *Evangelicals in the Public Square: Four Formative Voices in Political Thought and Action*, with responses by David L. Weeks et. al., an introduction by Michael Cromartie, and an afterword by Jean Bethke Elshtain (Grand Rapids: Baker Academic, 2006), 20.
43. Ibid., 21.
44. Ibid., 27.
45. Ibid., 28.

too much regarding the political, or in Budziszewski's words, it is the fact that "the Bible provides insufficient materials for the task."[46]

Budziszewski's proposed solution to Evangelical fallacies of this kind rests on the distinction between special and general revelation. While Budziszewski's conception of general revelation centers primarily on reason (the principles of noncontradiction and excluded middle, for example), as well as history and experience, he ultimately attributes general revelation, including reason, to "the divinely ordained design of the world."[47] This brings us back to O'Donovan's conception of a created order of ends and kind as a potential source of political knowledge. Budziszewski actually goes down the route of natural law and grace as the theological concepts that make general revelation operative. My proposal, while not incompatible with Budziszewski's, is to posit that the natural *ontology* of politics, and in particular political authority, licenses political theologians (Evangelical or otherwise) to employ the empirical methods of political science and the rational method of political philosophy as *supplements* and *augments* to the Bible as a resource for political knowledge. Employing this method for investigating the reality of the created world need not undermine the (Evangelical) biblical notion that God, as creator of natural ends and kinds, is the ultimate source of *all* political knowledge.

The virtue of Budziszewski's general revelation, or as I would put it, a creation ontology of politics, is that it allows the Christian political theologian to consider a wider range of political concepts and ideas than those explicitly found in Scripture. In practice, many, if not most, Christians embrace a range of political concepts found nowhere in Scripture, from democracy to the separation of powers, from conservatism to liberalism, from representation to self-determination, and many more besides. If Christian political theology is to attain the "full conceptuality" that O'Donovan rightly identifies as essential to its task, then it must have a theological rationale for incorporating both new concepts and old concepts not revealed in Scripture (such as democracy).[48]

There is an important analogy here to be made between the way that Christian scholars in secular fields use the Bible in support of their work that could be instructive for political theologians. Christian anthropologists, sociologists, and physicists, for example, do not restrict themselves to the conceptuality of Scripture in their respective inquiries. They do not expect to find ready-made anthropological, sociological, or scientific theories in Scripture, nor do they require that theories that can be empirically or experimentally verified also

---

46. Ibid., 30.
47. Ibid., 33.
48. O'Donovan, *The Desire of the Nations*, 2. As Bauckham notes, "a more imaginative and creative hermeneutic is necessary for the Bible to speak to modern political life." Richard Bauckham, *The Bible in Politics: How to Read the Bible Politically* (London: SPCK, 1989), 12. Walzer, who draws in places on O'Donovan's work in *Desire*, agrees, concluding that the Bible's "indifference" to politics is an asset because it "leaves politics free, open to prudential and pragmatic determinations" (*In God's Shadow*, 205).

be "authorized" from Scripture before they can be accepted. But nor do they disregard the illumination Scripture can potentially provide for their research. Scripture offers important insights into the origin and telos of the universe, and consequently into human life and history, and everything entailed therein. Why should we suppose that the political should be any different? Like anthropology, sociology, chemistry, and physics, political science seeks to understand a feature of empirical reality as humans experience it.

There is, on the other hand, something distinctive about political science (and political philosophy for that matter) of which O'Donovan is cognizant: the conceptuality of Scripture intersects with secular political vocabulary in a way that it does not in the case of sociology, anthropology, chemistry, or physics. The very basis for a Christian political theology, on O'Donovan's account, is Scripture's refrain: *Yhwh mālak*. So Scripture does uniquely bring God and political conceptuality into direct relation, making political theology an unavoidable professional hazard for the theologian rather than an extracurricular option. Still, there is no gainsaying the implications of the fact that while Scripture employs political vocabulary—"almost the whole vocabulary of salvation in the New Testament has a political pre-history of some kind"—it does not provide any obvious, unambiguous, or timeless political theory that can uncontroversially be expounded, let alone implemented.[49]

Thus, while political theology may be necessary for the Christian theologian by virtue of the convergence of the political vocabulary of Scripture and secular political discourse, as O'Donovan maintains, it is equally necessary that political theology extend its horizons beyond the limited, albeit important, convergent vocabulary so that at the very least it become conversant, if not enriched, by the much wider political conceptuality of political science and political philosophy. A virtue of this approach is that political science conceptuality has developed as a response to, and as a means of interrogating, empirical political realities. No matter how glorious one may be inclined to regard the political conceptuality found in Scripture, it will never be able to tell you what mechanisms make a representative democracy stable, nor myriad other questions regarding empirical political realities that humans are wont to decipher. But there should be no more shame in acknowledging this reality than acknowledging the obvious fact that Scripture tells us nothing about DNA.

Looking forward, the challenge for Christian political theology, one which O'Donovan uniquely recognizes, but is unable to navigate successfully, is to find a bridge (a methodology) that can bring the theological conceptuality of Scripture into fruitful concourse with the extra-biblical conceptuality of political science and political philosophy.

---

49. O'Donovan, *The Desire of the Nations*, 22.

CONCLUSION

In setting out the task of political theology in *Desire,* O'Donovan emphasized the need for "a unifying conceptual structure" and "an architectonic hermeneutic" in order to "connect political themes with the history of salvation as a whole."[1] I think architect is an apt metaphor for O'Donovan's contribution to political theology. His seminal works *Desire* and *Judgment* can be thought of, by way of analogy, as a building designed by O'Donovan (each a floor in a two-story building, perhaps). Throughout this study I have surveyed the building's structure and found some elements of its foundations wanting. But there is still much to admire and enjoy in the building.

To apply the analogy fully to the criticisms leveled in this book, we might say that, from the perspective of function, the building is in many ways a triumph. O'Donovan has developed a highly insightful conception of political authority that appears to be empirically valid and to be potentially efficacious for the kind of research conducted in political science. The fact that he arrived at this conception after a close reading of the Christian scriptures and reflection on the political and historical impact of the Christ-event demonstrates the fecundity of Christian sources, history, and thought not only for understanding our own present political context and moment, but also for theoretical understandings of the political reality we inhabit.

On the other hand, the design, though functional, has been built on the wrong foundations. The highly insightful conception of political authority developed by O'Donovan simply cannot be supported by the exegetical and theological foundations he has designed for his structure. That said, persevering with the analogy, these foundations can be remodeled using materials and designs from one of O'Donovan's other buildings, in this case his moral theology (*Resurrection*)— grounding the ontology of political authority in the natural ends and kinds of the created order and its redeemed normative expression in the Christian liberalism of providential history.

As a final word of appreciation, let me observe that O'Donovan triumphs in many ways as a Christian political philosopher, but falls short as a Christian

1. Ibid., 22.

political theologian. His most powerful insights regarding political theology are most appropriately described as philosophical, while his most tenuous claims tend to be theological. In fact, if we stripped out the tenuous theological claims of *Desire* and *Judgment*, O'Donovan would be left with a rather compelling and insightful *philosophy* of political authority. The root cause of his problems on the theological side all ultimately stem from his questionable method: using Scripture to adjudicate the validity of political concepts when Scripture itself offers no definition of "political," nor a fulsome enough conceptuality to construct a robust political theory of any kind.

BIBLIOGRAPHY

Anderson, Matthew Lee. "O'Donovan Contra Liberalism." *Mere Orthodoxy*. August 3, 2009. https://mereorthodoxy.com/odonovan-contra-liberalism/.
Aquinas, Thomas. *Summa Theologiae Prima Pars, 50–119*, translated by Fr. Laurence Shapcote, edited by John Mortensen and Enrique Alarcon. Lander, WY: The Aquinas Institute for the Study of Sacred Doctrine, 2012.
Aristotle. *The Politics*, translated by T. A. Sinclair, revised by Trevor J. Saunders. London: Penguin, 1992.
Armstrong, Charles K. "Trends in the Study of North Korea." *The Journal of Asian Studies* 70, no.2 (2011): 357–71.
Barth, Markus and Helmut Blanke. *Colossians: A New Translation with Introduction and Commentary by Markus Barth and Helmut Blanke*, translated by Astrid B. Beck. New York: The Anchor Bible, 1994.
Bartholomew, Craig and Jonathan Chaplin, Robert Song and Al Wolters, eds. *A Royal Priesthood? The Use of the Bible Ethically: A Dialogue with Oliver O'Donovan*. Carlisle, Cumbria: Paternoster, 2002.
Bartholomew, Craig G. "A Time for War, and a Time for Peace: Old Testament Wisdom, Creation and O'Donovan's Theological Ethics." In *A Royal Priesthood? The Use of the Bible Ethically: A Dialogue with Oliver O'Donovan*, edited by Craig Bartholomew, Jonathan Chaplin, Robert Song and Al Waters, 91–112. Carlisle, Cumbria: Paternoster, 2002.
Bauckham, Richard. *The Bible in Politics: How to Read the Bible Politically*. London: SPCK, 1989.
Bertschmann, Dorothea H. *Bowing Before Christ—Nodding to the State? Reading Paul Politically with Oliver O'Donovan and John Howard Yoder*. London: Bloomsbury T&T Clark, 2014.
Bertschmann, Dorothea H. "The Rule of Christ and Human Politics—Two Proposals: A Comparison of the Political Theology of Oliver O'Donovan and John Howard Yoder." *The Heythrop Journal* 56, no.3 (2015): 424–40.
Biggar, Nigel. "On Defining Political Authority as an Act of Judgment: A Discussion of Oliver O'Donovan's *The Ways of Judgment* (Part 1)." *Political Theology* 9, no.3 (2008): 272–93.
Bimson, John J. "Ezra." In *Theological Interpretations of the Old Testament: A Book-by-book Survey*, edited by Kevin J. Vanhoozer, 132–6. Grand Rapids: Baker Academic, 2008.
Blenkinsopp, Joseph. *David Remembered: Kingship and National Identity in Ancient Israel*. Grand Rapids: Eerdmans, 2013.
Blount, Brian K. "Response to *The Desire of the Nations*." *Studies in Christian Ethics* 11, no.2 (1998): 8–17.
Boring, Eugene M. *1 Peter*. Nashville: Abingdon Press, 1999.
Bretherton, Luke. *Christ and the Common Life: Political Theology and the Case for Democracy*. Grand Rapids: Eerdmans, 2019.
Bretherton, Luke. *Christianity & Contemporary Politics*. Oxford: Wiley-Blackwell, 2010.

Bretherton, Luke. "Coming to Judgment: Methodological Reflections on the Relationship between Ecclesiology, Ethnography and Political Theory." *Modern Theology* 28, no.2 (2012): 167–96.

Bretherton, Luke. "Introduction: Oliver O'Donovan's Political Theology and the Liberal Imperative." *Political Theology* 9, no.3 (2008): 265–71.

Brueggemann, Walter. *David's Truth: In Israel's Imagination and Memory*. 2nd ed. Minneapolis: Fortress Press, 2002.

Budziszewski, J. *Evangelicals in the Public Square: Four Formative Voices in Political Thought and Action*, with responses by David L. Weeks, John Bold, William Edgar and Ashley Woodiwiss, an introduction by Michael Cromartie and an afterword by Jean Bethke Elshtain. Grand Rapids: Baker Academic, 2006.

Burke, Edmund. "Reflections on the Revolution." In *Burke: Revolutionary Writings*, edited by Iain Hampsher-Monk. Cambridge: Cambridge University Press, 2014.

Calvin, John. "On Civil Government." In *On God and Political Duty*, edited with introduction by John T. McNeill, 83–7. Indianapolis: Bobbs-Merrill Educational Publishing, 1953.

Calvin, John. "Commentaries on Romans." In *On God and Political Duty*, edited with introduction by John T. McNeill, 83–7. Indianapolis: Bobbs-Merrill Educational Publishing, 1953.

Carson, D. A. *Divine Sovereignty and Human Responsibility: Biblical Perspectives in Tension*. London: Marshall, Morgan & Scott, 1981.

Carson, E. Ann. "Prisoners in 2019." *U.S. Department of Justice*. October 1, 2020. https://www.bjs.gov/content/pub/pdf/p19.pdf.

Cavanaugh, William T. *Migrations of the Holy: God, State, and the Political Meaning of the Church*. Grand Rapids: Eerdmans, 2011.

Cavanaugh, William T, Jeffrey W. Bailey and Craig Hovey, eds. *An Eerdmans Reader in Contemporary Political Theology*. Grand Rapids: Eerdmans, 2012.

Center for Pastor Theologians. "SAET Interviews in Politics and Theology #5: Oliver O'Donovan." October 29, 2010. Accessed April 24, 2016. http://www.pastortheologians.com/saet-interviews-in-politics-and-theology-5-oliver-odonovan/.

Chaplin, Jonathan. "Political Eschatology and Responsible Government." In *A Royal Priesthood? The Use of the Bible Ethically: A Dialogue with Oliver O'Donovan*, edited by Craig Bartholomew, Jonathan Chaplin, Robert Song and Al Waters, 265–308. Carlisle, Cumbria: Paternoster, 2002.

Chaplin, Jonathan. "Representing a People: Oliver O'Donovan on Democracy and Tradition." *Political Theology* 9, no.3 (2008): 295–307.

Chaplin, Jonathan. "Review of *The Ways of Judgment*, by Oliver O'Donovan." *Scottish Journal of Theology* 61, no.4 (2008): 477–93.

Chaplin, Jonathan. "Towards a Monotheistic Democratic Constitutionalism? Convergent Themes in Oliver O'Donovan, Sajjad Rizvi and Paul Heck." *Studies in Christian Ethics* 29, no.2 (2016): 169–76.

Cho, Sung Yoon. "The Judicial System of North Korea." *Asian Survey* 11, no.12 (1971): 1167–81.

Choi, Changyang. "'Everyday Politics' in North Korea." *The Journal of Asian Studies* 72, no.3 (2013): 655–73.

Chrysostom, John. "Twenty-fourth Homily on Romans." In *From Irenaeus to Grotius: A Sourcebook in Christian Political Thought 100–1625*, edited by Joan Lockwood O'Donovan and Oliver O'Donovan, 92–6. Grand Rapids: Eerdmans, 1999.

Clowney, Edmund P. *The Message of 1 Peter: The Way of the Cross*. Leicester: InterVarsity Press, 1988.
Cole, Graham A. *God the Peacemaker: How Atonement Brings Shalom*. Downers Grove, iL: InterVarsity Press, 2009.
Cole, Jonathan. "The Communo-centric Political Theology of Christos Yannaras in Conversation with Oliver O'Donovan." In *Mustard Seeds in the Public Square: Between and Beyond Theology, Philosophy, and Society*, edited by Sotiris Mitralexis. Wilmington, DE: Vernon, 2017, 61–92.
Cole, Jonathan. "Personhood, Relational Ontology, and the Trinitarian Politics of Eastern Orthodox Thinker Christos Yannaras." *Political Theology* 20, no.4 (2019): 297–310.
Cole, Jonathan. "Political Theology and Political Authority: Evaluating Oliver O'Donovan's Christian Liberalism." *ABC Religion & Ethics*. June 21, 2021. https://www.abc.net.au/religion/political-theology-oliver-odonovans-christian-liberalism/13401594.
Cole, Jonathan. "Towards a Christian Ontology of Political Authority: The Relationship between Created Order and Providence in Oliver O'Donovan's Theology of Political Theology." *Studies in Christian Ethics* 32, no.3 (2019): 307–25.
Cullman, Oscar. *The State in the New Testament*. London: SCM Press, 1957.
Cunning, Joseph. *A History of Medieval Political Thought 300–1450*. London: Routledge, 1996.
Doerksen, Paul. G. *Beyond Suspicion: Post-Christendom Protestant Political Theology in John Howard Yoder and Oliver O'Donovan*. Colorado Springs: Paternoster, 2009.
Doerksen, Paul. G. "Christology in the Political Theology of Oliver O'Donovan." *Mennonite Quarterly Review* 78, no.3 (2004): 433–47.
Donelson, Lewis. *I & II Peter and Jude: A Commentary*. Louisville: Westminster John Knox Press, 2010.
Dowding, Keith. *The Philosophy and Methods of Political Science*. London: Palgrave, 2016.
Eerdword: The Eerdmans Blog. "Five Questions with Oliver O'Donovan." March 17, 2015. http://eerdword.com/2015/03/17/five-questions-with-oliver-odonovan/.
Errington, Andrew. "Authority and Reality in the Work of Oliver O'Donovan." *Studies in Christian Ethics* 29, no.4 (2016): 371–85.
Errington, Andrew. "Between Justice and Tradition: Oliver O'Donovan's Political Theory and the Challenge of Multiculturalism." *Studies in Christian Ethics* 27, no.4 (2014): 417–30.
Errington, Andrew. *Every Good Path: Wisdom and Practical Reason in Christian Ethics and the Book of Proverbs*. London: T&T Clark, 2020.
Evans, G. R. "Henry Chadwick." In *Key Theological Thinkers: From Modern to Postmodern*, edited by Staale Johannes Kristiansen and Svein Rise, 475–86. Surrey: Ashgate, 2013.
Feiler, Therese. "From Dialectics to Theo-Logic: The Ethics of War from Paul Ramsey to Oliver O'Donovan." *Studies in Christian Ethics* 28, no.3 (2015): 343–59.
Fitzmyer, Joseph A. *Romans: A New Translation with Introduction and Commentary*. New York: Anchor Bible Doubleday, 1993.
Forsyth, P. T. *The Principles of Authority in Relation to Certainty, Sanctity and Society*. London: Independent Press, 1913.
Friedrich, Gerhard, ed. *The Theological Dictionary of the New Testament, Volume II*, translated and edited by Geoffrey W. Bromiley. Grand Rapids: Eerdmans, 1964.
Fukuyama, Francis. "The End of History?" *The National Interest* no.16 (1989): 3–18.
Ganas, Evaggelos. "Η πολιτική τοῦ Ἰησοῦ καὶ ἡ προσδοκία τῶν ἐθνῶν Θέτοντας τον Τζόν Χάουαρντ Γιόντερ καί τόν Ὀλιβερ Ο' Ντόνοβαν σέ διάλογο" [*The Politics of Jesus* and *The Desire of the Nations*: Bringing John Howard Yoder and Oliver O'Donovan into

Conversation]. In Θρησκεία καί πολιτική [*Religion and Politics*], edited by Stavros Zoumboulakis, 322–55. Athens: Artos Zois, 2016.

Gause, Ken E. "Coercion, Control, Surveillance, and Punishment: An Examination of the North Korean Police State." *The Committee for Human Rights in North Korea.* 2012.

Goedde, Patricia. "Law 'Of Our Own Style': The Evolution and Challenges of the North Korean Legal System." *Fordham International Law Journal* 27, no.4 (2003): 1265–88.

Goldingay, John. *Psalms: Volume 3; Psalms 90–150.* Grand Rapids: Baker Academic, 2008.

Gorman, Michael J. *Apostle of the Crucified Lord: A Theological Introduction to Paul & His Letters.* Grand Rapids: Eerdmans, 2004.

Gorringe, Timothy. "Anglican Political Thought." *The Expository Times* 124, no.3 (2012): 105–11.

Gottwald, Norman K. *The Politics of Ancient Israel.* Louisville: Westminster John Knox Press, 2001.

de Graaff, Guido. "To Judge and Not to Judge: Engaging with Oliver O'Donovan's Political Ethics." *Studies in Christian Ethics* 25, no.3 (2012): 295–311.

Gregory, Eric. *Politics and the Order of Love: An Augustinian Ethic of Democratic Citizenship.* Chicago: University of Chicago Press, 2008.

Gregory, Eric and Joseph Clair. "Augustinianisms and Thomisms." In *The Cambridge Companion to Political Theology*, edited by Craig Hovey and Elizabeth Phillips, 176–98. Cambridge: Cambridge University Press, 2015.

Haggard, Stephen and Marcus Noland. "Economic Crime and Punishment in North Korea." *Political Science Quarterly* 127, no.4 (2012): 659–83.

Hanson, Paul D. *Political Engagement as Biblical Mandate.* Eugene, OR: Cascade Books, 2010.

Hanson, Paul D. "Prophetic and Apocalyptic Politics." In *The Last Things: Biblical & Theological Perspectives on Eschatology*, edited by Carl E. Braaten and Robert W. Jensen. Grand Rapids: Eerdmans, 2002.

Hauerwas, Stanley and James Fodor. "Remaining in Babylon: Oliver O'Donovan's Defense of Christendom." *Studies in Christian Ethics* 11, no.2 (1998): 30–55.

Helyer, Larry R. "The Hasmoneans and the Hasmonean Era." In *The World of the New Testament: Cultural, Social, and Historical Contexts*, edited by Joel B. Green and Lee Martin McDonald. Grand Rapids: Baker International, 2013.

Hobbes, Thomas. *Leviathan*, edited with an introduction by C. B. Macpherson. London: Penguin, 1968.

Hovey, Craig and Elizabeth Phillips, eds. *The Cambridge Companion to Political Theology.* Cambridge: Cambridge University Press, 2015.

Hultgren, Arland J. *Paul's Letter to the Romans: A Commentary.* Grand Rapids: Eerdmans, 2011.

"Human Rights Watch World Report 2017." *Human Rights Watch.* http://www.hrw.org/sites/default/files/world_report_download/wr2017-web.pdf.

Jewett, Robert. *Romans: A Commentary.* Minneapolis: Fortress Press, 2007.

Johnson, Kristen Deede. *Sovereignty: An Inquiry into the Political Good*, translated by J. F. Huntington. Cambridge: Cambridge University Press, 1957.

de Jouvenel, Bertrand. *Sovereignty: An Inquiry into the Political Good*, translated by J. F. Huntington. Cambridge: Cambridge University Press, 1957.

Kang, David C. "They Think They're Normal: Enduring Questions and New Research on North Korea—A Review Essay." *International Security* 36, no.3 (2011/2012): 142–71.

Käsemann, Ernst. *Commentary on Romans*, translated by Geoffrey W. Bromiley. Grand Rapids: Eerdmans, 1980.

Keck, Leander E. *Romans*. Nashville: Abingdon Press, 2005.
Kelsey, David H. *The Uses of Scripture in Recent Theology*. London: SCM Press, 1975.
Kessler, Michael Jon. *Political Theology for a Plural Age*. Oxford: Oxford University Press, 2013.
Kim, Kipyo. *Introduction to Korean Law*, edited by the Korea Legislation Research Institute. New York: Springer, 2013.
Kim, Marie Seong-Hak. "Law and Custom under the Choson Dynasty and Colonial Korea: A Comparative Perspective." *The Journal of Asian Studies* 66, no.4 (2007): 1067–97.
Kirk, Russell. *The Conservative Mind: From Burke to Eliot*. 7th rev. ed. Introduction by Henry Regnery. Washington, DC: Gateway Editions, 1985.
Kirk, Russell. *The Roots of American Order*. 4th ed. Foreword by Forrest McDonald. Wilmington, DE: ISI Books, 2003.
Kirk, Russell. *Russell Kirk's Concise Guide to Conservatism*, introduction by Wilfred M. McClay. Washington, DC: Gateway Editions, 2019.
Knoppers, Gary N. "David's Relation to Moses: The Contexts, Content and Conditions of the Davidic Promises." In *King and Messiah in Israel and the Ancient Near East: Proceedings of the Oxford Old Testament Seminar*, edited by John Day, 91–118. London: Bloomsbury, 2013.
Kroeker, Travis. Foreword to *Beyond Suspicion: Post-Christendom Protestant Political Theology in John Howard Yoder and Oliver O'Donovan*, edited by Paul G. Doerksen. Colorado Springs: Paternoster, 2009.
Kroeker, Travis. "Why O'Donovan's Christendom Is Not Constantinian and Yoder's Voluntariety Is Not Hobbesian: A Debate in Theological Politics Re-defined." *The Annual of the Society of Christian Ethics* 20 (2000): 41–64.
de Kruijf, Gerrit. "The Function of Romans 13 in Christian Ethics." In *A Royal Priesthood? The Use of the Bible Ethically: A Dialogue with Oliver O'Donovan*, edited by Craig Bartholomew, Jonathan Chaplin, Robert Song and Al Waters, 225–37. Carlisle, Cumbria: Paternoster, 2002.
Larsen, Timothy. "Defining and Locating Evangelicalism." In *The Cambridge Companion to Evangelical Theology*, edited by Timothy Larsen and Daniel J. Treier, 1–14. Cambridge: Cambridge University Press, 2007.
Leithart, Peter J. "Good Rule." In *The Cambridge Companion to Political Theology*, edited by Craig Hovey and Elizabeth Phillips, 256–73. Cambridge: Cambridge University Press, 2015.
Lorish, Philip and Charles Mathewes. "Theology as Counsel: The Work of Oliver O'Donovan and Nigel Biggar." *Anglican Theological Review* 94, no.4 (2012): 717–36.
Markus, Robert A. "Political Order as Response to the Church's Mission." *Political Theology* 9, no.3 (2008): 319–26.
Marshak, Adam Kolman. *The Many Faces of Herod the Great*. Grand Rapids: Eerdmans, 2015.
Matera, Frank J. *Romans*. Grand Rapids: Baker Academic, 2010.
Mathewes, Charles. "A Response to Oliver O'Donovan's *Ethics as Theology* Trilogy." *Modern Theology* 36, no.1 (2020): 165–72.
Mawson, Mike. "The Understandings of Christendom in Yoder and O'Donovan." *The New Zealand Journal of Christian Thought and Practice* 15, no.3 (2007): 15–20.
McConville, J. Gordon. *God and Earthly Power: An Old Testament Political Theology Genesis–Kings*. London: T&T Clark, 2006.

McConville, J. Gordon. "Law and Monarchy in the Old Testament." In *A Royal Priesthood? The Use of the Bible Ethically: A Dialogue with Oliver O'Donovan*, edited by Craig Bartholomew, Jonathan Chaplin, Robert Song and Al Waters, 265–308. Carlisle, Cumbria: Paternoster, 2002.

McEvoy, James Gerard. "A Dialogue with Oliver O'Donovan about Church and Government." *The Heythrop Journal* 48, no.6 (2007): 952–71.

McIlroy, David H. "The Right Reason for Caesar to Confess Christ as Lord: Oliver O'Donovan and Arguments for the Christian State." *Studies in Christian Ethics* 23, no.3 (2010): 300–15.

McIlroy, David H. *A Trinitarian Theology of Law: In Conversation with Jurgen Moltmann, Oliver O'Donovan and Thomas Aquinas*. Carlisle, Cumbria: Paternoster, 2009.

McLean, Iain and Alistair McMillan, eds. *Oxford Concise Dictionary of Politics*. 3rd ed. Oxford: Oxford University Press, 2009.

Michaels, J. Ramsey. *1 Peter: World Biblical Commentary Volume 49*. Waco, TX: Word Books, 1988.

Milbank, John and Adrian Pabst. *The Politics of Virtue: Post-Liberalism and the Human Future*. London: Rowman & Littlefield, 2016.

Miller, Maxwell J. *A History of Israel and Judah*. 2nd ed. Louisville: Westminster John Knox Press, 2006.

Moberly, R. W. L. "The Use of Scripture in *The Desire of the Nations*." In *A Royal Priesthood? The Use of the Bible Ethically: A Dialogue with Oliver O'Donovan*, edited by Craig Bartholomew, Jonathan Chaplin, Robert Song and Al Waters, 46–64. Carlisle, Cumbria: Paternoster, 2002.

Moo, Douglas J. *The Letters to the Colossians and to Philemon*. Grand Rapids: Eerdmans, 2008.

Moore, Megan Bishop and Brad E. Kelle. *Biblical History and Israel's Past: The Changing Study of the Bible and History*. Grand Rapids: Eerdmans, 2011.

Morrow, William S. *An Introduction to Biblical Law*. Grand Rapids: Eerdmans, 2017.

Neufeld, Justin. "Just War Theory, the Authorization of the State, and the Hermeneutics of Peoplehood: How John Howard Yoder Can Save Oliver O'Donovan from Himself." *International Journal of Systematic Theology* 8, no.4 (2006): 411–32.

Neuhaus, Richard John. "Commentary on *The Desire of the Nations*." *Studies in Christian Ethics* 11, no.2 (1998): 56–61.

Noll, Mark A. *Between Faith and Criticism: Evangelicals, Scholarship, and the Bible in America*. 2nd ed. Grand Rapids: Baker Book House, 1991.

Novak, David. "Oliver O'Donovan's Critique of Autonomy." *Political Theology* 9, no.3 (2008): 327–38.

O'Brien, Peter T. *Colossians, Philemon: World Biblical Commentary Volume 44*. Waco, TX: Word Books, 1982.

O'Donovan, Joan Lockwood. "Nation, State, and Civil Society in the Western Biblical Tradition." In *Bonds of Imperfection: Christian Politics, Past and Present*, edited by Oliver O'Donovan and Joan Lockwood O'Donovan, 277–95. Grand Rapids: Eerdmans, 2004.

O'Donovan, Joan Lockwood. "Subsidiarity and Political Authority in Theological Perspective." In *Bonds of Imperfection: Christian Politics, Past and Present*, edited by Oliver O'Donovan and Joan Lockwood O'Donovan, 225–45. Grand Rapids: Eerdmans, 2004.

O'Donovan, Joan Lockwood. *Theology of Law and Authority in the English Reformation*. Atlanta: Scholars Press, 1991.

O'Donovan, Oliver. *Common Objects of Love: Moral Reflections and the Shaping of Community*. Grand Rapids: Eerdmans, 2002.

O'Donovan, Oliver. "Deliberation, History and Reading: A Response to Schweiker and Wolterstorff." *Scottish Journal of Theology* 54, no.1 (2001): 127–44.

O'Donovan, Oliver. *The Desire of the Nations: Rediscovering the Roots of Political Theology*. Cambridge: Cambridge University Press, 2003.

O'Donovan, Oliver. *Entering into Rest: Ethics as Theology; Volume 3*. Grand Rapids: Eerdmans, 2017.

O'Donovan, Oliver. "Evangelicalism and the Foundation of Ethics." In *Evangelical Anglicans: Their Role and Influence in the Church Today*, edited by R. T. France and A. E. McGrath. London: SPCK, 1993.

O'Donovan, Oliver. *Finding and Seeking: Ethics as Theology Volume 2*. Grand Rapids: Eerdmans, 2014.

O'Donovan, Oliver. "Government as Judgment." *First Things* 92 (1999). https://www.firstthings.com/article/1999/04/004-government-as-judgment.

O'Donovan, Oliver. "Judgment, Tradition and Reason: A Response." *Political Theology* 9, no.3 (2008): 395–414.

O'Donovan, Oliver. *The Just War Revisited*. Cambridge: Cambridge University press, 2003.

O'Donovan, Oliver. "The Justice of Assignment and Subjective Rights in Grotius." In *Bonds of Imperfection: Christian Politics, Past and Present*, edited by Oliver O'Donovan and Joan Lockwood O'Donovan, 167–203. Grand Rapids: Eerdmans, 2004.

O'Donovan, Oliver. "Karl Barth and Paul Ramsey's 'Uses of Power.'" In *Bonds of Imperfection: Christian Politics, Past and Present*, edited by Oliver O'Donovan and Joan Lockwood O'Donovan, 246–75. Grand Rapids: Eerdmans, 2004.

O'Donovan, Oliver. "The Language of Rights and Conceptual History." *Journal of Religious Ethics* 37, no.2 (2009): 193–207.

O'Donovan, Oliver. "The Loss of a Sense of Place." *The Irish Theological Quarterly* 55, no.1 (1989): 39–58.

O'Donovan, Oliver. *On the Thirty Nine Articles: A Conversation with Tudor Christianity*. Exeter: Paternoster Press, 1986.

O'Donovan, Oliver. *Peace and Certainty: A Theological Essay on Deterrence*. Grand Rapids: Eerdmans, 1989.

O'Donovan, Oliver. "Political Theology, Tradition, and Modernity." In *The Cambridge Companion to Political Theology*, edited by Christopher Rowland, 235–47. Cambridge: Cambridge University Press, 1999.

O'Donovan, Oliver. "The Political Thought of the Book of Revelation." *Tyndale Bulletin* 37 (1986): 61–94.

O'Donovan, Oliver. "The Political Thought of *City of God* 19." In *Bonds of Imperfection: Christian Politics, Past and Present*, edited by Oliver O'Donovan and Joan Lockwood O'Donovan, 48–72. Grand Rapids: Eerdmans, 2004.

O'Donovan, Oliver. "The Possibility of a Biblical Ethic." *Theological Students Fellowship Bulletin* 67 (1973): 15–23.

O'Donovan, Oliver. *The Problem of Self-Love in St. Augustine*. Eugene, OR: Wipf & Stock, 1980.

O'Donovan, Oliver. "Representation." *Studies in Christian Ethics* 29, no.2 (2016): 135–45.

O'Donovan, Oliver. "Response to Craig Bartholomew." In *A Royal Priesthood? The Use of the Bible Ethically: A Dialogue with Oliver O'Donovan*, edited by Craig Bartholomew, Jonathan Chaplin, Robert Song and Al Waters, 113–15. Carlisle, Cumbria: Paternoster, 2002.

O'Donovan, Oliver. "Response to Gerrit de Kruijf." In *A Royal Priesthood? The Use of the Bible Ethically: A Dialogue with Oliver O'Donovan*, edited by Craig Bartholomew, Jonathan Chaplin, Robert Song and Al Waters, 238–40. Carlisle, Cumbria: Paternoster, 2002.

O'Donovan, Oliver. "Response to Gordon McConville." In *A Royal Priesthood? The Use of the Bible Ethically: A Dialogue with Oliver O'Donovan*, edited by Craig Bartholomew, Jonathan Chaplin, Robert Song, and Al Waters, 89–90. Carlisle, Cumbria: Paternoster, 2002.

O'Donovan, Oliver. "Response to the Respondents: Behold, the Lamb!" *Studies in Christian Ethics* 11, no.2 (1998): 91–110.

O'Donovan, Oliver. *Resurrection and Moral Order: An Outline for Evangelical Ethics*. 2nd ed. Grand Rapids: Eerdmans, 1994.

O'Donovan, Oliver. *Self, World, and Time: Ethics as Theology Volume 1*. Grand Rapids: Eerdmans, 2013.

O'Donovan, Oliver. *The Ways of Judgment: The Bampton Lectures, 2003*. Grand Rapids: Eerdmans, 2005.

O'Donovan, Oliver. *The Word in Small Boats: Sermons from Oxford*, edited by Andy Draycott. Grand Rapids: Eerdmans, 2010.

O'Donovan, Oliver and Joan Lockwood O'Donovan, eds. *From Irenaeus to Grotius: A Sourcebook in Christian Political Thought, 100–1625*. Grand Rapids: Eerdmans, 1999.

O'Donovan, Oliver. "Political Theology." In *God's Advocates: Christian Thinkers in Conversation*, edited by Rupert Shortt. London: Darton, Longman and Todd, 2005.

Oh, Kongdan. "Understanding North Korea." *Brookings Institution*. April 1, 2013. https://www.brookings.edu/articles/understanding-north-korea/.

Open Doors. "About North Korea." opendoorsusa.org. https://www.opendoorsusa.org/christian-persecution/world-watch-list/north-korea/.

Phillips, Elizabeth. *Political Theology: A Guide for the Perplexed*. New York: T&T Clark, 2012.

Preuss, Horst Dietrich. *Old Testament Theology Volume 1*, translated by Leo G. Perdue. Louisville: Westminster John Knox Press, 1995.

"Prison Camps of North Korea." US Department of State. Humanrights.gov. https://www.humanrights.gov/dyn/news/features/prison-camps-of-north-korea/.

Provan, Iain, V. Philips Long and Tremper Longman III. *A Biblical History of Israel*. Louisville: Westminster John Knox Press, 2003.

Ramsey, Paul. *Basic Christian Ethics*. Louisville: Westminster/John Knox Press, 1993.

Ramsey, Paul. "The Uses of Force." In *The Essential Paul Ramsey: A Collection*, edited by William Werpehowski and Stephen D. Crocco, 84–95. New Haven: Yale University Press, 1994.

Rasmusson, Arne. "Not All Justifications of Christendom Are Created Equal: A Response to Oliver O'Donovan." *Studies in Christian Ethics* 11, no.2 (1998): 69–76.

Rist, John M. "Judgment, Reaction and the Common Good." *Political Theology* 9, no.3 (2008): 363–72.

Robinson, Michael Edson. *Cultural Nationalism in Colonial Korea, 1920–1925*. Seattle: University of Washington Press, 1988.

Rowland, Christopher. "Response to *The Desire of the Nations*." *Studies in Christian Ethics* 11, no.2 (1998): 77–85.

Sanders, E. P. *Paul: The Apostle's Life, Letters, and Thought*. London: SCM Press, 2016.

Schmitt, Carl. *Political Theology: Four Chapters on the Concept of Sovereignty*, translated and edited by George Schwab, new foreword by Tracy B. Strong. Chicago: University of Chicago Press, 1985.

Schreiner, Thomas R. *Romans*. Grand Rapids: Baker Books, 1998.
Schweiker, William. "Freedom and Authority in Political Authority: A Response to Oliver O'Donovan's *The Desire of the Nations*." *Scottish Journal of Theology* 54, no.1 (2001): 110–26.
Scruton, Roger. *The Meaning of Conservatism*. 3rd ed. Basingstoke: Palgrave Macmillan, 2001.
Shanks, Andrew. "Response to *The Desire of the Nations*." *Studies in Christian Ethics* 11, no.2 (1998): 86–90.
Shepsle, Kenneth A. *Analyzing Politics: Rationality, Behavior, and Institutions*. 2nd ed. New York: W. W. Norton, 2010.
Shortt, Rupert, ed. *God's Advocates: Christian Thinkers in Conversation*. London: Darton, Longman and Todd, 2005.
Skillen, James W. "Acting Politically in Biblical Obedience?" In *A Royal Priesthood? The Use of the Bible Ethically: A Dialogue with Oliver O'Donovan*, edited by Craig Bartholomew, Jonathan Chaplin, Robert Song and Al Waters, 398–417. Carlisle, Cumbria: Paternoster, 2002.
"Socialist Constitution of the Democratic People's Republic of Korea." *Foreign Languages Publishing House*. Pyongyang: North Korea, 2014.
Song, Robert, and Brent Waters, eds. *The Authority of the Gospel: Explorations in Moral and Political Theology in Honor of Oliver O'Donovan*. Grand Rapids: Eerdmans, 2015.
Soulen, Richard N., and R. Kendall Soulen. *Handbook of Biblical Criticism*. 4th ed. Louisville: Westminster John Knox Press, 2011.
Spoorenberg, Thomas and Daniel Schwekendiek. "Demographic Changes in North Korea: 1993–2008." *Population and Development Review* 38, no.1 (2012): 133–58.
Stott, John R. W. *The Message of Romans: God's Good News for the World*. Leicester: Inter-Varsity, 1994.
Talbert, Charles H. *Romans*. Georgia: Smyth & Helwys, 2002.
Tharoor, Ishaan. "The Man Who Declared the 'End of History' Fears for Democracy's Future." *The Washington Post*, February 9, 2017.
Toews, John E. *Believers Church Bible Commentary: Romans*. Scottdale, PN: Herald Press, 1989.
Tranter, Samuel. *Oliver O'Donovan's Moral Theology: Tensions and Triumphs*. London: T&T Clark, 2020.
"Understanding North Korea." *Institute for Unification Education, Ministry of Unification*. 2014.
van der Toorn, Jojanneke, and John T. Jost. "Twenty Years of System Justification Theory: Introduction to the Special Issue on 'Ideology and System Justification Processes.'" *Group Processes & Intergroup Relations* 17, no.4 (2014): 413–19.
VanDrunen, David. *Politics after Christendom: Political Theology in a Fractured World*. Grand Rapids: Zondervan Academic, 2020.
Walzer, Michael. *In God's Shadow: Politics in the Hebrew Bible*. New Haven: Yale University Press, 2012.
Wannenwetsch, Bernd. "Soul Citizens: How Christians Understand Their Political Role." *Political Theology* 9, no.3 (2008): 373–94.
Waters, Brent. "*The Desire of the Nations*: An Overview." *Studies in Christian Ethics* 11, no.2 (1998): 1–7.
Williams, Rowan. Foreword to *The Authority of the Gospel: Explorations in Moral and Political Theology in Honor of Oliver O'Donovan*, edited by Robert Song and Brent Waters, vii–viii. Grand Rapids: Eerdmans, 2015.

Williams, Rowan. "Liberalism and Capitalism Have Hollowed Out Society—So Where Do We Turn Now?" *New Stateman America*. October 18, 2016. https://www.newstatesman.com/culture/books/2016/10/liberalism-and-capitalism-have-hollowed-out-society-so-where-do-we-turn-now.

Williams, Rowan. "Obituary: Henry Chadwick." *The Guardian*. June 19, 2008. https://www.theguardian.com/world/2008/jun/19/religion.

Witherington III, Ben, with Darlene Hyatt. *Paul's Letter to the Romans: A Socio-Rhetorical Commentary*. Grand Rapids: Eerdmans, 2004.

Wolterstorff, Nicholas. "A Discussion of Oliver O'Donovan's *The Desire of the Nations*." *Scottish Journal of Theology* 54, no.1 (2001): 87–109.

Wright, G. Ernest. *God Who Acts: Biblical Theology*. London: SCM Press, 1966.

Wright, N. T. *Colossians and Philemon: Tyndale New Testament Commentaries Volume 12*. Downers Grove, IL: InterVarsity Press, 1986.

Yannaras, Christos. Ἡ ἀπανθρωπία τοῦ δικαιώματος [*The Inhumanity of Rights*]. Athens: Domos, 1998.

INDEX

Adam 18–19, 74, 112, 126, 130
Antichrist 2, 105
apocalypse 105
Aquinas, Thomas 124
architectonic hermeneutic 22, 137
Aristotle 104
Armstrong, Charles 97
Assyria 52
Augustine 9–12, 16, 106
Augustinianism 10–11, 14
authority (*see also* political authority) 2, 7–8, 11, 15, 18–21, 23–5, 29–31, 34, 40, 43, 47, 57, 59, 61, 64–6, 76, 79–85, 87, 98, 102, 107, 112–13, 115–17, 124, 127–8, 132–3
    Christ's 25
    definition of 79, 81
    demonic 132
    divine 54, 117
    dual 10, 47, 53
    God's 45, 73, 80
    governing 61–3, 65, 86, 133
    of government 29, 59
    informal 86
    institutions of 133
    judicial 90
    legitimate 86
    mediates divine 24
    mediatory nature of 127
    moral 19, 82, 86, 113, 115, 127
    natural 18–19, 112–16, 124–6, 129–31
    of order 115, 115
    of the risen Christ 58
    Scriptural 33, 76
    of secular government 28, 35, 57
    secular 58
    social 114
    of tradition 32

Babylon 47–8, 52, 64
Barth, Karl 11–12, 15–16, 106
Bebbington, David 14, 16

Bertschmann, Dorothea 4, 64
Boring, Eugene 133
Bretherton, Luke 9, 11, 13
Budziszewski, J. 134–5
Burke, Edmund 107

Calvin, John 14, 63, 66–7, 99, 125
Carson, Don 80
Catholic 13–16
Cavanaugh, William 9
Chadwick, Henry 15
Chaplin, Jonathan 3, 7, 13, 27–8, 43–4, 111, 126
Choi, Changyang 90
Choson dynasty 88–92
Christendom 7–8, 15, 82, 99, 101, 105–9
Christ-event 24–6, 49, 53–5, 57–9, 61
Christological 11, 57–62, 67, 103, 125–6
Christ's triumph 25, 57–8, 102, 105, 126, 129–31
Chrysostom, John 66–7, 125
church 8, 16, 21, 26–7, 58, 61–2, 67, 101–3, 105, 108
Church
    Anglican 14
    Broad 14
    of England 13, 15
citizen 19, 30, 85–7, 93–4, 97, 105, 121
Cole, Graham 68
Coleridge, S. T. 14
common good 31, 66–7, 84–5, 124–5, 129
communication
    covenanted sphere of 117
    social 31, 127
community 18–20, 23, 25–7, 31–2, 54, 58–9, 61, 74, 85–8, 90–2, 98, 103, 112–13, 124
concepts, true political 32–3, 39, 43, 51, 75, 80
Confucianism 89, 92

conscience 65–6
conservatism 106–8, 110, 135
contractarianism 72, 76, 104
covenant 42, 44–5, 47, 49, 51, 55, 70, 74–7, 128–9, 134
created order 18, 112–17, 119, 124–8, 131, 135, 137
creation 20, 45, 51–2, 81, 90, 117, 121, 124–7, 131–5
   Christ's vindication of 126
   God's 113, 133
   good 123–5
   ontology of 127
   universal 73

David 25, 46, 48, 52–3, 73–4
democracy 1, 49, 90, 92, 105, 135–6
divine kingship (*see also* kingship) 22–5, 37–45, 46, 48–50, 65, 73, 76–7, 79–80, 100, 128, 132, 134
   as salvation, judgment, and possession paradigm 37–41, 45–6, 48, 128
Doerksen, Paul 4
dominion 18, 126, 132
Dowding, Keith 118

ecclesiological 57–9, 61, 67
ecumenism 15–16
Egypt 46–7, 81
eschatological 57, 60, 105
ethics
   Christian political 28
   political 27
Evangelicalism 13–14, 16
exaltation, Christ's 26, 28, 42, 57, 73, 102, 130–1
exegesis 14, 25–6, 32, 40–1, 43–4, 62, 66, 114, 120, 122
Exodus 23, 46, 76
Ezra 47

Fitzmyer, Joseph 61
Fodor, James 9, 106
Forsyth, P. T. 117
freedom 30, 94, 99–100, 102–4, 107, 130
   Christian 102
   conception of 30, 102

ontology of human 116
   of speech 102
Fukuyama, Francis 1

Gause, Ken 97
God 2, 7, 18, 20–3, 26–7, 37–8, 41–2, 45–54, 57–8, 61, 64–6, 70–7, 80–1, 98–9, 102–3, 105, 113, 117, 126, 128–9, 131–3, 135–6
   action of 127
   activity of 21, 117
   acts of 21, 119
   judgments of 66
   reign of 7, 20, 28
   rule of 25, 58
   Trinitarian Christian 121
   triumph of 28, 70
   will of 44, 64
Goedde, Patricia 90–1, 93–4
good 65–5, 68, 84, 87, 96, 130
   God's servant for your 61, 65–6, 129
   public 66
   social 96
goods (*see also* common good) 87
   of creation 20, 126
   political 11
Gorman, Michael 62
Gorringe, Timothy 14, 106
Gottwald, Norman 51
government (*see also* government-as-judgment) 9, 25–6, 29, 31, 42, 44, 46, 58–67, 74–5, 81, 85–6, 88, 90, 97, 108, 124, 126, 129
   church's 26
   function of 26, 63, 66–7, 129
   Israelite 52
   legitimate 81
   purpose of 26, 65–6
   responsible 99
   secular 27–8, 35, 57–8, 61, 68, 75, 80, 108, 114, 119, 121–2, 124
   theory of 63, 67
government-as-judgment 17, 65, 101, 134
Grant, George 13
Gregory, Eric 10
Grotius, Hugo 12, 16

Haggard, Stephan 94
Hanson, Paul 51

Hauerwas, Stanley 9, 106
history (*see also* salvation-history) 1–2, 21–2, 24, 26, 32, 44–6, 48–9, 53, 65, 70–3, 75, 79–80, 87, 90–1, 97–8, 113–16, 123, 125, 127–31, 135–7
    Christian 15, 28, 100
    covenantal 46
    end of 1
    of God's reign 20
    of God's rule 20
    human 24, 81, 128
    intellectual 9, 11, 15–16, 106
    Israel's 20, 44, 47–9, 51, 54, 71–2, 74, 76, 100–1, 127–9
    Jewish 42
    meaning of 72
    one public 119
    political 20, 22, 128
    post-exilic 53
    providential 114–15, 126
    recorded 51, 81
    redemptive 105, 126
    revealed 20, 44
    sacred 52–3
    of salvation 22, 32, 39
    secular 52
    universal 20, 72
Hobbes, Thomas 76
Holy Spirit 35, 125–6, 130
Hooker, Richard 14
Hultgren, Arland 61–2, 64
human rights abuses 94–5, 97

Il-sung, Kim 90–2, 97
institution 19–20, 26, 31, 54, 73–4, 90–1, 124, 133
    political 31, 49, 133
    social 51
Israel (*see also* history, Israel's) 20, 22–6, 37–8, 41–2, 44–55, 64, 70–7, 87, 100, 116, 127–9
    ancient 38, 44, 71, 107–9
    post-exilic 53
    state of 48, 52

Japan 89–91, 94
Jesus 22, 25, 54, 71, 73–5, 128–9, 132
Jewett, Robert 62

Josephus 64
Judah 47–8, 51–2
Judaism 53, 64
Judges, book of 47–8
judgment (*see also* government-as-judgment) 22–3, 25–9, 32, 37–42, 45–6, 48, 57–8, 62–3, 65–7, 83–4, 88, 90, 100, 104–5, 113, 123, 125, 127–9
    acts of 29, 31, 84
    concept of 29
    definition of 83–4
    execution of 65, 123–4
    exercise of 25, 58, 81, 108
    of God 23, 74, 99, 114
    government's 31
    judicial 124
    merciful 99–100, 102–3, 130
    moral 122
    performance of 59, 67
    political 83, 126
    practice of 28–9, 35, 57
    secular 102
    task of 27, 59–60
    tradition of 83
justice 19–20, 43, 48, 75, 85, 93–5, 112, 124
    absolute 83
    relative 84, 86, 92, 94, 96, 103

Käsemann, Ernst 60, 62, 64–5
Keck, Leander 60, 62, 64
Kelsey, David 33–4, 39, 44, 58–60
Kessler, Michael 118
Kim, Kipyo 89
kingdom 25, 58, 70
    God's 26–7, 58, 73
    human 64
    Jesus' 73
    northern 52–3
    post-political 105
    southern 52–3
kingship (*see also* divine kingship) 23, 40, 64, 104
    Christ's 69, 77
    covenantal 45–6, 48–9
    God's 22–3, 46, 48, 73
    mediated Davidic 46, 48
    universal 45–6
    Yhwh's 22, 41
Kirk, Russell 107

Klink, Edward 70–1
Kroeker, Travis 11
de Kruijf, Gerrit 62

Larsen, Timothy 16
law 23, 43, 48, 89, 93, 103, 124
  alien 91
  constitutional 86
  land and 26, 42
  natural 135
  tradition of 37, 42
  unjust 85, 92
Leithart, Peter 9
liberalism 1–2, 8, 10, 102, 104–6, 109–10, 131
  Augustinian 10
  Christian 2, 99–105, 107–9, 130–1
  conservative Christian 106, 109
  definition of 102
  future of 110
  modern 20
  secular 2, 102, 104–5, 107
  Western 1, 100, 130
liberation theology 22
Lockett, Darian 70–1
Lockwood O'Donovan, Joan 12–13, 16, 107
Lorish, Philip 3, 8, 24

Matera, Frank 64–5
Mathewes, Charles 3, 8, 24
Maurice, F. D. 14
McConville, Gordon 75
McEvoy, James 4
McIlroy, David 4, 10
McLean, Iain 118
McMillan, Alistair 118
mediation
  of divine kingship 49, 50
  of God's authority 73
  of God's judgments 74
  of God's kingship 45
  of God's rule 53
  of his rule 51
  of Yhwh's kingship 48
  unitary 46
method
  empirical 135
  normative 121

O'Donovan's 33
  for political theology 32
  rational 135
  theopolitical 32, 43
Michaels, J. Ramsey 133
Milbank, John 1, 105
mission, church's 27, 58, 101, 105, 108
Moberly, R. W. L. 75
modernity 104–5
monarchy 46–8, 51–2, 74, 87, 128
  Choson 92
  Davidic 26, 37, 46, 48–51, 53–5, 65, 69, 73, 75, 77, 81, 99–100, 121, 128
  divided 52
  Hasmonean 52–3
  Israel's 49, 51–2
  Jewish 53
  Saudi 88
  united 52–3
moral discriminations 29, 32, 83–5, 95, 123–6
morality 18, 82, 125
Morrow, William 75
Moses 46–7, 73, 75

Nehemiah 47
Neuhaus, Richard 3
Noland, Marcus 94
Noll, Mark 14
North Korea 79, 82–4, 88–99, 131
Novak, David 3

obedience 7, 30, 85–7, 98, 125, 127
obligation 19, 30–1, 63, 81, 85–6, 102, 116
Oh, Kongdan 83, 90
oligarchy 49
openness of speech 99–100, 102–4, 130
order (*see also* created order) 23, 26, 42–3, 54, 105, 115, 117
  Christian 105
  civil 66
  constitutional 108
  God's 18
  international 46
  liberal 105–6
  moral 18, 117, 129
  natural 19, 45, 112, 114, 133
  political 1, 28, 45–6, 61, 75, 80, 88, 90, 96, 100–1, 104–6, 116, 130

providential 113–15, 126
social 2, 29, 65

Pabst, Adrian 1, 105
Paul 58–67, 81, 121, 129
Persia 41
political authority 2, 17, 19–20, 23–4,
    26–8, 30, 33–5, 37, 40–2, 44–5,
    49–53, 55, 57–8, 60–1, 64–6,
    74–6, 79–88, 91, 94–5, 97–8,
    106, 108, 111–17, 121–3, 125–7,
    129–30, 132–5
  alien 129
  bene esse of 49, 100, 131
  of the Bible 108
  conception of 8, 13, 30, 53, 96, 114,
    121, 128, 137
  definition of 28, 43, 48, 99, 113
  esse of 25, 100, 125–6
  essence of 37, 45, 49–51, 55, 59–60,
    64, 67, 69, 72–3, 75–6, 77, 80, 83,
    88, 98–100, 111, 113, 115, 123,
    127–31
  function of 25, 58–60, 65, 98, 127
  human 62, 80, 133
  nature of 23, 30–1, 42, 62, 73, 75,
    124–5
  ontology of 112, 117, 125, 128, 137
  philosophy of 138
  purpose of 19, 25
  re-authorization of 26, 57, 60, 101,
    103
  reconception of 63
  redemption of 126–7, 129
  secular 25, 58, 61, 102, 105
  theology of 2, 16–17, 28, 30, 34–5,
    40–1, 64, 69, 77, 98, 111, 115, 117,
    121–3, 126, 128, 134
  theory of 8, 24, 121
political philosophy 27–8, 118, 128,
    135–6
political psychology 97
political science 98, 118, 121, 128,
    135–7
political theology 1–5, 9, 20–2, 27, 32–3,
    41, 54, 62, 72, 76, 108, 118–19, 121,
    125, 129, 134, 136, 137–8
  applied 82
  Barth's 11

Christian 8, 27, 44, 52, 109, 118, 121,
    128, 135–6
  conservative 106
  definition of 118–19
  evangelical 24
  government-centric 134
  O'Donovan's 4, 6, 9–13, 15, 17, 26, 39,
    75, 105–6, 109, 120
  revived Augustinian 9
  Western Christian 3
  Yoder's 6
political thought 16, 77
  Anglican 14
  Augustine's 9
  Christian 12, 15
  contemporary 20, 109
  early modern period of 76
  High Tradition of Christian 20, 101,
    104, 130
  late medieval Christian 105
  liberal 72
  normative 107
  O'Donovan's 9
  secular 106, 118
politics 3, 9, 20, 28, 43, 51, 70, 73, 75, 102,
    114, 118–23, 125–6
  centralized 51
  decentralized 51
  definition of 119, 124–5
  modern 30
  natural ontology of 135
  North Korean 82
  post-Easter 77
  of Western liberalism 1
power 23, 25, 28, 30, 35, 37, 39–44, 47, 49,
    52–3, 57–60, 63, 67, 79–83, 85–7,
    89–90, 94, 98–100, 108, 112–13,
    116, 127–30, 132–3, 135
Preuss, Horst Dietrich 76
Protestantism 72
providence 24, 35, 44–6, 49, 79–82, 82–3,
    87–8, 97–9, 114–17, 123–4, 126,
    128, 130–

Ramsey, Paul 10, 12, 16, 43–4, 54, 123,
    128
redemption 8, 70, 102, 125, 127
  Christological 126
  Christ's 18, 125, 131

history of 70, 127
of political authority 129
Reformed 14
revelation
    divine 116
    of Jesus Christ 116
    general 135
    God's 71
    nature of 71
    special 135
right (*see also* authority of right)
    of a community 32, 84, 86, 92, 124
    execution of 23, 25, 28, 31, 35, 37, 39,
        41–2, 45, 47, 49, 53, 57, 59, 79,
        81–8, 92, 94, 97–9, 108, 124
    individual 102
    injured 19–20, 31, 41, 43, 82, 85, 98,
        112, 123, 125
    natural 100, 102–4, 130
rights
    human 84–5, 94–7, 103
Robinson, Michael 88–9
Rowland, Christopher 106
rule 26, 45, 49, 51–3, 80–1, 90, 92, 97, 130
    Adamic 130
    Christ's 75
    colonial 51, 89, 91
    divine 20, 22, 24, 44–6, 106, 126
    God's 20–2, 25–6, 37, 42, 48, 53, 58, 74,
        77, 128
    God's kingly 2, 38
    God's providential 45
    Hellenistic 53
    history of God's
    human 59
    kingly 22, 50, 75
    monarchical 90
    priestly 46–7
    Roman 53

salvation-history 25–6, 28, 36, 50, 59,
    69–77, 104–5, 122, 126, 128–9
Samuel 50
Sanders, E. P. 63
Saul 52–3
Schreiner, Thomas 61–2, 64–5
Schweiker, William 4
Scripture
    authorized from 13, 32–3, 37–41, 43–4,
        54, 68, 75, 80, 119–21, 129, 136

Scruton, Roger 108
Shanks, Andrew 8
Shortt, Rupert 10, 13
Skillen, James 66
society 8, 18–19, 21, 26–7, 31, 44, 58, 66,
    82–4, 91–2, 102–3, 112, 126–7, 133
    church and 26
    North Korean 90
    political 26, 130
    secular 26
    socialist 94
Solomon 46, 52–3
Song, Robert 4
South Korea 90–1
state 26, 38, 48, 52–3, 61, 65, 85–6, 92–3,
    96–7, 133
    church and 62
    failed 96, 99
    socialist 89–91
    theory of 62–3
Stott, John 62, 64
Sumer 81

Talbert, Charles 62, 64
theocracy 51
theodicy 79, 82, 98, 99, 116
theology (*see also* political theology *and*
    liberation theology) 7, 13, 15, 20–1,
    24, 32, 34, 53, 61–2, 71–2, 114, 118,
    120–1
    biblical 21, 70–2
    moral 2, 12, 137
    O'Donovan's 16, 23–4, 28
    systematic 63
Toews, John 61
tradition (*see also* authority of tradition
    and political thought, High
    Christian tradition of) 14, 16, 20,
    23, 25, 37, 39–44, 47, 49, 52–3, 60,
    63–4, 67, 82–3, 85, 87–8, 90, 91–2,
    97, 99, 103, 107–9, 111, 113, 128–30
    Augustinian 9
    authoritarian 90
    Catholic 15–16
    classical liberal 108
    Davidic 53
    definition of 87
    Evangelical 114
    exegetical 66
    Hellenistic 64

Jewish 64
Korean 91
legitimate 87–8, 90, 95
medieval 16, 45
perpetuation of 25, 28, 31, 35, 37, 39, 41–2, 45, 48, 53, 59, 79, 81–3, 86, 88, 94, 98–9, 108
political 44, 90
representative 32, 49, 92, 94, 98
revolutionary 91
Roman 15
Western 20, 23, 40
Western liberal 99, 101, 104, 109, 130
tyranny 102, 104

unifying conceptual structure 22, 32–3, 39, 73, 137

van der Toorn, Jojanneke 97
victory
    Christ's 27
    military 37, 41
    won by Christ over the nations' rulers 101, 104, 130

Wannenwetsch, Bernd 65
Waters, Brent 4, 9
Williams, Rowan 8, 14
Witherington, Ben 62
Wolterstorff, Nicholas 3–4, 48, 59
Wright, G. Ernest 69–70, 72–6, 128, 134
Wright, N. T. 133

Yannaras, Christos 103, 120–1
Yoder, John Howard 6

www.ingramcontent.com/pod-product-compliance
Lightning Source LLC
Chambersburg PA
CBHW051812230426
43672CB00012B/2712